OUT
OF THE
WHIRLWIND

MeOtzar HoRav SERIES:
SELECTED WRITINGS OF RABBI JOSEPH B. SOLOVEITCHIK

The *MeOtzar HoRav* series
has been made possible
by a generous grant from
Ruth and Irwin Shapiro.

The publication of *Out of the Whirlwind*
has been made possible by a grant
in memory of
Clarence and Irma Horwitz.

Volume One
Family Redeemed
Edited by David Shatz and Joel B. Wolowelsky

Volume Two
Worship of the Heart
Edited by Shalom Carmy

Volume Three
Out of the Whirlwind
Edited by David Shatz, Joel B. Wolowelsky and Reuven Ziegler

OUT
OF THE
WHIRLWIND

Essays on Mourning, Suffering and the Human Condition

by
Rabbi Joseph B. Soloveitchik

Edited by
David Shatz, Joel B. Wolowelsky
and Reuven Ziegler

Published for
TORAS HORAV FOUNDATION
by KTAV Publishing House

Library of Congress Cataloging-in-Publication Data

Soloveitchik, Joseph B.
  Out of the whirlwind: essays on mourning, suffering and the human condition / by
Joseph B. Soloveitchik
      p. cm. (Meotzar horav; v.3)
Includes index.
  ISBN 0-88125-772-9
1. Grief—Religious aspects—Judaism. 2. Suffering—Religious aspects—Judaism.
3. Man (Jewish theology) I. Title.

BM645.G74 S65 2002
296.3'2—dc21

2002028927

Printing year: 2017

ISBN 978-0-88125-772-4

Published for
THE TORAS HORAV FOUNDATION by

KTAV PUBLISHING HOUSE
527 Empire Blvd.
Brooklyn, NY 11225

Website: www.ktav.com
Email: orders@ktav.com
ph: (718)972-5449 / Fax: (718)972-6307
Price $26.95

• Table of Contents •

• Preface •

*O*ut *of the Whirlwind: Essays on Mourning, Suffering and the Human Condition* is the third volume of the *MeOtzar HoRav Series: Selected Writings of Rabbi Joseph B. Soloveitchik*. Rabbi Soloveitchik *zt"l* (1903-1993) was not only one of the outstanding talmudists of the twentieth century, but also one of its most creative and seminal Jewish thinkers. Drawing from a vast reservoir of Jewish and general knowledge, "the Rav," as he is widely known, brought Jewish thought and law to bear on the interpretation and assessment of the modern experience. On the one hand, he built bridges between Judaism and the modern world; yet at the same time he vigorously upheld the integrity and autonomy of the Jew's faith commitment, and in particular the commitment to a life governed by Halakhah, Jewish law.

For over four decades, Rabbi Soloveitchik commuted weekly from his home in Brookline, Massachusetts to New York City, where he gave the senior *shiur* (class in Talmud) at the Rabbi Isaac Elchanan Theological Seminary (RIETS), affiliated with Yeshiva University, and, in his early years there, also taught

Jewish Philosophy at the University's Bernard Revel Graduate School. Generations of rabbinical students were taught and inspired by him—among them many of the future leaders of the Orthodox and broader Jewish community. By his extensive personal teaching and influence, as well as by serving locally as the chief rabbinic figure in Boston, where he founded the Maimonides School, he contributed vitally to the dynamic resurgence of Orthodox Judaism in America. The thousands of people who regularly flocked to his public lectures in Boston and New York on halakhic, philosophical and biblical topics were consistently enthralled and inspired. Rabbi Soloveitchik stands, indeed, as one of the great religious leaders of our time. Even now, after his passing, his teachings—"the Rav's Torah"—are always eagerly sought, and his words continue to ring with relevance and authority.

Although many of Rabbi Soloveitchik's writings and discourses have been published over the years, much additional material, rich and evocative, remains in handwritten manuscripts. THE TORAS HORAV FOUNDATION was established by family members and former students to disseminate these and other works, with the aims of enhancing both our grasp of Rabbi Soloveitchik's philosophy and our understanding of the diverse topics he addresses. Rabbi Reuven Ziegler of Yeshivat Har Etzion, Director of the MeOtzar HoRav Archives, joins us as a co-editor of the present volume.

Alas, it is impossible to read the Rav's powerful and challenging essays without an accompanying sense of the profound loss we have all incurred with the passing of this giant. But the reader who experiences these essays, who absorbs and appreciates their rare blend of intellectual sweep and energizing passion, will find them to be an invaluable, integral part of his or her own spiritual quest.

David Shatz
Joel B. Wolowelsky

❧ Introduction

The essays in this volume articulate a Jewish response to the phenomena of death, crisis and suffering—topics on which Rabbi Soloveitchik wrote and lectured frequently. Perhaps the reader's best point of entry into the essays is an understanding of the role that the confrontation with tragedy plays in Rabbi Soloveitchick's larger philosophy and hence an appreciation of why he returns to it time and again.

The simplest explanation of his focus on evil is the one the Rav suggests in "A Halakhic Approach to Suffering:" "The Halakhah could not avoid the problem of evil; no religion could." Evil is a formidable and inevitable challenge, both intellectually and emotionally. However, the Rav confronts the issue not only as a philosopher of religion, but as a Torah master as well. He roots his discussions in the Bible and the larger corpus of Aggadah and Halakhah, while simultaneously drawing upon his vast knowledge of Western philosophy, literature and science to arrive at a striking understanding of those sources. His analyses of the laws of mourning and the inner experience of mourning display in a striking fashion his remarkable synthesis of a penetrating halakhic mind with a profound understanding of the human personality. Brilliant formal analysis of halakhic regulations and texts fuses in these pages with a subtle, powerful philosophical and psychological portrait of man in distress and despair.

The Rav's understanding of halakhic mourning is rooted in his understanding of the dynamics of *mitzvah* performance. In general, people fulfill their obligation to perform a *mitzvah* merely by doing certain physical acts. Thus, one fulfills the biblical commandment to eat *matzah* on the first night of Passover by simply eating the unleavened bread, irrespective of one's mental state or attitude. But in the case of other commandments, the inner experience is essential. For example, the commandment to repent requires certain physical acts such as recital of the *vidduy* (verbal confession to God of past sins), but clearly the essential obligation is the transformation of one's inner self. Other such examples are prayer, in which the recital of a set text must be accompanied by a certain focus and orientation; and festival rejoicing (*simhat yom tov*), in which physical feasting alone is not enough, but rather must be accompanied by inner rejoicing as well. To use technical halakhic language, there are commandments in which the *kiyyum ha-mitzvah*, the fulfillment of the *mitzvah*, is obtained not through the *ma'aseh mitzvah*, the physical performance of the *mitzvah*, but rather through an inner experience. In these *mitzvot*, the inner component is not the product of pietistic, extra-legal motivation, but rather constitutes an essential component of the formal halakhic definition of the *mitzvah*. For the Rav, mourning is a sterling example of this sort of *mitzvah*, and the critical question for him is how to characterize the state of *kiyyum*.

The Rav's focus on *mitzvot* in which *ma'aseh* and *kiyyum* are distinct is paralleled by his interest on a philosophical plane in the relationship between outer deed and inner person. As he states in *Family Redeemed* (speaking of another *mitzvah*, reverence for parents, which likewise requires both an inner fulfillment and an outer performance):

> A novel element is injected into the performance—the motivation, the causative inner situation of man, the all-pervading mood. The deed becomes the agency through which experience speaks, the objectified intimate feeling which reveals the very recesses of personal existence. The good will becomes externalized, noble desire presses into action, and the organs of acting are inspired by restlessness. The tense muscle is then an experience concretized, the feverish movements of the hand are a thought turned into nerve-tissue and the whole of external man—an ecstatic soul made visible. The deed in such a stage consists not just of acting but of acting out something deep-seated, hidden in the inaccessible recesses of the human personality. The *pe'ulat mitzvah,* the *mitzvah* performance, becomes a dramatic gesture, a soliloquy— or rather a colloquy—telling a marvelous tale of the boundless existential distances and unexplored spaces of man, his dilemma, contradiction and self-redemption.

Thus, the Rav opens his discussion in *"Aninut* and *Avelut"* with the question, "What are the experiential and halakhic distinctions between these two stages of mourning?" For him, the examination of the halakhic distinction demands an investigation of the mourner's inner dynamics. The halakhah reflects this inner experience; indeed, in a sense, the halakhah flows from the realities of the human situation.

Likewise, in *"Avelut Yeshanah* and *Avelut Hadashah,"* Rabbi Soloveitchik contrasts the structure and dynamics of the halakhic norms that govern an individual who recently has lost a loved one with those that govern *Kelal Yisrael,* the community of Israel, during the three-week period between the Seventeenth of Tammuz and the Ninth of Av (*Tish'ah be-Av*), the period in which the community mourns an ancient tragedy, the loss of the Temple. In the case of individual mourning, the halakhic restrictions become progressively more lenient. In the case of communal mourning, the restrictions intensify and become more stringent as *Tish'ah be-Av* approaches. To understand the opposite movements in individual and communal mourning, Rabbi Soloveitchik enters the inner world of the mourner. The person who confronts the death of a close relative reacts with shock. Gradually, he or she leaves the trauma behind, and, with that movement, the restrictions of mourning recede. But the individual who mourns the destruction of the Temple as a member of the community is far removed temporally from the event. Such people need time to capture the intensity of a mourner, and therefore a process is necessary to gradually and progressively translate the intellectual awareness into an emotional awareness. Hence the restrictions of mourning build up to *Tish'ah be-Av*.

The contrast between an intellectual and an emotional response to tragedy is presented somewhat differently in "Abraham Mourns Sarah." Here the Rav focuses on the mourning dynamics of an individual, distinguishing between *bekhi* (crying) and *hesped* (eulogizing). The former is a spontaneous, overwhelming and uncontrollable grief; the latter is rooted in logical judgment, where clear analysis of the disastrous event and its consequences replaces the sudden and confusing emotional confrontation with disaster.

In "The Redemption of Death," Rabbi Soloveitchik offers a summary response to the question of how man can redeem himself from death. It is a double procedure, he says. First, man must make his own organized effort to limit death's power as much as possible. Second, he must place his trust in the Almighty. In the end, man cannot solve the mystery of death—only God can explain to us this awesome mystery. "Death is the great marvel, the unintelligible experience, the *hok*, the Torah no one can grasp."

"The Essential Nature of Mourning" approaches the issues at hand from an entirely different perspective. The only essay in this volume which is a translation from the Hebrew, it proceeds as a traditional talmudic/halakhic *shiur*. The Rav assembles a series of seemingly contradictory texts and then proceeds to work out a resolution and synthesis. The emphasis seems to be textual and technical—how, for example, is it that the mourner and biblical leper have many of the same normative mourning-type restrictions and yet differ in other details. Yet the solution, while following the traditional talmudic methodology of reconciliation, is in its essence phenomenological, because it sees the differences and contradictions explained by the differing experiences required.

Indeed, in each of these essays, the Rav's approach is phenomenological rather than metaphysical. That is, he tries to capture the inner world of the believer rather than deal with the metaphysical question of how God could allow such evil to exist. He treats evil as a given of human experience, not as a conundrum to be explained away.

Turning from mourning to suffering generally, the Rav argues in "A Halakhic Approach to Suffering" that practical Halakhah eschews the metaphysical question and focuses instead on action. A person can react to suffering passively and allow it to defeat him, or he can respond actively by combating evil and by using suffering as an opportunity to purify his personality. Modern man is not yet reconciled to the fact that evil is unconquerable in its entirety. He is therefore vulnerable to disillusionment when disaster strikes. The Halakhah, however, trains man in all aspects of his life to retreat, thereby fortifying him to confront the unconquerable. Man was summoned to defy evil and try to eliminate it. However, if he fails temporarily to defeat evil he must see to it that the confrontation be a courageous one, heroic and useful. In a word, instead of philosophizing about the nature of evil within the framework of a theodicy, Judaism wants man to fight it relentlessly and to convert it into a constructive force.

"Out of the Whirlwind" specifies two ways in which a person can use suffering to elevate and purify his personality. The feeling of loneliness, of being singled out, can press one into a closer relationship with God. By awakening man to his own mortality, suffering can also force him to assess his mission in life and compel him to utilize his time on earth to further this end. Judaism believes each person has a unique assignment from God. If he does not hear God's call when times are good, employing divinely-provided bounty in the service of God, then God will summon him "out of the whirlwind," through catastrophe and suffering.

In the Rav's view, catastrophe imposed by external events is not the only kind of crisis man confronts; rather, crisis is intrinsic to human existence. "The Crisis of Human Finitude" shows why this is so. Man is finite; hence, both he and his victories are incomplete: life is bounded by death, knowledge by ignorance, etc. Halakhah provides a means of coping with this crisis, advocating the raising of one's conflicting emotions to an encompassing dialectical experience of life—one which acknowledges both man's greatness and his limitations. By submitting one's emotions to critical review in light of the dialectical experience—which entails both an ability to relinquish perceived goods and a realization of one's ultimate dependence on God alone—one can avoid the neurotic anxiety so characteristic of modern man. The Rav was well-known for his dialectical treatments, and this essay, along with the next, affords a much-needed glimpse into the significance of dialectic and why he made it so central.

As elaborated in the above essays, Judaism takes for granted man's control over his emotional realm; "A Theory of Emotions" provides philosophic backing for this notion. Far from being just a collection of fleeting moods, man's personality can have depth, wholeness and constancy. It attains this by remaining ever mindful of the dialectical experience of life (presented in the previous essay), an awareness fostered by the

Halakhah. Maintaining a critical attitude towards one's emotional responses and incorporating them into a broader perspective, one can shape them according to his values. This critical interpretation of the emotions also engenders more complex responses, both in terms of one's range of emotions and their multi-dimensionality. Finally, the dialectical perspective can ethicize emotion by helping one's emotions leave their self-reflecting, egotistical shell, thereby discovering the "other" and promoting an expanded existence, or *hesed*. Although this essay and its predecessor contain some passages of dense philosophical analysis, they also shimmer with penetrating psychological insights, revealing new depths of meaning in a host of Judaic sources.

For all its focus on suffering, crisis and "the tragic destiny of man," Rabbi Soloveitchik's is not a pessimistic vision. It proceeds from and affirms a sense of the value of each individual and the meaningfulness of his life. In fact, it is only in light of the meaningfulness of a person's life that the Rav pronounces death absurd by contrast. As the Rav frequently pointed out, the halakhic requirements of mourning and eulogizing are predicated upon a recognition of each person's uniqueness, for only this recognition permits a proper assessment of the irreplaceable loss we have suffered with his or her passing. Studying Judaism's attitude towards mourning therefore enhances our esteem for man, notwithstanding his inevitable and tragic end. Furthermore, reflecting on one's mortality awakens a person's sensitivity to the flow of time, pressing him to assess the nature of his own unique mission and to strive to accomplish it.

The very act of creative confrontation with the subjects of mortality and human vulnerability can help one overcome his fear of them. In *Halakhic Man*, Rabbi Soloveitchik explains that by subjecting these topics to creative analysis, by making them into materials for one's mind to act upon, one in effect becomes their master, and his fear of them dissipates. He relates that his grandfather, the illustrious scholar Rabbi Hayyim of Brisk, would overcome his dread by studying the laws of corpse defilement: "And these laws . . . would calm the turbulence of his soul and would imbue it with a spirit of joy and gladness . . . The act of objectification overcomes the subjective terror of death." Analogously, the Rav continues, Tolstoy conquered his fear of death by "transforming death into an object of his artistic creativity" when writing *The Death of Ivan Illich (Halakhic Man*, p. 73 and n. 86). Thus, the very study of the subjects of these essays can be a constructive, cathartic and redemptive act.

* * *

Before turning to the individual essays in greater detail, we repeat a note made in the introduction to *Family Redeemed*. The reader unfamiliar with philosophical terms may be somewhat unnecessarily intimidated by some of the technical language that appears in the text of this volume. The Rav treated hashkafic discussions with the same rigor and exactness of language that he used in halakhic ones. In general, difficult terms in this book are subsequently explained, and therefore the reader who meets up with a hard term should not, in frustration, overlook these clarifications. But most fundamentally, it must be said that the Rav—not only in Halakhah but also in philosophy—expected effort from his audience. The difficulty of the essays is a function of the high level of the discussion; edification, learning from genius, comes with—to invoke a theme of the Rav's writing—labor and struggle. At the same time, those who meet Rabbi Soloveitchik's expectations are invariably rewarded. Master teacher that he was, the Rav goes on to explain his core concepts in a manner that is clear and accessible even to readers who are not familiar with every word of the presentation.

The summaries that follow are, of course, no substitute for *experiencing* the essays themselves. In *Family Redeemed*, at the end of "Torah and *Shekhinah*," the Rav establishes that Torah study has not only an intellectual dimension but an experiential one as well. Rabbi Soloveitchik's profound, passionate, textured exposition must be experienced first-hand, so that one can fully appreciate his remarkable ability to plumb a point to its very depths, to tap textual subtleties, and to construct a world-view from a linguistic nuance.

Although many of the themes in these essays have parallels in other writings of the Rav, our focus here is the essays themselves.

Aninut and Avelut

The halakhic distinctions between the two initial phases of mourning, *aninut* and *avelut*, are well-known. *Aninut*, which begins at death and ends with burial, is marked by an exemption from all *mitzvot aseh*, the positive commandments. The mourner may not pray, is exempted from putting on *tefillin* and, indeed, from fulfilling any positive halakhic obligation unconnected with the funeral arrangements. *Avelut*, on the other hand, which commences after burial, is marked by a sudden imposition of halakhic obligations.

The Rav opens his discussion of the these two stages with a characteristic question, "What is the halakhic and the experiential distinction between these two phases of mourning?" The human psyche confronts the world with different, even contradictory, perceptions. Halakhah, insistent on a truthful and realistic appreciation of these human reactions, gives expression to all of them. An understanding of Halakhah, then, requires an understanding of human nature.

Allegiance to Halakhah requires an appreciation of human self-worth, an awareness of the significance and importance of one's actions. A confrontation with death, however, undermines that self-conception. How can our existence have significance over that of the animals when death makes us realize that we are just another one of the living creatures, like the beasts in the field, facing the same cruel end?

In a word, man's initial response to death is saturated with malice and ridicule toward himself. He tells himself: If death is the final destiny of all men, if everything human terminates in the narrow, dark grave, then why be a man at all? Then why make the pretense of being the choicest of all creatures? Then why lay claim to singularity and *imago Dei* (the Divine image)? Then why be committed, why carry the human-moral load?

The Halakhah does not try to gloss over these "crazy" torturing thoughts and doubts that contradict the basic halakhic doctrine of man's election. Instead, it insists on giving expression to "the spontaneous human reaction to death." For the Rav, the rule that the mourner is exempt from performing positive *mitzvot* flows naturally from the realities of life, not the exegesis of texts.

If the exemption from *mitzvot* is a natural reaction, the immediate reimposition of obligation when *aninut* abruptly comes to an end with burial is an imposed reaction. Free will extends not only to actions, says the Rav, but to thoughts as well. A healthy person can reorient himself at will. "Man, the Halakhah maintains, does not have to wait patiently for one mood to pass and for another to emerge gradually. He disengages himself, quickly and actively, and in a wink replaces a disjunctive frame of mind with a cathartic-redemptive one." Just as the Halakhah demands that people give expression to their devastation in confronting the inevitable end of life, so too it demands that they give expression to their strength and their ability to triumph in their encounter with the "self-devastating black despair" that accompanies the "hideous darkness" of a confrontation with death.

In the stage of *aninut*, man mourns "in total darkness and confusion," unable to acknowledge his greatness and chosenness. But after burial, in *avelut*, he mourns "in an enlightened mood" in which he can acknowledge his unique human status. This is not a return to the pre-*aninut* stage wherein man might have been oblivious to the possibility of the bottom falling out of the meaningfulness of life. Rather, "death gives man the opportunity to display greatness and to act heroically; to build even though he knows that he will not live to enjoy the sight of the magnificent edifice in whose construction he is engaged."

The ceremonial turning point at which *aninut* becomes *avelut* is the recital of *Kaddish*. This prayer is a praise of God, an awareness that, far from being insignificant like the beasts of the field, man is important enough for God Himself to be concerned with his praise. Saying *Kaddish*, then, is a defiance of death, a statement not only about the greatness of God, but about the greatness of man. "Through the *Kaddish* we hurl defiance at death and its fiendish conspiracy against man," as "grief asserts itself in the awareness of human greatness and human election."

This self-awareness is also tied to repentance, and, indeed, many of the *shiv'ah* prohibitions (such as those against washing, the use of cosmetics and ointments, wearing shoes, and sexual relations) are reminiscent of Yom Kippur. The act of mourning becomes an act of expiation. "The Halakhah commands the mourner to expiate his guilt by observing those prescribed rites which are also observed on the Holy Day of Atonement when man is questing for forgiveness."

It is loss that makes us aware of what we had. The consequence of sin is God's departure from our lives. Only then do we realize the opportunities lost and potential unfulfilled. The same holds true for the death of a loved one. "During the mourning stage we ask the questions we should have asked before: Who was he? Whom did we lose? His image fascinates us from afar, and we ask with guilt and regret the questions that are now overdue, the questions to which only our lives can provide the answers."

Avelut Yeshanah and *Avelut Hadashah: Historical and Individual Mourning*

In "*Avelut Yeshanah* and *Avelut Hadashah*: Historical and Individual Mourning," the Rav continues the discussion of man's freedom of will in the area of mourning. Just as people can disown emotions which their conscience assesses as unworthy of being integrated into their personality, they can assimilate constructive noble feelings.

In this essay, the Rav applies this policy on the communal level, indicating how the Jewish people respond to national catastrophe, in this case the destruction of the Temple, which is mourned formally on *Tish'ah be-Av*, the ninth day of the month of Av. There are two types of mourning, one which affects the individual and the other the community. The first, *avelut hadashah*, is "a primordial, instinctual, spontaneous response of man to evil, to the traumatic confrontation with death, to the impact of catastrophe and disaster. It is an existential response, not one that evolves by the application of artificial stimuli." The second category, *avelut yeshanah*, is man-made. "There is no spontaneous reaction to some new event which has just transpired, for nothing new has happened which should justify grief. The *avelut* is a result of recollection of events."

Both forms of mourning come in stages, but their process is reversed. Individual mourning begins with the most intense, most poignant and highest state of grief, *aninut*, and slowly recedes into *shiv'ah*, *sheloshim*, and *yod-bet hodesh*—the seven-day, thirty-day, and year-long periods that follow *aninut*—"until it fades into a lingering melancholy." *Avelut yeshanah* follows a reverse course. It starts out with the mildest form of mourning and gradually turns into mourning of increased intensity.

Thus the Rav sets up an inverse parallel between the stages of individual mourning and those of communal grief. The time between the Seventeenth of Tammuz and *Rosh Hodesh Av* is devoted to remembrance, to meditation, to reliving and reexperiencing. Only on *Rosh Hodesh Av* does the inner *avelut* begin to be recorded on the register of objective mourning and the first signs of observance become visible. "When Av begins, we lessen our happiness" (Mishnah *Ta'anit* 1:7). This parallels the twelve-month period of mourning for one's parents, as both share the avoidance of participation in any festive events, receptions, and so forth.

Shavua she-hal bo, the week during which *Tish'ah be-Av* falls, corresponds to *sheloshim*, the thirty-day mourning period, as both include the prohibitions of cutting one's hair (*tisporet*) and pressing one's clothes (*gihutz*). The mourning of *Tish'ah be-Av* itself is like that of *shiv'ah*. The *baraita* says that "all the restrictions that are observed during *shiv'ah* are observed on *Tish'ah be-Av*" (*Ta'anit* 29b).

The parallelism is not exact, notes the Rav. For example, washing one's clothes and commerce are prohibited in the week before *Tish'ah be-Av* and permitted during *sheloshim*, while betrothal is handled in the opposite manner: betrothals are permissible during the week of *Tish'ah be-Av* and forbidden, according to Ri and Ramban, during *sheloshim*.

This distinction can be explained by the fact that there is one aspect of historical public mourning which has almost no application to personal mourning, namely, *heseah ha-da'at*, any distraction or diversion of attention. The inner mourning of an individual grieving over the loss of a relative expresses itself in sharp, unbearable pain. With communal mourning, however, the pain is not as severe as in the case of recent disaster, nor is the grief as sharp and distressing as in the individual's encounter with death. However alive the experience of *hurban* (destruction) might be, it is the intellect which commands the emotions to respond to the historical memories of a community. Any distraction, any diversion of attention, any *heseah ha-da'at* breaks up the *avelut*.

That, explains the Rav, is why the mourning of the week in which *Tish'ah be-Av* falls revolves around the concept of *heseah ha-da'at.* Whatever may cause diversion or dissipation of emotional tension has been prohibited. This includes engaging in commerce, which is a steady occupation, and washing one's clothes, which in olden times meant continuous public work at the river. *Avelut yeshanah* is stricter with regard to those matters which are public and continuous.

On the other hand, the prohibition of betrothal (an act which requires only two witnesses and is therefore not considered public) is not rooted in *heseah ha-da'at.* The individual *avel* is enjoined from betrothal for a different reason entirely, namely, the apparent worthlessness of life and its irrational, absurd vicissitudes. He simply cannot engage in any act which is related to the survival and continued existence of man. *Heseah ha-da'at* plays no role in the personal encounter with individual grief, because intellectual concentration or even emotional fixation are not responsible for the emergence of the mourning. The latter leaps out of nowhere, it befalls, overpowers and breaks man unexpectedly.

Similarly, the Rav examines the differing laws regarding *tefillin* on *Tish'ah be-Av* and the beginning of *shiv'ah.* There are, he explains, two components of the laws of mourning. One pertains to *nihug avelut*—the practical observance of *avelut*, the compliance with various injunctions. Then there is another *halakhah* which applies to the *gavra*, to the person who is called *avel.* Being an *avel* is an attribute of the *gavra*, an adjectival description of the person, and the *gavra* can be an *avel* even without the *nihug avelut.*

With regard to historical mourning, *avelut yeshanah*, Jews can engage in *nihug avelut* and comply with its prohibitions, but they are not *avelim* with respect to their *gavra*, their personhood. The prohibition against putting on *tefillin* as a mourner is not part of *nihug avelut* but rather is a result of the *gavra* being an *avel.* The *gavra* as an *avel* is relieved of *tefillin* on the first day of mourning. A *gavra* who is an *avel* somehow cannot be crowned with *tefillin*, cannot adorn himself with them. *Avelut yeshanah*, historical mourning, imposes observance of *avelut*, but it cannot change the *gavra* into an *avel*. Therefore *tefillin* are worn on *Tish'ah be-Av*.

A final distinction between *Tish'ah be-Av* and *avelut* relates to *kefiyyat ha-mittah*, turning the bed upside down. Death impinges upon the worth of human dignity and the human divine nature. The symbol of humiliated man, of man who goes down in defeat, insult and shame, is an overturned bed. The bed is a metaphor for the moral integrity of the family (we say, "*mittato shelemah*") or the human personality in general ("*mittato porahat ba-avir*"). We no longer do this during *avelut*, and instead cover mirrors as a substitute. This whole manifestation is alien to *avelut yeshanah*. All this cannot fit into the context of historical grief, as the *hurban* did not deprive us of our dignity.

In individual mourning, betrothal is forbidden, but it is permissible to betroth on *Tish'ah be-Av*. The dimension of despair and resignation, the notion of the mourner being unworthy of his own existential experience, is contrary to the very essence of *avelut de-rabbim*. "There, the mourner is not the individual but the nation, the covenantal community, which must never lose hope or faith. No matter how difficult times are, no matter how great the loss is, however dreary and bleak the present seems, the future shines with a brilliant glow full of promise. The messianic hope has never vanished; the people have never been enveloped by the dark night of despair."

Abraham Mourns Sarah

The Bible tells us that when his wife died, "Abraham came *lispod le-Sarah ve-livkotah*" (Gen. 23:2), indicating two verbs, *lispod* and *livkot*. The latter, says the Rav, refers to *bekhi*, crying, indicative of a spontaneous, overwhelming and uncontrollable grief. The former, *sepod*, refers to eulogizing and is related to another kind of reaction, one rooted in logical judgment. The mourning at the stage of *bekhi* cannot be verbalized. The grief at the stage of *hesped*, the eulogy, lends itself to objectification through words.

The natural order always leads from *bekhi* to *hesped*, yet here the Torah reverses the order, indicating that Abraham came first to eulogize Sarah and then to cry for her. This reversal gives expression to Abraham's relationship with Sarah. Both of them had suffered together, praying and waiting for God's promise of a child to come true. Abraham loved Sarah; she lived through all the adventures and crises that Abraham had to face. Their life was rich in common experiences; two lives merged into one. The blow to Abraham as an individual was almost unbearable. It was not *hesped*, logical interpretation, which described Abraham's state of mind most precisely in this respect, but *bekhi*, crying, feeling the desolation.

However, Sarah was not only Abraham's mate but his partner as well. Together they discovered God; together they discovered a new morality, together they joined the covenant and started the *Masorah*, the communal tradition handed down from generation to generation. Now the mother is dead and the *Masorah* will be incomplete. The Torah tells us that Abraham first mourned the death of the mother of the *Masorah*, and then the death of a lovely wife, without whom his life will be desolate, bleak and dreary.

Abraham's sequence of mourning reflects a philosophy expressed in the fact that the Halakhah demands thirty days mourning for a child and twelve months of mourning for parents. This is the case despite the fact that the death of a parent is not as devastating psychologically as the death of a child. Parents who have lost a child will never forget their grief. Their distress is endless; nothing can offer them solace. A son and a daughter, on the other hand, can usually get past the death of a parent. Yet the Halakhah has decreed otherwise.

Apparently, says the Rav, the Halakhah here is guided not by psychological, emotional reality but by concerns about the *Masorah*. The mourning is great for a parent because it is he or she who introduces the child to the *Masorah*. The death of a person who extended the chain of tradition to an individual must precipitate greater formalized mourning than the death of a child, to whom one does not owe any debt of gratitude as far as the *Masorah* is concerned.

Mourning, if observed with restraint and in compliance with the Halakhah, enhances the status of man. It is an experience of great dignity, a sacrificial act enlightening the sufferer about the meaning of life as well as the destiny of mankind. He must at a certain moment be capable of rising from the mourner's stool, no matter how difficult it is. Abraham realized that he could not afford to continue to cry hysterically and mourn forever. People watched him; they observed his conduct in his hour of crisis. When disaster struck, he had to demonstrate faith in God and act with fortitude and dignity. "And Abraham rose up from before his dead and spoke to the Hittites" (Gen. 23:3). Abraham rose from the ashes, straightened his back, lifted his eyes to heaven and whispered: "Yes, as long as I have You with me I feel strong. I am faithful to You."

Abraham controlled his emotions; he regained his dignity, his freedom and particularly his inner strength and firmness because he had to speak to the Hittites about important matters. He did not want the Hittites to see him low in spirit, completely displaced by endless, bleak despair.

No matter how great the suffering, one must not make a public exhibition of his emotional world. Abraham mourned for Sarah endlessly. However, the grieving took place in the privacy of his house, not in public. When he had to negotiate with the Hittites in public, when he had to acquire the field in the presence of the entire community, he got up from his dear Sarah and regained his strength, since the history of a covenant was dependent upon the outcome of his performance.

His transaction with the Hittites was of great importance because Abraham finally disclosed to them his strange identity and his unique way of life.

The Hittites suggested to Abraham two things: the grave-yards will be integrated and the grave will not belong to Abraham. "In the choicest of our sepulchers shall you bury your dead; none of us shall withhold from you his sepulcher" (Gen. 23:6). The interment will be in the finest of *our* sepulchers; Sarah's grave will be an integral part of *our* cemetery; the place will not belong to you: it will be our property. We will just permit you to use "the choicest of *our* sepulchers"; no one will withhold "*his* sepulcher."

Abraham graciously acknowledged the kindness of the people of the land, who were anxious to see that the stranger be assimilated into the general society and who offered leadership to the newcomer. Yet he declined the offer and explained precisely what he had in mind.

I am a part of the civilized, scientifically trained and progress-minded society, he said. I work with you in laboratories, study in the same academia. I participate in industry and commerce, help support the poor, pay taxes and am ready to defend the land. However, I am also a stranger; I am different as far as my covanental relationship with God is concerned. I worship differently, I celebrate my holidays in a unique fashion, I rejoice as well as mourn in a singular way. I share with you the laboratory but not the place of worship. I will attend the same school but will insist upon a separate *ahuzat kever*, a grave-inheritance. Please speak to Ephron, let him sell me the Makhpelah Cave, and it will become not just a grave but an *ahuzat kever* that is exclusively mine, something that I will pass on to my descendants. It will be the symbol of the commitment of my people to the land.

Yet Abraham wanted more than that: the land must not be given to him as a gift. He demanded that Ephron sell him the land for its full price. Ephron argued that he does not want to take money. He agreed with Abraham pertaining to separation of sepulchers and unrestricted ownership, but insisted that the land be given to Abraham as a grant, that is, *free*. But Abraham declines to accept the gift; he wants to pay. Money represents labor, the sweat and fatigue of the worker. Therefore the goods I buy are absolutely mine, while a gift which I received, lacking the catharsis of work and exhaustion, lacks the redemptive quality. That is why Abraham certainly did not want Sarah to be put to her eternal rest in a grave which was given to him as a present, a gratuity, a grave which was not hallowed by sweat.

There are two kinds of property, *sedeh ahuzah* and *sedeh mikneh*. *Sedeh mikneh* is property that one buys easily and sells easily. Usually such property is purchased and sold for the sake of gain. There is no emotional attachment. There is also *sedeh ahuzah*, property which one inherits from his ancestors, property with which one gets emotionally involved, to which one is bound inwardly. *Ahoz* conveys being held and passed on from generation to generation, never to be given up.

When Abraham paid money, he acquired legal rights. The relationship remained that of a *sedeh mikneh*, formal-juridic. Once Sarah was put to rest in the Makhpelah Cave, Abraham reacquired not only the field, but the whole land of Canaan as the place of the first Jewish grave, that of Sarah. "And the field and the cave that is therein were made sure unto Abraham for an *ahuzat kever*" (Gen. 23:20).

The Redemption of Death

The laws concerning the *parah adumah*—the Red Heifer which plays an essential part in "purifying" a person who came into contact with a dead body (Numbers, chapter 19)—are considered the epitome of unintelligible and mysterious "*hukkim*," laws which the human mind is incapable of comprehending. As a result of the purification process, the individual who became *tamei*—ritually "impure" or "defiled"—by contact with death becomes "purified," and the priest who performed the ritual becomes *tamei*.

While the Rav agrees that it is beyond us to understand the

logic of the law, he insists on the legitimacy of searching for the spiritual message of the *hok*. "Of course," he writes, "I must never say that the message I detected in the *mitzvah* explains the *mitzvah* and answers the illegitimate question of why the Almighty commanded us to act in such an unintelligible way. However, I am permitted to raise the question of what this *mitzvah* means to me. How am I to understand, not the reason for the *mitzvah*, but the essence of the latter as an integral part of my service of God?" The Rav finds in this particular *hok* an approach to the challenges created by a confrontation with death.

The focal point for the Rav's discussion is the fact that the "impurity" that results from contact with the dead is different from all other forms of *tum'ah*. Generally, all that is required to remove one's impurity is *tevillah*—immersion in a *mikvah* or the "living water" of a spring, river or ocean. But while this applies to a person who becomes impure by contact with, say, the carcass of a dead animal, it does not apply to the *tamei met*, the individual who became impure by contact with a dead human body. The sprinkling of the *mei hattat* (water containing the ashes of the red heifer) is indispensable for the *tamei met* to regain his previous status of *tahor*, pure; immersion alone does not suffice. The real question for the Rav, then, is: why did the Torah single out the *tamei met*?

The entire zoological kingdom experiences death, but not as a monstrosity; death simply destroys the functionality of the organism.

> Human death, however, terminates a personality, an ontological dimension, a spiritual individuality—someone who was self-aware, self-conscious, driven by vision, hoping, despairing, rejoicing, grieving, anticipating events and remembering occurrences, building fantasy worlds and destroying them . . . Death denies the very worth of human existence. Hence the *tum'ah* is due not

to organic but to spiritual destruction. It is the expression of human anxiety and terror, human helplessness in the face of a mocking Satan. *Tum'at met* is the result of the traumatic experience that dislocates man's self, I-awareness and existential security.

His suggestion is that the peculiar method of cleansing the *tamei met* is indicative of the existential metaphysic of man.

> The basic difference between immersion and sprinkling lies in the fact that the *tevillah* is accomplished by the impure person himself. No one can help the *tamei* to immerse . . . However, as regards sprinkling, the situation is the reverse: the *tamei met* cannot sprinkle the water upon himself; another person must do it.

Man must struggle with death and try to defeat it on two levels. On the one hand, man must respond with his own dignified and significant gesture in reducing the power of death and of prolonging life—and this is expressed in the cleansing requirement of *tevillah*. However, Judaism does not have unrestricted faith in human capability to eliminate death and make the human immortal. Sprinkling, *haza'ah*, represents our trust that at some point in the future the Almighty will redeem us, "and the clean person shall sprinkle upon the unclean" (Num. 19:19).

> "The clean person" who will free the unclean from the bondage of defilement is the Almighty, as the prophet says, "Then I will sprinkle water upon you, and you shall be clean" (Ez. 36:25). Only He will heal man from the threat and terror of nihility. Man cannot solve the enigma or mystery of death. Only God will elucidate and explain to us this awesome mystery. Death is the great marvel, the unintelligible experience, the *hok*, the Torah

no one can grasp — "This is the Torah: when a man dies in a tent . . ." (Num. 19:14).

The Essential Nature of Mourning

The next chapter derives from a *yahrzeit* address delivered by the Rav in memory of his father and has the form of a traditional *shiur* rather than a lecture. Its focus seems to be purely textual, as the Rav surveys halakhic texts, mostly passages from the Talmud and its medieval commentators. He relates specifically to exceptional instances of *avelut*: the mourning, if any, of the High Priest; mourning during a festival; the mourning-like rituals followed by lepers and the excommunicated. Those uninitiated in halakhic studies might see in this material some superfluities as details are listed and reviewed. But the Rav will draw conclusions about the nature of ordinary halakhic mourning and its theological underpinnings from the Halakhah's handling of these atypical situations. The essay follows the "Brisker" method of talmudic study, with its emphasis on incisive analysis, exact definition, and precise, almost scientific, classification of halakhic categories.

The Rav begins by enumerating a series of difficulties issuing from the various talmudic discussions of the laws of *avelut*, usually in the form of textual anomalies and apparent contradictions. Specifically, he questions: (1) how is it that Rambam (Maimonides) could consider the High Priest "subject to the laws of mourning" even though a passage in the Talmud likens him to "an ordinary Jew on a festival," for whom mourning is suspended; (2) how could medieval commentators maintain a leper's mourning-like regimen on a festival (thereby indicating that it is compatible with festival joy), while the analogous mourner's regimen gives way to the holiday's primacy; (3) why does the Halakhah see simultaneous observance of both mourning and festival joy as impossible when, in fact, nothing of the mourning ritual prevents the bereaved from partaking of meat

and wine, the ritual elements of festival joy; (4) how can Rabbi
Yehiel of Paris' student claim that festival joy is not possible for
a leper because he is isolated from the Camp of Israel, while it
is somehow achievable for a bereaved mourner; (5) how can
some of the Tosafists—who maintain that though public mourning ceases on a festival, private aspects of *avelut* are observed,
just as they are on the Sabbath—justify excluding the festival
as a day of *shiv'ah*, while at the same time allowing the Sabbath
to be reckoned as one of the days of *shiv'ah*; (6) how, finally,
could the Talmud consider that a festival count toward the period of *sheloshim*, when, again, a festival cancels mourning?

The Rav attempts to deal with these difficulties by offering
a broad analytical thesis about the nature of mourning, through
which the anomalies and contradictions are ultimately resolved.
The mourner's ritual, we know, is composed of specific demands
and prohibitions enumerated by the Halakhah. The mourner
may not, for instance, shave or launder clothing, among other
rules. Now these rules, says the Rav, are merely *details*; they do
not constitute the whole of mourning itself. For halakhic
mourning is not simply an assortment of duties, it is rather a
positive halakhic undertaking that the mourner is called to fulfill, what the Rav calls a *kiyyum*. The specific laws of the mourning regimen are but the particulars of the larger, essential
halakhic task of *kiyyum*.

The Rav adduces preliminary proof for the existence of this
kiyyum by observing the halakhic weight given to mourning in
its intersection with another sphere of Halakhah. A priest is
scripturally enjoined from encountering the ritual impurity of a
corpse, but when the deceased is a close relative, the priest is
told to become *tamei*, ritually defiled, in order to ensure proper
interment and observance of mourning rites. It is only because
of the larger framework of *kiyyum avelut* that the priest is
allowed—nay, obligated—to violate his standing prohibition.
Were *avelut* simply a handful of scattered laws, they would not
license him to become *tamei* and thus defile his priesthood.

Moreover, this *kiyyum*—and here we arrive at the thrust of the Rav's thesis—is fulfilled primarily within the human heart, through grief and broken-heartedness. The obligatory observances are but an instrument toward, and expression of, the personal experience that is the essential fulfillment of halakhic mourning. Both elements are normative, but it is the experiential aspect which subtly underlies halakhic discussions of mourning practice, as the Rav proceeds to demonstrate.

He does so, first, by noting the Halakhah's willingness, in certain circumstances, to do away with the practices of mourning—the willingness to imagine mourning without its concomitant regimen. Relatives of criminals put to death by a Jewish court or of those who commit suicide are told to mourn only inwardly, while refraining from external expressions of mourning. Biblically-ordained *avelut* seems to last for all seven days of *shiv'ah*, according to Rambam, since he rules that the mourner's exclusion from offering sacrifices lasts for the duration of the seven-day period. The regimented laws, however, are required on the level of biblical law only for the first day of mourning. If *avelut* exists for six days independent of its accompanying *halakhot*, clearly its center is outside the realm of pure procedure, and rather inside the human heart.

The Rav then returns to the array of questions with which he began his lecture, and goes on to show how, in view of his concept of *kiyyum*, the initial difficulties are answerable.

Certainly *avelut* is thoroughly incompatible with festival joy, even though the mourner may partake of the ritual meat and wine, as festival joy, too, is an experience above and beyond its halakhic particulars (a point the Rav goes to great length to demonstrate). The two emotions are too much at variance with each other to reside jointly in the Jew's heart, and one *must* give way, though the associated regimens are technically compatible. And it is joy, a communal imperative, which is given priority over the individual obligation to mourn.

The regimen of the leper, on the other hand (for those who see it as operative on festivals), may *resemble* the regimen of *avelut*, but it is not meant to urge or represent an inner *kiyyum*. Thus, the outward observance of its laws should not interfere with the experience of festival joy. (The Rav later adds that, in any case, the leper is exempt from festival joy, since he is excluded from the community, and festival joy is in its essence communal.)

Understandable, too, is Tosafot's exclusion of festival days from the *shiv'ah* count. On the Sabbath, mourning is not really suspended. Public acts of mourning are adjourned in respect for the dignity of the day, but in no way is *avelut* itself—its *kiyyum*—interrupted, and the Sabbath thus counts toward the tally of seven. On festivals, however, *avelut* is offset altogether by the joy of the day (*simhat ha-yom*) and thus cannot possibly count as a day of *shiv'ah*. (Tosafot require that private *avelut* be upheld on a festival only because of their concurrence with Semak [*Sefer Mitzvot Katan*], who maintains the practices of *avelut* even in the absence of their *kiyyum*.)

Likewise clear, with one additional qualification, is the possibility that the *sheloshim* period may in fact include the days of a festival. The Rav here notes that it is only the biblically-ordained *shiv'ah* period that calls for *kiyyum*; the mourning of *sheloshim* and *yod-bet hodesh* involve certain *halakhot*, but do not demand *kiyyum*. It is for that reason festivals may count toward the tally of thirty.

The concluding sections of the essay synthesize many of the ideas that appeared previously, via a penetrating depiction of festival joy as an expression of God's nearness to man, and of mourning as an expression of God's distance from man.

A Halakhic Approach to Suffering

This essay discusses the Halakhah's recommendations on maintaining mental health in the face of suffering. In approaching the subject, the Rav first distinguishes two forms that halakhic creativity can take. One is the *topical* Halakhah, the term deriving from the Greek word *topos*, meaning surface. At this level, the Halakhah posits formal, articulated categories and rules that relate to the human mind and will, will that translates into action. In its topical mode, Halakhah is a formal cognitive and normative system.

But there is a second form of halakhic creativity, the *thematic*, from the Greek word for root. The thematic Halakhah is addressed not to the human's ability to engage in conceptual thinking, as is the topical Halakhah, but to man's "axiological gesture," that is, his apprehension of values and metaphysical themes. The topical Halakhah is understood; the thematic Halakhah is beheld (intuitively), tasted or confronted.

(Perhaps a convenient way for the reader to think about the thematic Halakhah is to identify it, at least roughly, with what we would call Aggadah or *mahshavah*, that is, Jewish thought and philosophy. The Rav often uses the term "Halakhah" in contexts where we would say "Judaism," and this terminological preference on his part is reflected in his use of the term thematic Halakhah rather than Jewish philosophy.)

Thus, on the one hand, Halakhah is "a reasoned, clearly defined, precise system of thought," which is applied via concrete actions; but on the other hand Halakhah is "a singular, unreasoned order of experiential themes." For example, when the topical Halakhah addresses the Sabbath, it formulates legal categories of, and rules about, the prohibited forms of *melakhah* (work) on that day; but the thematic Halakhah treats the Sabbath as a living reality, as a great experience of a sacred, blessed time. The Rav maintains that whereas the topical Halakhah deals exclusively with the physical universe, the world known to science and to our senses, the thematic "envelops Being in its majestic totality." The thematic Halakhah enters into the realm of a transcendent reality unfettered by the bounds of time and space—the realm of the infinite.

Accordingly, the topical and the thematic Halakhah treat the phenomena of suffering and evil in profoundly different ways. The thematic Halakhah views evil, or rather what we call evil, as something that we can transcend after death (transcendentalism) or as something that is swallowed up in the totality of boundless Being (universalism). But the topical Halakhah, grounded as it is in the world of the physical, the transient, the here-and-now, could not accept the idea that evil can be explained. For this reason we grieve and engage in practices of mourning: death is real. For the topical Halakhah, which is practically oriented, there is no metaphysic of suffering, no grand picture that makes evil inconsequential or unreal. Instead there is only an ethic of suffering, a way of responding to it. This ethic regards evil as real, as something to which we must never acquiesce. "Man is summoned by God to combat evil, to fight evil, and to try to eliminate it as much as possible." We must marshal for this battle all scientific resources at our disposal. We will lose from time to time, but the war is long, and the time will come when "He will swallow up death forever, and the Lord God will wipe off the tears from all faces" (Isa. 25:8).

The conquest of evils such as illness through scientific means is modern man's project as well as Judaism's. But Judaism goes beyond modern man. Whereas the latter accepts distress with Stoic *equanimity*, Judaism turns suffering into a great experience of *dignity*. Man's ability to commune with God confers upon him dignity, which asserts itself in victory and conquest. And yet being confronted by God results in recoil and withdrawal, which is also an expression of dignity. "The dialectical movement of surging forward and falling back is the way of life ordained by God for Jews." Thus the Rav asserts that we must experience defeat at the aesthetic-hedonic, intellectual and emotional levels, an assertion he develops in his 1978 *Tradition* essay "Catharsis." This is why the Halakhah requires retreat from sexual pleasure at certain times. And that is why Abraham had to be ready to sacrifice his child at God's request.

What is the moral to draw about suffering? That to preserve our dignity, we must learn to take defeat. Jewish law, as we saw, requires us to take defeat at our own hands, this occurring when we recoil and withdraw. By learning to take, or more accurately, administer defeat at our own hands, we become able to bear with dignity defeat by external enemies, even when we did not summon it.

This approach was conveyed by the Rav with concise beauty in a letter (dated April 15, 1965) to Dr. Dan Vogel, then Dean of Stern College for Women, Yeshiva University, in which he himself summarizes this lecture.

> The gist of my discourse was that Judaism did not approach the problem of evil under the speculative-metaphysical aspect. For such an inquiry would be a futile undertaking. As long as the human mind is unable to embrace creation in its entirety and to gain an insight into the very essence and purposiveness of being as such, it would not succeed in its attempt to resolve the dilemma of evil. The latter is interwoven into the very fabric of reality and cannot be understood outside its total ontological configuration. Job was in error because he tried to grasp the nature of evil. Therefore, Judaism has recommended that the metaphysical inquiry be replaced by the halakhic ethical gesture. Man should not ask: Why evil? He should rather raise the question: What am I supposed to do if confronted with evil; how should I behave *vis-à-vis* evil? The latter is a powerful challenge to man and it is the duty of man to meet this challenge boldly and courageously. Suffering, in the opinion of Judaism, must not be purposeless, wasted. Out of suffering must emerge the ethical norm, the call for repentance, for self-elevation. Judaism wants to convert the passional frustrating experience into an integrating, cleansing and redeeming factor.

Out of the Whirlwind

Many of the essays in this volume clearly grow out of the Rav's personal experiences, which imbue them with power and authenticity; consider, for example, the echoes of Rabbi Soloveitchik's own mourning for his wife that are discernible in "Abraham Mourns Sarah." Yet "Out of the Whirlwind" is the only essay in this volume in which he specifically alludes to his own encounter with suffering. This essay was written shortly after his own bout with cancer (in late 1959 through early 1960), and the impact of this encounter with his own mortality is sharply felt.

Anticipating a theme he was later to develop in "The Lonely Man of Faith," Rabbi Soloveitchik posits two orders of human experience: the cosmic and the apocalyptic, or the natural and the revelatory. The question of theodicy highlights the difference between them. In the cosmic order, man encounters God primarily at the intellectual level; within this frame of reference, we can say that pain is part of a larger good. By contrast, the revelatory confrontation with God is meta-logical, and within it intellectual explanations are insufficient. Rather, in confronting God on this plane, man seeks to know how to respond to suffering. And in order to respond properly, he must be able to interpret the message of suffering.

At this point, Rabbi Soloveitchik makes a key argument. Not only is the revelatory experience initially catastrophic, since it exposes man to his own nihility and shakes him loose from his fixed attachments, but the catastrophic experience is revelatory as well. God reveals Himself in the whirlwind of catastrophe, and man must be sensitive to the messages God wishes to impart. (Note that the message contained in suffering does not explain *why* the suffering occurs, but rather relates to how man can *use* the suffering.) Thus, suffering can be not only a traumatic but a redemptive experience as well.

How does suffering shake man out of his complacency? The Rav now adds substantively to his other discussions of the halakhic response to evil (in *"Kol Dodi Dofek"* and "A Halakhic Approach to Suffering") by specifying two lessons of suffering, or two ways suffering can be used to purify the human personality. (In his other treatments, the Rav focused on the need to combat evil and the lesson of sympathy for fellow-sufferers.) First, the confrontation with nihility, with the reality of one's own end, should shock a person out of his illusions of immortality. Although everyone knows intellectually that he will die, this does not often enter a person's consciousness. Consequently, desires assume overblown proportions and the significance of frustrations is similarly exaggerated. Shifting to an awareness of temporality relieves one of his petty worries and anxieties and allows him to focus on what is truly significant. Furthermore, it reawakens his time-awareness and sensitizes him to his unique role, the mission that only he can fulfill in the here-and-now. The Rav illustrates this point with an account of the crisis in his own mindset at the time he was admitted for cancer surgery.

The second existential dimension opened by suffering is that of loneliness. The person who suffers, like the person who has been granted Divine revelation, feels singled out from the crowd and cut loose from his social moorings. On the eve of his operation, the Rav recounts, he felt alienated from his friends and family, for he alone faced death and they could not participate in that confrontation. Yet realizing the ultimately limited connection one can have with others strengthened his feeling of the absolute, unlimited and solitary connection to God.

If one integrates the experiences of non-being and loneliness into his selfhood, he thereby responds actively and constructively to his experience of suffering. Although suffering is of course traumatic, we must not repress it in our consciousness, for it contains a summons from God and can lead to religious growth, increased closeness to the Divine, and a heightened sense of personal mission. Repression leads to wasting the experience of suffering, which would be doubly tragic.

God reveals Himself not just in the catastrophic experience, but in the majestic experience of nature and being (the ontic experience) as well; He appears within both negation and affirmation, chaos and order. The paradoxical alternation between these two disclosures is a basic motif in our experience. (Therefore, as explained in "A Theory of Emotions," one must avoid absolutizing only one of these experiences, and instead maintain in each emotion an awareness of its opposite.) While the sense of God's "absence" at times of crisis often leads one to try to regain His presence through prayer and repentance, the sense of God's "presence" during times of joy and success also demands a response. If one fails to appreciate God as the source of all bounty, if he fails to use God's gifts in the service of a good cause, then the ontic revelation will be supplanted by the nihilitic revelation.

Job is a prime example of this phenomenon. He did not use God's blessings to further his Divine destiny; he did not appreciate that every Divine gift entails a summons. (The rabbis of the Aggadah highlighted this by placing Job at various destiny-charged junctures of Jewish history, where he could have helped, but didn't.) When, consequently, the cosmic revelation was replaced by the catastrophic revelation, Job cried out to God. Once again, God appeared to him in the whirlwind, in the catastrophic, and disclosed to him the meaningfulness of the cosmic drama.

Isaiah and Ezekiel both beheld visions of God's numinous presence and His functioning in the cosmos. For Isaiah, who lived at a time of peace and prosperity, this vision was ontically affirmative; God addressed him through the joyous cosmic experience. Yet for Ezekiel, who lived during a time of exile and suffering, the vision of heavenly functioning was strange and frightening. Like a person struck by catastrophe, at first he beheld only mechanical forces—wheels, creatures, torches—and missed God. This grisly vision was projected against an icy void, indifferent and unresponsive. Suddenly God disclosed Himself to Ezekiel, speaking to him in a meaningful voice, not an absurd noise or a mighty tumult.

> God spoke out of the catastrophic event, out of the seeming void and emptiness, from above the icy firmament, from nowhere. It took Ezekiel a long time to make the great leap . . . from the absurdity of a historical cataclysm to the great dialogue with the hidden, numinous, mysterious God, abiding behind the heavens. Suddenly a new light was shed over everything he beheld before. The weird creatures, the wheels, the great noise, the host, the mighty waters—this did not fill him with grisly fear any more . . .

From within the catastrophic revelation, Ezekiel beheld a vision of the meaningfulness of the cosmos and received a personal mission.

So, too, God summons each of us to His service. Our existence is not a caprice but a meaningful assignment, abounding in responsibility and commitment. This is Judaic humanism or democracy: each person has a unique mission and is equally worthy. When one lives in an illusory eternity, he may miss the message; but when sensitized to the flow of time, one becomes vigilant, anticipates the future and regards each moment as precious. God placed each person at a specific time and place for a reason. A person's creation implies a twofold message: his service is required, and he has the ability to act. He must not ignore or misread this message.

The Crisis of Human Finitude

There are two types of crisis in human life. Surface crisis, such as a disease or a natural disaster, is shared by others and is visible to all. Judaism adopts an activist and optimistic posture with regard to this type of crisis. Depth crisis, however, cannot be fought; moreover, it is a private experience, and the mature personality must freely choose to confront it. What is the nature of this crisis? "The incompleteness of our existential experience at all levels is rooted in the nature and destiny of man. He is a creature and, as such, a part of a finite reality— and finitude is incomplete, deficient and impregnated with paradoxes and absurdities." Everything we desire is ultimately bounded by its antithesis, such that none of our victories is complete: life is bounded by death, knowledge by ignorance, beauty by ugliness and morality by evil.

We can relieve ourselves of the burden of despair brought on by this realization "by consecrating this incompleteness as an offering to God . . . We find dignity and majesty not in the madness of 'draining' one conquest 'to the dregs' in order pass on to another, but in self-conquest and self-giving; in the quest for catharsis, for redemption by returning my existence to its Owner; in the heroic sacrifice." This can be accomplished in two ways: "first, at the subjective experiential level, as a crisis-awareness spelled out in prayer; second, at the objective level, as a sacrificial decision." The latter refers to our ability to accept limitations upon ourselves, thereby hallowing all our actions (a theme developed in other essays, such as "A Halakhic Approach to Suffering" and "Catharsis"). As for the former, the Rav explains that, "The prayer consecrates the defeat, redeems the misery and elevates it to the level of sacrifice . . . The supplication imparts meaning and directedness to the crisis experience." The remainder of this essay is devoted to spelling out the nature of the crisis experience, which leads to the dialectical experience of life.

Two types of personalities avoid confronting the depth crisis and lack the dialectical awareness of man as both "king and pauper" (in the words of the midrash): the philistine personality, represented by Job, and the daemonic, represented by

Kohelet (Ecclesiastes). Job remained oblivious of the depth crisis, instead focusing all his energies on self-preservation through the avoidance of surface crisis. In order to maintain a life lived solely at the plane of victory without ever having to experience defeat, he entered into a self-centered and mercantile relationship with God. All this was shattered by the cataclysm that struck him.

Ultimately, a new Job emerged out of the crisis. "The tempest that swept him out of his complacency and egotism raised him to a new level of dialectical existence, where triumph is interwoven with defeat, success with failure, and receiving serves a higher end—relinquishing." The turning point was Job's prayer. How so? First, he abandoned egotism and learned to pray for his friends. Second, true prayer is an expression of *tzarah*, distress; it sweeps away man's security and self-satisfaction, forcing him to admit his bankruptcy and total dependence on God.

Kohelet, on the other hand, recognized the incompleteness of life; however, he proudly thought it possible to overcome this through the sheer force of a boundless will. He, too, denied the reality of defeat. "Fundamentally, Kohelet did not grasp the essence of the depth crisis, since he believed in complete self-realization and in the possibility of resolving the existential crisis." His eventual realization of the unattainability of his dream led him to vast disappointment, to a pessimistic and skeptical attitude—"All is vanity."

Rabbi Soloveitchik takes pains to distinguish between a mood and an experience. The depth crisis is not "a *mood* of defeat and forlornness, but . . . an *experience* in which the affirmation is indissolubly bound up with the negation, the thesis with the antithesis." Moods are shallow and uncontemplative emotional reactions, lacking "intellectual insight, intuition of higher values and direction of spiritual energy into the right channels." An experience, on the other hand, is consciously chosen and constructed out of desirable emotions.

Judaism disapproves of all unrestrained affective responses, and instead tries to discipline emotion and convert it into an experience which, in contrast with the mood, is assimilated into one's character and possesses personal value . . . When emotion is raised to the level of experience, we gain the upper hand or control over our own emotions. We acquire the freedom to integrate feelings or to disown them . . . We gather up in our experience those emotions whose worth is meaningful to us, and we reject the feelings which are disjunctive and negating as far as our existential adventure is concerned . . . Freedom of will, according to Judaism, is not limited to external action. Its application extends to the inner life of man. Man freely forms his living experience by selecting ennobling and worthwhile emotions out of a pile of unorganized and amorphous moods, and molds them into a great experience, endowed with constancy and directedness.

Accordingly, Judaism does not value religious moodiness, such as sudden conversion; instead, it views the religious experience as the product of a long inner development. Therefore Judaism does not try to allure man with charming externals, since this would produce merely a fleeting mood.

While moods are subject to the principle of contradiction—e.g., a person cannot feel both a happy and a sad mood at the same time—an experience, when properly constructed, can contain dichotomies. This is what enables the dialectical experience advocated by Judaism. "The experience of life is ambivalent because existence itself abounds in dichotomies and contradictions . . . The existential awareness must not mirror ideal conditions, but everyday realities. Therefore, it should not reflect only one or two of the multiple aspects, but the total adventure of man, which contains both affirmation and negation, triumph and loss."

By maintaining such a perspective, one will be able to subject his emotions to critical review, and perhaps even be strengthened by the contradiction itself. The dialectical experience of the reality of finitude (and the ability to relinquish that accompanies it) can help man cope with both unexpected loss and the paradox of his existence. Furthermore, by not giving himself over wholeheartedly to any earthly good, one can avoid the neurotic anxiety characterizing so much of modern society, brought about by the shaking of one's faith in a limited value to which one had committed himself unreservedly. All bonds are finite, save that between man and God; so long as the latter is maintained, there is hope for man.

A Theory of Emotions

In the previous chapter, Rabbi Soloveitchik asserted that Judaism requires that man control his emotional life, integrating into his personality those emotions he finds worthy and rejecting those he finds unworthy. As we shall soon note, this does not require dampening his emotional responses, but rather approaching them with a critical eye. What are the criteria according to which one should evaluate the worthiness of his emotional responses?

If I love my neighbor, that entails two components: first, an intellectual assertion that there exists a person I call my neighbor; second, a value judgment that this person is worthy of my love. (It is because of this second component that Rabbi Soloveitchik says, "Emotions are the media through which the value-universe opens up to us," thus highlighting the importance of emotions and of the employment of our critical faculties with regard to them.) A worthy and character-building emotion would be one where both the cognitive and the value judgments are accurate; an unworthy and damaging emotion would be one generated by a false perception of reality (e.g., the object of my fear does not really exist) or by a mistaken value judgment (e.g., this person is really not worthy of my friendship). Thus, the worthiness of an emotion is to be assessed not by its intrinsic qualities, but by the context in which it arises.

This leads to the first principle Judaism derives from its broad and dialectical vision of reality. The principle, which Rabbi Soloveitchik calls *the totality of emotional life*, states that we must not absolutize one emotion and disqualify others. Christianity, for instance, declares that it bases itself solely on love, but this curtailment of man's emotional activity both impoverishes human creativity and distorts one's view of the world. Life, according to Judaism, is too rich and multifaceted to be captured by a single emotional response; as the Rav puts it, "A changing destiny cannot be appreciated by an unalterable emotional activity." Hate is sometimes as necessary as love—for example, when the need arises to fight entrenched evil.

The second principle derived from our polar existential awareness—in other words, our perception that man is both majestic and abject, both king and pauper, both capable of self-transcendence and bound by finitude—is the *continuity of our emotional experience*. Primarily, this refers to the fact that, when raised to the plane of critical interpretation, each of our emotional experiences embraces the antithetic state of mind. At this point, it is important to clarify an important distinction. An emotion is one-dimensional: it does not take into account past or future, nor does it incorporate its antithetical feeling. However, the opposite is true of our *emotional awareness*, where we use intellectual tools to subject our emotions to *critical interpretation*, assimilating some and disowning others, and "where one discovers the freedom of self-formation and self-actualization."

As an example, take the by-now-familiar distinction between *aninut* and *avelut*. While *aninut* represents raw emotion, focused only on the present and feeling only pain, *avelut* denotes the critical stage of mourning, and it therefore contains elements of consolation and hope. The latter do not replace grief, but rather interpenetrate with it to form a broader, more integrated experience. The Rav draws similar distinctions between hilarity and joy, and between destructive, one-dimensional guilt and constructive guilt that is linked with faith in one's ability to change. The entire continuum of emotion is especially present in the religious experience, whose objective reference extends to the totality of being.

After distinguishing the Judaic dialectical emotional experience from Freudian ambivalence, Rabbi Soloveitchik also distinguishes it from the Aristotelian Golden Mean. Aristotle wished to keep emotion manageable and bounded; however, this tends "to dampen the emotional expressiveness of man and to dull the richness and iridescent beauty of our affective life." Creative emotion must be overpowering and dynamic, like Isaiah's passion for justice or man's love for God. Judaism wants not a *restrained* but a *critical* emotional experience. We do not stem the onrush of primordial emotions but rather raise them to the plane of critical interpretation, at which they are connected with events beyond the present and with their antithetic emotion. Thus we achieve an integrated experience.

The main reason for Judaism's dialectical approach to emotion is ethical. Feelings focus on oneself: How do I feel about this, what does this mean to me? Judaism believes that emotions must leave their egotistic shell. For example, instead of a young lover becoming totally wrapped up in his beloved and erecting walls between himself and his parents, his love should rather tear down the barriers and enable him to understand how much and how unselfishly his parents love him, and how important his reciprocation is to them. The means to accomplish this is the critical awareness, which shifts emotion into the perspective of one's total life experience and directs a person's attention to the feelings of others. One of several halakhic examples: Joy at a successful harvest should not lead a person to self-centered satisfaction, but rather to a desire to share one's bounty with those less fortunate. Through the critical awareness a person discovers the "other," and emotion is thus ethicized.

"The critical interpretation of our emotional experiences and their ethicization expresses the most uniquely Jewish ethical idea, namely, *hesed*." In Hebrew, *hesed* denotes excess or overflow; when raised to the existential level, this means opening a closed-in existence, or self-transcendence. While the norm of *hesed* is demonstrated first via deeds, it also extends to cultivating an all-inclusive awareness, sharing others' feelings and sharing one's own feelings with others—in other words, expanding one's own existential sphere. Maimonides bases both his theory of education and of prophecy on this notion: the teacher or prophet is impelled by an inner drive to impart his message; his personality is so full that it overflows to others.

However, prior to such reaching out, one must retreat within himself to perfect his personality, contracting his egotistic existence and moving his ego from the center of reality to its periphery. Only then will *hesed* express regard for others and not just self-glorification. This movement of contraction and expansion is "the great ethical drama which the dialectical experience unfolds before us."

* * *

We express our profound appreciation to the TORAS HORAV FOUNDATION for affording us the opportunity to prepare these manuscripts so that a long-awaiting public can gain further understanding and appreciation of the Rav's Torah.

The first stage in preparing the book consisted of deciphering, organizing and ultimately transcribing the Rav's handwritten manuscripts. This task was coordinated by Rabbi Reuven Ziegler, Director of the MeOtzar HoRav Archives, who pieced together the manuscripts, assembled and supervised an able and devoted staff of transcribers and then reviewed all the material. Rabbi Yair Kahn also reviewed a number of the transcriptions against the manuscripts.

To produce this volume, the three editors selected materials from the manuscripts and divided them into chapters and sections. The Rav had not readied these manuscripts for publication, and editing was required. The editors also provided section headings, in some cases titles for the chapters, and finally the title *Out of the Whirlwind* for the collection as a whole. When necessary, they inserted references, furnished transliterations and translations of Hebrew and other foreign-language terms and sources, and, to aid readers' comprehension without interrupting the flow of the material, added synonyms for some technical philosophical terms (generally set off by brackets).

The manuscripts, all undated, were used by the Rav in presenting his public lectures, and in some cases tapes of these presentations are available. Some of the essays in this volume include material added by the Rav in the oral presentation.

These essays show the Rav's ability, as master Torah teacher of his generation, to address with equal effectiveness audiences of differing backgrounds, proclivities, and levels of observance. Rabbi Soloveitchik was a *rosh yeshiva*, the traditional lecturer to advanced students who had a rich background in Talmud and Halakhah. "The Essential Nature of Mourning" was presented from that perspective and represents a distinctive genre of presentation, one to which non-specialists generally do not have access. "*Avelut Yeshanah* and *Avelut Hadashah*," a less complex presentation in that genre, reflects the Rav's interest in maintaining an ongoing relationship with his former students. It was a lecture to the members of the Rabbinical Council of America, then comprised mostly of his former students.

The Rav was also a community rabbi, and "Abraham Mourns Sarah" is taken from his Saturday night *shi'urim* at Maimonides, which were regularly attended by hundreds of university students and community laypersons. It and "The Redemption of Death" represent a different genre, that of *derush*, homiletics, drawing contemporary messages through an examination of biblical themes and texts. *"Aninut* and *Avelut"* is part of a eulogy for the Talner Rebbe *zt"l*, one of the other leading rabbinic personalities in Boston and father of the Rav's son-in-law, Rabbi Yitzhak Twersky *zt"l*.

"A Halakhic Approach to Suffering," "Out of the Whirlwind," "The Crisis of Human Finitude" and "A Theory of Emotions" display yet a different genre, the philosophical discourse, which reached a broad audience that included not only Reform and Conservative rabbis, but Jewish and non-Jewish academics as well, reflecting the fact that the Rav's stature extended well beyond the Orthodox community. This versatility in style and genre testifies to his remarkable pedagogic gifts.

"Aninut and *Avelut"* is taken from Rabbi Soloveitchik's eulogy for the Talner Rebbe, Rabbi Meshulam Zusha Twersky *zt"l*, in 1972. The eulogy was prepared for publication by Rabbi Abraham R. Besdin *z"l*, with corrections and elaborations suggested by Rabbi Soloveitchik. It originally appeared in the *Boston Jewish Advocate* on June 22, 1972, and was reprinted in *Shiurei Harav*, edited by Joseph Epstein and published by *Hamevaser* in 1974 (reissued by Ktav in 1994).

"Avelut Yeshanah and *Avelut Hadashah:* Historical and Individual Mourning" was presented as a lecture to the Rabbinical Council of America on June 25, 1969.

"Abraham Mourns Sarah" is taken from a lecture on *parashat Hayyei Sarah* delivered in Boston on November 5, 1977. It also contains material from a lecture on the same *parashah* on November 25, 1978.

"The Redemption of Death" was presented as part of a lecture on *parashat Hukkat* to the Rabbinical Council of America on June 1, 1974. It contains a number of corrections and elaborations suggested to Rabbi Shalom Carmy by Rabbi Soloveitchik.

"The Essential Nature of Mourning" is a translation, with small modifications, by Joel A. Linsider of a memorial lecture for Rabbi Soloveitchik's father, Rabbi Mosheh Soloveitchik *zt"l*. The Hebrew version appears in volume two of Rabbi Soloveitchik's *Shiurim le-Zekher Abba Mari z"l*, Jerusalem 5745 (1985), pages 182-196.

"A Halakhic Approach to Suffering" was presented at the Symposium on Religion and Mental Health, sponsored by the National Institute of Mental Health, at the Hotel Biltmore in New York City on December 6, 1961.

"Out of the Whirlwind" was presented as a series of lectures between April and June 1960 at the conclusion of the three-year Yeshiva University Mental Health Project.

"The Crisis of Human Finitude" and "A Theory of Emotions," presented between November 1957 and January 1958, are taken from the beginning of the same three-year lecture series entitled "Judaism's Conception of Man." The lecture series was held at the Federation Building in New York City under the sponsorship of the New York Board of Rabbis and the National Institute of Mental Health, and was attended by a small group of Orthodox, Conservative and Reform rabbis. The beginning of this manuscript was missing, and the editors had to reconstruct the first four and a half sentences of "The Crisis of Human Finitude" on the basis of notes and context.

Several rabbis, educators and laypersons were generous in sharing their expertise with us by responding to various queries. It is a pleasure to extend thanks to them here: David Berger, Michael S. Berger, David Billet, Shalom Carmy, Joseph J. Feit, Samuel P. Groner, Warren Zev Harvey, Pinchas Kahn, Abraham Kurtz, Mosheh Lichtenstein, Joel A. Linsider, Bob Sandmeyer, Benjamin Sharfman, Avigdor Shinan, Richard Steiner, Josef Stern, and Avner Taler. Atara Graubard Segal again collaborated on the index. Shifra Schapiro copy-edited the material and made many valuable suggestions. Finally, we are deeply grateful to Rabbi Aharon and Tovah Lichtenstein for their guidance during the editorial process, and for reviewing our work at various stages, including the final manuscript.

David Shatz
Joel B. Wolowelsky
Reuven Ziegler

OUT
OF THE
WHIRLWIND

🐾 *Aninut* and *Avelut*

There are two distinct phases in the process of mourning, and the Halakhah has meticulously insisted upon their strict separation. The first phase begins with the death of the relative for whom one is obliged to mourn and ends with the burial. The second commences with burial and lasts seven, or with regard to some aspects, thirty days. The first we call *aninut*, the second *avelut*. What is the halakhic and the experiential distinction between these two phases of mourning?

Aninut

Aninut represents the spontaneous human reaction to death. It is an outcry, a shout, or a howl of grisly horror and disgust. Man responds to his defeat at the hands of death with total resignation and with an all-consuming, masochistic, self-devastating black despair. Beaten by the fiend, his prayers rejected, enveloped by a hideous darkness, forsaken and lonely, man begins to question his own human singular reality. Doubt develops quickly into a cruel conviction, and doubting man turns into mocking man.

At whom does man mock? At himself. He starts downgrading, denouncing himself. He dehumanizes himself. He arrives at the conclusion that man is not human, that he is just a living creature like the beasts in the field. In a word, man's initial response to death is saturated with malice and ridicule toward himself. He tells himself: If death is the final destiny of all men, if everything human terminates in the narrow, dark grave, then why be a man at all? Then why make the pretense of being the choicest of all creatures? Then why lay claim to singularity and *imago Dei* [the Divine image]? Then why be committed, why carry the human-moral load? Are we not, the mourner continues to question himself, just a band of conceited and inflated daydreamers who somehow manage to convince themselves of some imaginary superiority over the brutes in the jungle?

The Halakhah has displayed great compassion with perplexed, suffering man firmly held in the clutches of his archenemy, death. The Halakhah has never tried to gloss over the sorrowful, ugly spectacle of dying man. In spite of the fact that the Halakhah has indomitable faith in eternal life, in immortality, and in a continued transcendental existence for all human beings, it did understand, like a loving, sympathetic mother, man's fright and confusion when confronted with death. Therefore the Halakhah has tolerated those "crazy," torturing thoughts and doubts. It did not command the mourner to disown them because they contradict the basic halakhic doctrine of man's election as the king of the universe. It permitted the mourner to have his way for a while and has ruled that the latter be relieved of all *mitzvot*.

"One whose dead relative lies before him is exempt from the recital of the *Shema*, and from prayer, and from *tefillin*, and from all the *mitzvot* laid down in the Torah" (Mishnah *Berakhot* 3:1 at 17b). The Jerusalem Talmud (*Berakhot* 3:1), quoted by Tosafot (*Berakhot* 17b), derives this law from the verse in Deuteronomy (16:3): "So that you may remember the day of your departure from the land of Egypt all the days of your life." The commitment accepted in Egypt is applicable to man who is preoccupied with life and not to one who has encountered death.

What is the reason behind this law exempting the mourner from the performance of *mitzvot*? Because our commitment to God is rooted in the awareness of human dignity and sanctity.

Once the perplexed, despairing individual begins to question whether or not such distinctiveness or choiceness exists, the whole commitment expires. Man who has faith in himself, who is aware of his charisma, was chosen and burdened with obligations and commandments. Despairing, skeptical man was not elected. How can man pray and address himself to God if he doubts his very humanity, if speech is stripped by his doubts of its human characteristics and turned into mere physical sound? How can the mourner pronounce a benediction or say "amen" if he is "speechless"? He is still capable of producing sounds, but a benediction consists of spiritual words and not just of physical sounds.

In a word, the motto of *aninut* is to be found in the old pessimistic verse in the book of Ecclesiastes (3:19): "So that man has no preeminence over the beast, for all is vanity."

Avelut

At this point, the dialectical Halakhah, which has masterfully employed both the thesis and the antithesis in her treatment of antinomies, makes an about-face. The Halakhah is firmly convinced that man is free and that he is master not only of his deeds but of his emotions as well. The Halakhah holds the view that man's mastery of his emotional life is unqualified and that he is capable of changing thought patterns, emotional structures and experiential motifs within an infinitesimal period of time.

Man, the Halakhah maintains, does not have to wait patiently for one mood to pass and for another to emerge gradually. He disengages himself, quickly and actively, and in a wink replaces a disjunctive frame of mind with a cathartic-redemptive one. Hence, the Halakhah, which showed so much tolerance for the mourner during the stage of *aninut*, and let him float with the tide of black despair, now—forcefully and with a shift of emphasis—commands him that, with interment, the first phase of grief comes abruptly to a close and a second phase—that of *avelut*—begins.

With the commencement of *avelut*, the Halakhah commands the mourner to undertake a heroic task: to start picking up the debris of his own shattered personality and to reestablish himself as man, restoring lost glory, dignity and uniqueness. Instead of repeating to himself time and again that man has no preeminence over the beast and that all is vanity, he is suddenly told by the Halakhah to be mindful of the antithesis: "Thou hast chosen man at the very inception and Thou hast recognized him as worthy of standing before Thee" (Yom Kippur *Ne'ilah Amidah*).

Yes, the Halakhah tells man, death is indeed something ugly and frightening, something grisly and monstrous; yes, death is trailing behind every man, trying to defeat him, his ambitions and aspirations; all that is true. Nevertheless, the Halakhah adds, death must not confuse man; the latter must not plunge into total darkness because of death. On the contrary, the Halakhah asserts, death gives man the opportunity to display greatness and to act heroically, to build even though he knows that he will not live to enjoy the sight of the magnificent edifice in whose construction he is engaged, to plant even though he does not expect to eat the fruit, to explore, to develop, to enrich—not himself, but coming generations.

Death teaches man to transcend his physical self and to identify with the timeless covenantal community. Death, the Halakhah warns the mourner, not only does not free man from his commitment but, on the contrary, enhances his role as a historic being and sensitizes his moral consciousness. The day is short, the workload is heavy, the Master is strict and demanding (cf. *Avot* 2:20), and the commitment therefore is great.

Before burial, in the stage of *aninut,* man mourned in total darkness and confusion, and his grief expressed itself in an act of resignation from his greatness and chosenness. After burial, in stage two, man mourns in an enlightened mood, and his grief asserts itself in the awareness of human greatness and human election.

The ceremonial turning point at which *aninut* is transformed into *avelut,* despair into intelligent sadness, and self-negation into self-affirmation, is to be found in the recital of *Kaddish* at the grave.

The *Kaddish* marks the beginning of a new phase of courageous and heroic mourning to which the message of salvation is addressed. What is the relationship between the proclamation of the solemn doxology and burial? Through the *Kaddish* we hurl defiance at death and its fiendish conspiracy against man. When the mourner recites "Glorified and sanctified be the Great Name . . . ," he declares: No matter how powerful death is, notwithstanding the ugly end of man, however terrifying the grave is, however nonsensical and absurd everything appears, no matter how black one's despair is and how nauseating an affair life is, we declare and profess publicly and solemnly that we are not giving up, that we are not surrendering, that we will carry on the work of our ancestors as though nothing has happened, that we will not be satisfied with less than the full realization of the ultimate goal—the establishment of God's kingdom, the resurrection of the dead, and eternal life for man.

Teshuvah

A question arises: What is the experiential substance of *avelut* in this second phase? The latter is intrinsically an experience of *teshuvah,* of repentance. The aching heart is a contrite heart, and a contrite heart is, of course, an atoning heart. Enlightened *avelut* contains a feeling of guilt. In fact, the laws concerning the observance of *shiv'ah*, the seven-day period of mourning, express not only a mood of grieving but also, and perhaps mainly, a mood of repenting. Quite a few of the injunctions governing the observance of *shiv'ah*, such as the prohibitions against washing, the use of cosmetics and ointments, wearing shoes, and sex life, are reminiscent of Yom Kippur. Somehow, we arrive at a strange equation: The act of mourning equals the act of expiation. The Halakhah commands the mourner to expiate his guilt by observing those prescribed rites which are also observed on the Holy Day of Atonement when man is questing for forgiveness.

What is the feeling of guilt which is implied in *avelut* and with which the Halakhah is concerned?

First, death *per se* is a consequence of sin or human imperfection. If man were perfect, if the ultimate moral law were within his reach, if he had not fallen away from his Maker, man could combat death. As a matter of fact, we do believe that in the eschatological world where man will attain absolute perfection, death will finally be defeated. The equation of mourning and repentance is expressed in the passage in Tractate *Mo'ed Katan* (15a-b): "A mourner is bound to overturn his bed, because Bar Kappara taught: 'God says: I have set the likeness of My image in them, and through their sins have I upset it. Let your beds be overturned on account of this.'" The passage becomes intelligible if we take into consideration that according to talmudic and midrashic symbolic semantics the term *mittah*—couch or bed—represents man as parent and teacher, as link between past and future, at both a natural and a spiritual level. If man fails to discharge his twofold duty, his image is tarnished and death follows. The overturned couch represents a desecrated image of man, and the mourning rites represent an act of expiation.

Second, the aspect of guilt is interwoven into the human time-consciousness. Man is a tragic as well as a comic figure in a variety of ways. However, his peculiar way of forming value judgments is the saddest of all his experiences and at the same time the most ludicrous of all his comical performances.

Man is always a latecomer as far as the formation of value judgments is concerned. His axiology [value system] or appreciation of persons, things and events is always a product of hindsight. In retrospection man discovers the precise value of something which, or somebody who, was but is no longer with us. This kind of tardiness in understanding and appreciating is tragic as well as comic. While the somebody was near, while I could communicate with the somebody, I was unaware of him, as if he were nobody. He comes into existence and turns into somebody important and precious at the very moment he departs from me and is lost in the mist of remoteness. Only after he has gone do I begin to ask: Who was he? What did he mean to me?

All these questions which descend in droves upon the grieving, expiating individual are extremely painful, since they are saturated with a feeling of guilt. One torturing, cruel question stands out: Why didn't I ask all these questions yesterday while the somebody was still here? The Talmud tells a strange story:

> Rav died. His disciples followed his bier. On their trip back home they stopped and ate a meal by the River Danak. When they were about to say Grace, they became involved in a question which they could not resolve. Whereupon Rav Adda bar Ahabah rose and made a second tear in his garment, which he had already torn once, and he said: "Rav is dead and we have not learned even the rules about Grace" (*Berakhot* 42b).

They discovered the greatness of their master and the degree of their dependence on him on the day on which they buried him.

How sad and how ironic! They studied under him, he trained their minds, fashioned their outlook, and opened up to them new worlds of thought, and yet he remained unknown to them. They all looked upon him as "the Great Master of the Diaspora," and they all admired and revered him, and yet even they failed to see Rav's real stature and his full greatness until he had vanished from their midst.

This tragic as well as comic aspect of man is often the source of sin. The latter is precipitated by human harshness and insensitivity to the Divine presence. Man does not feel the secret vigor, joy and bliss that flow spontaneously from God's nearness. Man is unaware of God's working and acting through him while God uses him as the instrument of His will. Consequently, man sins; God departs and leaves man alone. Only then does lonely man comprehend the magnitude of his loss and nostalgically reach out for God. However, by the time man decides to turn to God, God is gone and man has nobody to turn to. All he finds then is an empty space and a mechanical, indifferent world. "From afar the Lord appeareth unto me" (Jer. 31:2). God becomes visible to man only from a distance, not when God wants to be really close to man. God allures and fascinates man from the infinite, uncharted lanes of the beyond, not while God is ready to be in immediate, intimate contact with him.

Many a time the Bible, while telling us about sin, adds significantly either "and it came to pass on the morrow" or "early next morning." Only on the morrow, following the night of insensitivity and hardness to God, does man begin to value Divine comradeship and friendship, the happiness which he could have enjoyed if he had opened up his heart to God just a few seconds prior to God's departure.

Avelut during *shiv'ah* or *sheloshim*, which ends on the thirtieth day after burial, is an act of atonement or expiation for both these sins, for man's insensitivity *vis-à-vis* God and *vis-à-vis* his fellow man, for not having realized who they were until they were gone.

During the mourning stage we ask the questions we should have asked before: Who was he? Whom did we lose? His image fascinates us from afar, and we ask with guilt and regret the questions that are now overdue, the questions to which only our lives can provide the answers.

❧ *Avelut Yeshanah* and *Avelut Hadashah:* Historical and Individual Mourning

Man and His Emotional World

I would like to try in this presentation to interpret the halakhic terms and concepts that relate to mourning in philosophical and also, perhaps, psychological categories. I want to try to derive from dry, formal, abstract terms experiential materials which can be utilized in formulating an understanding of Judaism's view of the mourning experience. People speak about religious experiences today, trying to stimulate religious experiences with drugs or all kinds of acrobatics while actually engaging in idolatrous practices. But one cannot get a religious experience—that is, a Jewish religious experience—without utilizing the materials of Halakhah. There can be no philosophy of science or nature unless one is an expert in the fields of physics, chemistry and biology, the sciences of animate and inanimate objects. So, too, it is impossible for one to philosophize about Judaism and speak about its experiential universe without having the Halakhah at his fingertips. I am suggesting a modest experiment here: to try to translate a halakhic discussion into the idiom of modern man without doing any harm or inflicting any damages, without restricting or limiting the depth and the sweep of Halakhah.

The whole concept of *avelut*, mourning, at both an individual and a historical level, is nurtured by a unique doctrine about man and his emotional world. It actually represents, I would say, the Judaic philosophy of man and his relationship to both God and the world. Man, Judaism maintains and insists, is capable of determining the kind of emotional life he wants to live. Man has both actions and emotions at his disposal. Man must never be overwhelmed by his emotions. He can invite emotions as well as reject them, opening the door and inviting feelings and sentiments if they are worthy, and slamming the door on those which are degrading and unworthy of attention. In the same manner in which man has the freedom to abstain from engaging in an act to which his conscience objects on moral grounds, he can also disown emotions which the same conscience assesses as unworthy of being integrated into his personality. Likewise, he can assimilate such emotions which bear the stamp of moral approval—constructive noble feelings.

Emotions can be subjected to the scrutiny of our moral consciousness, examined and evaluated as to whether they are worthy and dignified ones which enrich, redeem and exalt man's life. Bahya ibn Pakuda wrote a famous book called *Hovot ha-Levavot*, in which he discriminates between *hovot ha-evarim*, the duties of our limbs, and *hovot ha-levavot*, the duties of the heart. But how can one speak about *hovot ha-levavot* if the heart succumbs hysterically to emotions, such as love for a person, object, goal or idea which is in reality unworthy of one's love and appreciation?

Actually, many precepts in the Torah deal exclusively with human emotional attitudes and not physical actions: "Love your neighbor" (Lev. 19:18), "You shall not covet" (Ex. 20:14, Deut. 5:18), "You shall rejoice on your holiday" (Deut. 16:14), "You shall not hate your brother" (Lev. 19:17), "You shall love the stranger" (Deut. 10:19), etc. We all know the question which Ibn Ezra raised *vis-à-vis* the command of *lo tahmod*, not to covet the property of one's neighbor. Coveting is an emotion, a feeling. How then can one be commanded to not covet, desire, or be envious? But in truth one can be called upon to exclude an emotion in the same way one must abstain from a certain act which is considered unworthy. Ibn Ezra (in his commentary to Ex. 20:14) introduces a famous fable or simile. The ignorant peasant, he says, will never desire or fall in love with the daughter of the king, the princess. Ibn Ezra wants to show that emotions are guided by human reason. One desires only what is possible; whatever is impossible is not desired. Pascal spoke about the *logique de couer*, the reasons of the heart (*Pensees* #277). The freedom to adopt and accept emotions or to reject and disown them is within the jurisdiction of man.

Avelut and the Control of Emotions

The precept of *avelut*, as I indicated above, rests completely upon this Jewish doctrine of human freedom from emotional coercion. However, man's task *vis-à-vis avelut* is not always the same. At times man is told to respond emotionally to disaster, to yield to the emotional hurricane and not master his feelings. He must not take evil as something inevitable, which warrants no emotional outburst, just because such a response would be an exercise in futility.

Judaism says with admirable realism: Of course every event, good or bad, is planned by the Almighty. So too is death. Man can do little to change the course of events; he rather must surrender to God's inscrutable will. Yet submission to a higher will must not prevent man from experiencing those emotions which are precipitated by a confrontation with existential absurdity, with the total disregard for and complete indifference to human interests manifested, *prima facie*, by natural law.

Judaism does not want man to rationalize evil or to theologize it away. It challenges him to defy evil and, in case of defeat, to give vent to his distress. Both rationalizing and theologizing harden the human heart and make it insensitive to disaster. Man, Judaism says, must act like a human being. He must cry, weep, despair, grieve and mourn as if he could change the cosmic laws by exhibiting those emotions. In times of distress and sorrow, these emotions are noble even though they express the human protest against iniquity in nature and also pose an unanswerable question concerning justice in the world. The Book of Job was not written in vain. Judaism does not tolerate hypocrisy and unnatural behavior which is contrary to human sensitivity. Pain results in moaning, sudden fear and shrieking. The encounter with death must precipitate a showing of protest, a bitter complaint, a sense of existential nausea and complete confusion. I want the sufferer to act as a human being, God says. Let him not suppress his humanity in order to please Me. Let him tear his clothes in frustrating anger and stop observing *mitzvot* because his whole personality is enveloped by dark despair and finds itself in a trance of the senses and of the faculties. Let him cry and shout, for he must act like a human being.

The Mishnah relieved the mourner who has not buried his dead "from the recital of the *Shema* . . . and from all the [positive] *mitzvot* laid down in the Torah" (*Berakhot* 3:1 at 17b). Rashi (s.v. *patur*) says that the reason is that a person who is engaged in performing one *mitzvah* is exempt at that time from other *mitzvot*. But Tosafot (s.v. *patur*), quoting R. Bon in the Jerusalem Talmud (3:1), disagree, saying that the reason is that "the Torah says '. . . that you may remember the day of your departure from the land of Egypt all the days of your life'—days during which you are concerned with the living, not those days during which you are concerned with the dead." That means that the mourner is relieved of his obligation in *mitzvot* because he is incapable of performing them. He has simply lost his own sense of dignity; the focus of his personality has been lost. He is like a *heresh, shoteh ve-katan,* the deaf-mute, imbecile and minor who are all exempt from *mitzvot.* This is what Tosafot and all the *rishonim* [medieval halakhic authorities] mean when they say that it is completely forbidden to perform a *mitzvah* during this first stage of mourning: the mourner is incapable of performing *mitzvot.* Judaism understands that bitterness, grief and confusion are noble emotions which should be assimilated and accepted by man, not rejected at the time of distress. Of course, emotions, like the tide, reach a high mark, make an about face, and begin to recede. The Torah has therefore recommended to man not only to submit himself to the emotional onslaught, but gradually and slowly to redeem himself from its impact.

Therefore, the Halakhah divided mourning into various stages: First, "*meto muttal lefanav,* when his dead lies before him." This is the period of *aninut,* extending from the time of death until the time of burial. Then, commencing with burial, *avelut shiv'ah,* the week-long period, which extends into *sheloshim,* the thirty-day period. Finally, for one's parents, *yod-bet hodesh,* the twelve-month mourning period. We have during these stages an imperceptible transition from a depressed, desolate, bitter consciousness of catastrophe to a redeemed higher consciousness.

Two Types of Mourning

The *Gemara* (*Yevamot* 43b) distinguishes between *avelut hadashah* and *avelut yeshanah,* "new" mourning and "old," historical mourning—or, expressing the same thought in a different idiom, between *avelut de-yahid* and *avelut de-rabbim,* private and national-communal mourning. The first, *avelut hadashah,* is caused by a death or disaster which strikes a family or an individual. It is a primordial, instinctual, spontaneous response of man to evil, to the traumatic confrontation with death, to the impact of catastrophe and disaster. It is an existential response, not one that evolves by the application of artificial stimuli.

The second category, *avelut yeshanah,* is due to a historic disaster that took place 1,900 years ago. This category is the handiwork of man. There is no spontaneous reaction to some new event which has just transpired, for nothing new has happened which should justify grief. The *avelut* is a result of recollection of events. Judaism here introduced a strange kind of memory, a very unique and singular memory. Thousands of years later, Henri Bergson (*Matter and Memory*) came very close to describing the kind of memory of which Judaism spoke so long ago.

A Unitive Time Experience

Judaism developed a very peculiar philosophy of memory—indeed, an ethics of memory. Memory and forgetfulness are subject to ethical determination. Memory is not just the capacity of man to know events which lie in the past. Memory is experiential in nature; one does not simply recollect the past or just remember bygones, but reexperiences that which has been, and quickens events that are seemingly dead.

Many *mitzvot* are based upon this idea. The Passover *seder* is, of course, the prime example: "In each generation a person is required to see himself as if he had gone out of Egypt" (Haggadah). So too is *keri'at ha-Torah,* the institution of the public reading of the Torah, which is not simply *limmud*—study and instruction—but an experiential event meant to restage and re-enact *mattan Torah*, the giving of the Torah. The proof of this is to be found in the use of the *ta'amei elyon*, the special cantillation (*trope*) used for the public reading of the *Aseret ha-*

Dibberot (Decalogue). These *ta'amei elyon* combine together the units of the Decalogue in its reading, rather than separating them into the actual verses. But the division would be determined by the verses if instruction were the sole purpose of *keri'at ha-Torah*.

This shows that actually the reading of the *Aseret ha-Dibberot* is not only a didactic performance of *limmud*, but a restaging, a dramatic reenacting of *mattan Torah*. That is why people rise when it is read. Rambam asked in his responsum (no. 263, Blau ed.), Why should they rise? *Aseret ha-Dibberot* is no more sacred than the *parashah* which speaks of Timnah, the concubine of Elifaz (Gen. 36:12)! But the *Aseret ha-Dibberot* is read not only as a text which is being studied, but as a text which is being promulgated and proclaimed by God Himself.

When Rambam speaks about the obligation of *Hakhel*, the public reading of the Torah performed by the king in Jerusalem every seven years, he writes that the king is the representative of the *kahal*, the congregation, and the entire *kahal* must pay close attention to the *keri'at ha-Torah*. Even the wise and great, as well as converts who do not understand the Hebrew text, must concentrate and hearken with dread and trepidation in the same manner as the Jews hearkened to the words of God when the Torah was given at Sinai—as if the law were being proclaimed now for the first time, as if the person were hearing it from the Almighty, listening to the voice of God Himself (*Hilkhot Hagigah* 3:6). Rambam actually has spelled it out in plain terms. The rubric of "In each generation a person is required to see himself as if he had gone out of Egypt" is applicable not only to the Exodus, but to all events which the Torah has commanded us to remember and not forget.

Experiential memory somehow erases the borderline separating bygone from present experiences. It does not just recollect the past, but *reexperiences* whatever has been. It quickens events which man considered dead and it actually merges past with present—or shifts the past into the present. Judaism has

recommended what I would call a "unitive time consciousness"—unitive in the sense that there is a tightening of bonds of
companionship, of present and past.

Many modern experiences can be understood only if we look
upon them from the viewpoint of the unitive time awareness.
Our relationship to the Land of Israel is very strange. After a
gap of 1900 years, our relationship is a very weak one in historical terms. I have no doubt that had a Jewish state arisen in
Africa or South America, Jews would not feel so committed or
dedicated to it. Our commitment is not to the state *per se*, but to
Eretz Yisrael, the Land of Israel. This is because of our very distant and remote experiences, which usually would have vanished into oblivion over the years.

Since Jews have a unitive time consciousness, the gap of
centuries simply cannot separate them from the past. They do
not have to relive the past, as the past is a current living reality. Memory opens up new vistas of the time experience, and the
companionship of the present and past is tightened, growing in
intimacy and closeness. As a matter of fact, our relationship to
our heroes—such as Rabbi Akiva and Rabbi Yohanan ben
Zakkai, or even the Patriarchs and the Prophets—is completely
different from that which the nations of the world have to their
heroes. To us, they are not just ancient heroes. Usually history
is divided into antiquity, the Middle Ages, and the contemporary
period. However, the word "antiquity" does not exist in our history. The story of Joseph and his brothers, the story of the
destruction of the Temple, the story of Moses' death—all used to
move me to tears as a boy. It was not just because I was a child;
it was not an infantile reaction on my part. It was very much a
human *gestalt* reaction. These stories do not lie in antiquity;
they are part of our time awareness, part of our historical experience. Similarly, there is no archaeology in Judaism. There is
history but not archaeology. Archaeology refers to something
remote, a dead past of which I am no part. It arouses my curiosity; I am inquisitive to know about the origins. But history to us

means something living, past integrated into present and present anticipating future.

We all know the aphorism, "*He-avar ayyin* (the past is no more), *ve-he-atid adayyin* (the future has not yet come), *ve-ha-hoveh ke-heref ayin* (the present is fleeting)." However, in my opinion this is wrong. The past is not gone; it is still here. The future is not only anticipated, it is already here, and the present connects the future and the past. That is what I mean by a unitive time consciousness.

Tish'ah be-Av, the Ninth of Av, would be a ludicrous institution if we did not have the unitive time consciousness. We say in the *Kinnot*, "On this night, *be-leil zeh*, my Temple was destroyed." "This night" means a night 1900 years ago; "*be-leil zeh*" means tonight. Apparently, that night nineteen hundred years ago is neither remote nor distant from us; it is living—as vibrant a reality as this fleeting moment in the present. The unitive time consciousness contains an element of eternity. There is neither past nor future nor present. All three dimensions of time merge into one experience, into one awareness. Man, heading in a panicky rush toward the future, finds himself in the embrace of the past. Bygones turn into facts, pale memories into living experiences and archaeological history into a vibrant reality.

Of course, historical mourning is based upon this unitive time consciousness. Without that experiential memory it would be ridiculous to speak of mourning due to an event which lies in antiquity. It would be contrary to human nature. *Avelut hadashah* is a spontaneous response—neither premeditated nor planned—to the sudden attack or onslaught of evil, catastrophe, disaster or death. *Avelut yeshanah* is cultivated, gradually evolving through recollection and through the unitive time awareness. The main distinction between these two types of mourning expresses itself in the reversal of the order of the stages. *Avelut hadashah* commences with the most intense, most poignant and highest state of grief—*aninut*—and slowly recedes into *shiv'ah, sheloshim* and *yod-bet hodesh*, until it fades into a lingering melancholy. *Avelut yeshanah* follows a reverse course. It starts out with *avelut* of *yod-bet hodesh*, the mildest form of mourning, which represents a sadness that is usually non-conative and non-explosive. It gradually turns into *avelut sheloshim* and grows in intensity until it reaches the pitch of *shiv'ah*.

The Three Weeks

Although R. Moshe Isserles (*Shulhan Arukh Orah Hayyim* 551:2,4) rules that the minimum mourning preceding *Tish'ah be-Av* commences on the Seventeenth of Tammuz, R. Joseph Karo (ibid., 551:1) rules that it commences only on *Rosh Hodesh Av*, the first day of the month of Av: "When Av begins we lessen our happiness." Does that mean that the whole idea of *bein ha-metzarim*, the three weeks before *Tish'ah be-Av*, is not of halakhic origin? If it is, in what does it express itself? What are the prohibitions which the Seventeenth of Tammuz initiates?

In fact, the Talmud does not mention *bein ha-metzarim* at all. The Midrash refers to the period in its interpretation of Lamentations 1:3: "'. . . all her persecutors overtook her *bein ha-metzarim*, within the straits'—these are the days between the Seventeenth of Tammuz and *Tish'ah be-Av*" (*Eikhah Rabbah* 1:29). Interestingly, the Yerushalmi (end of *Ta'anit* 4:5) says that if the walls of Jerusalem in the time of the First Temple were breached on the ninth of Tammuz instead of the seventeenth, as occurred in the time of the Second Temple, then the date of the destruction of the First Temple must have been the first of Av; the interim period consists of only twenty-one days. The Yerushalmi derives this from the verse, "I see a rod of an almond tree" (Jer. 1:11): it takes the almond tree twenty-one days to blossom and bud. Yet all this does not answer our question: Does this interim period of three weeks have halakhic significance?

The key to the answer is to be found in the fact that during these three weeks we suspend the recital of the *haftarot* which are concerned with the same motif as the weekly Torah reading and read instead the *sheloshah de-pur'anuta*, the three chapters from Jeremiah and Isaiah which speak of destruction and exile. Apparently, we consider the theme of catastrophe and *hurban* (destruction) to be *me-inyana de-yoma*, "from the topics of the day." Otherwise, the elaboration of such a theme in the *haftarah* would be out of context. In other words, halakhically, the twenty-one days are linked up with *hurban* and *avelut*.

Even though the mourning of an individual constitutes a *kiyyum she-ba-lev*, an inner, experiential fulfillment of the obligation to mourn, it must be translated into deeds, into technical observance. The inner experience cannot be divorced from objective aspects. The Halakhah demanded that feeling be transposed into deed, subjective emotions into solid objective data, that fleeting, amorphous moods be crystallized into real tangible symbols. The individual does not invite sorrow; the latter strikes him hard and mercilessly. His immediate response is a dual one—subjective and objective. He reacts to disaster with everything he has at his command—thought and deed, feeling and action.

Avelut yeshanah does not establish itself at one bang; the process is generally slow. It begins with the awakening of the unitive time awareness of a memory which not only notes and gives heed to bygone days but also reexperiences, relives, restages and redramatizes remote events which seem to have forfeited their relevance long ago. The Halakhah could not decree observance of mourning at once. The reawakening takes time; it transpires gradually. It would be absurd, therefore, to start out with the practical observance of mourning before the experience has been reproduced and relived in all its tragic, frightening magnitude. The time between the Seventeenth of Tammuz and *Rosh Hodesh Av* is exclusively devoted to remembrance, to meditation, to reliving and reexperiencing. Only on

Rosh Hodesh Av does the *avelut she-ba-lev* begin to be recorded on the register of objective mourning and the first signs of observance become visible.

When Av Begins

The period of mourning for the Temple which parallels that of the twelve-month period of mourning for one's parents begins on the first day of the month of Av. Both share the avoidance of participation in any festive events, receptions, and so forth. The mishnah (*Ta'anit* 1:7) states in general terms that "When Av begins we lessen our happiness." The *baraita* says as follows:

> From the first day of the month until the fast, *ha-am mema'atim*, the people must restrict their activities in trade, building and planting, betrothals and marriages. During the week in which the ninth of Av occurs, it is *asur*, forbidden, to cut one's hair and wash one's clothes (*Yevamot* 43b).

When the *baraita* spoke of *Rosh Hodesh Av*, it used the term *mema'atim*, whereas within the week in which *Tish'ah be-Av* falls, the term *asur* was used. Why this change in terminology? Apparently, there is a basic difference between the *avelut* which commences with *Rosh Hodesh Av* and that of the week in which *Tish'ah be-Av* falls. If one violated the law pertaining to the mourning of the latter, he or she has committed a *ma'aseh averah*, an illicit act which itself is culpable and is considered to be sin—like a mourner who failed to observe the laws of mourning. However, in the days preceding the week, there are separate injunctions against certain activities. The *baraita* did not speak of *issurim*, of prohibitions. The positive aspect, not the negative, was formulated. If one abstains from all those pursuits, as suggested in the *baraita*, the result is a *kiyyum avelut*, a fulfillment of the obligation to mourn. However, the failure to comply results not in a commission of a sin, but in a forfeiture of a *kiyyum mitzvah* and the guilt of *shev ve-al ta'aseh*, of an omission.

The positive aspect is emphasized—it is important to withdraw temporarily from those activities: "The people must restrict their activities in trade, building and planting, betrothals and marriages." The term *avelut* is not employed. As a matter of fact, the *baraita* speaks of reducing, of doing less. If a prohibition were attached to such activities, the amount and volume of business and construction would not matter at all. This type of work is either prohibited or sanctioned; the amount, how much, would not be an important factor. However, if the activity *per se* is not culpable, then only the *avelut she-ba-lev* is robbed of an opportunity to express itself in deed. Partial abstention is also important because through it *avelut she-ba-lev* is realized and consummated. If this be true, even restricted activity is relevant.

Maimonides omitted the *baraita* in *Yevamot* from his Code. He quoted *(Hilkhot Ta'anit* 5:6) only the mishnah in *Ta'anit*: "When Av begins we lessen our happiness." He did not, however, specify or enumerate the forbidden activities; *per se* they are legitimate. They serve only as media through which the mourning expresses itself. Hence, the *kiyyum avelut she-ba-lev*, the fulfillment of inner mourning, can also be realized through other means and by abstaining from such activities which usually please the doer and give him a certain amount of contentment. In fact, the *baraita* says "*ha-am*, the people"—those activities which have been classified by the people as joyous. However, they are not the only ones from which one must refrain. Any engagement which results in joy and satisfaction is to be avoided. That is why Rambam omitted those specific pursuits. They are not the only ones which come under the rubric of *simhah*, of happiness. There is no objective criterion; the choice is subjective and varies with the times.

The Week of Tish'ah be-Av

Shavua she-hal bo, the week during which *Tish'ah be-Av* falls, corresponds to *sheloshim*, the thirty-day mourning period, as both include the prohibitions of cutting one's hair (*tisporet*) and pressing one's clothes (*gihutz*). The two periods differ, however, with regard to three other specific actions, washing one's clothes (*kibbus*), commerce (*massa u-mattan*), and betrothals (*erusin*), as the *Gemara* (*Yevamot* 43a) discusses.

Washing one's clothes and commerce are prohibited in the week before *Tish'ah be-Av* and permitted during *sheloshim*, while betrothal is handled in the opposite manner: betrothals are permissible during the week of *Tish'ah be-Av* and forbidden, according to Ri and Ramban (*Yevamot* 43b, s.v. *shanei*), during *sheloshim*.

This distinction can be explained by the fact that there is one aspect of historical public mourning that has almost no application to personal mourning, namely, *heseah ha-da'at*, any distraction or diversion of attention. The content of *avelut she-ba-lev*— the inner mourning of the heart—for an individual grieving over the loss of a member of the household expresses itself in sharp unbearable pain, black despair and bitter protest against evil and absurdity in the universe. One has the impression that God has absented Himself from human destiny and delivered man into the hands of laughing Satan. In a word, *avelut she-ba-lev* expresses itself in the experience of the dark night.

With communal mourning, however, no matter how imaginative the person, and no matter how powerful his intuitive time awareness and experiential memory, the pain is not as severe as in the case of recent disaster, the grief not as sharp and distressing as in the private encounter with death. Since there is no sudden plunge into the night of mourning, the emotional loss is not complete. However alive the experience of *hurban* (destruction) might be, it is nurtured by human reflection and meditation. It is the intellect which commands the emotions to respond to the historical memories of a community. The emotions are aroused not spontaneously but rather by meditation and concentration. They do not explode under the impact of disaster; they are just lit by the fire which memory brought forth. It is measured pain, rational grief, whose cause lies outside of the emotional sphere. Any distraction, any diversion of attention, any *heseah ha-da'at* breaks up the *avelut*.

That is why the mourning of the week in which *Tish'ah be-Av* falls revolves around the concept of *heseah ha-da'at*. Whatever may cause diversion or dissipation of emotional tension has been prohibited. Engaging in commerce is a steady occupation. If you engage in commerce for only a quarter of an hour each day, you'll go bankrupt—just as you cannot become a scholar by studying only fifteen minutes a day. In addition, as Tosafot note (*Yevamot* 43b, s.v. *shanei*), commerce is done publicly, so people will say that the community does not care about the destruction of Jerusalem. The same reasoning is also applicable to washing one's clothes. In olden times, washing one's clothes meant continuous public work at the river. *Avelut yeshanah* is stricter with those matters which are public and continuous.

On the other hand, *heseah ha-da'at* plays no role in the personal encounter with individual grief, because intellectual concentration or even emotional fixation are not responsible for the emergence of the mourning. The latter leaps out of nowhere, it befalls, overpowers and breaks man—unexpectedly and completely. In fact, the mourner cannot concentrate and is unable to relax or to think of something else. He cannot think or rationalize at all because he loses the focus of his personality, and his inner life, including his intellectual capacity, is in disarray. The prohibitions pertaining to private mourning are concerned not with the possibility of *heseah ha-da'at* but with different aspects such as untidiness (*nivvul*), feeling pain *(tza'ar)*, etc.

The prohibition of betrothal (an act which requires only two witnesses and is therefore not considered public) is not rooted in *heseah ha-da'at.* The private mourner is enjoined from betrothal for a different reason entirely, namely, the apparant worthlessness of life and its irrational, absurd vicissitudes. There is no need to engage in any act which is related to the survival and continued existence of man. He is not worth the effort he himself makes in order to assure his survival. This prohibition is symbolic of the experience of human failure and full bankruptcy through which one lives during the days of mourning.

Matrimony is in fact related to the bitter human destiny which ends in death. There is no doubt that the procreative urge in man reflects his anxiety over and fear of death. In the child he finds continuity and immortality. He sees himself redeemed from the curse of nihility by continuing to live through the child. However, when man reaches the state of resignation and utter insensibility, when he finds himself in a stage of total deprivation, when everything that used to matter is not worth one's attention—then the urge to live and to persevere and to defeat evil vanishes. That is the foundation of the prohibition of betrothal.

In light of the above, we understand yet another distinction between *avelut de-rabbim* and *avelut de-yahid*: that which involves white and colored clothes. Maimonides writes, "Just as it is forbidden for a mourner to wash his clothes, so too it is forbidden to wear white, new ironed, clothing, etc. . . ." (*Hilkhot Avel* 5:3). Maimonides limits the prohibition of wearing new clothes to white ones. However, in his *Hilkhot Ta'aniyyot* 5:6, he did not distinguish between white and colored clothes. The answer again is the same. The prohibition of washing one's clothes and wearing newly ironed ones during the week of *avelut de-yahid* is motivated by the law of untidiness, the requirement that grief should express itself in the neglect of one's appearance, in carelessness as to dress—and a distinction between colored and white clothes is relevant.

The identification of *avelut* with untidiness is an outgrowth of the traumatic experience of death as destroying human distinction and chosenness, as testimony to the pessimistic statement, "Man has no preeminence over the beast" (Eccl. 3:19). Neatness in dress and appearance is inseparably associated with the dignity of man who was created in the image of God. Man bears a resemblance to God, a likeness to Him, and therefore cleanliness, tidiness and neatness are worthwhile qualities. When his disciples asked Hillel where he was going, he answered that he was going to perform a *mitzvah*, for he was on his way to the baths (*Lev. Rabbah* 34:3). One serves God by respecting his own personality and observing *kevod ha-beriyyot*, human dignity. Therefore, after one's encounter with death, which erases human dignity and leaves man deprived of all those traits, the grief over the loss of humanity manifests itself in a state of neglect in appearance, dress, etc.

All this cannot fit into the whole context of historical grief; the *hurban* did not deprive us of our dignity. What we are worried about is *heseah ha-da'at*, that the mind should not be distracted, that the passional meditation about the historical destiny of our people—about its past and future—not be discontinued. As far as this aspect is concerned, there is no difference between white and colored clothes; the activity was forbidden, the color matters not at all. Thus in *Hilkhot Ta'aniyyot* 5:6, Maimonides does not distinguish between colored and white clothes in noting the prohibition of washing and wearing them during the period of *avelut de-rabbim*.

Tish'ah be-Av

The mourning of *Tish'ah be-Av* itself is like that of *shiv'ah*. The *baraita* says, "All the restrictions which are *noheg* (observed) during *shiv'ah* are observed on *Tish'ah be-Av*" (*Ta'anit* 30a). "All" should not be taken literally, as there are a number of basic distinctions between the two. First, according to the *Gemara* (*Mo'ed Katan* 15a), the mourner does not put on *tefillin* on the first day, while we do don *tefillin* on *Tish'ah be-Av*.

(In this connection there is no significance to the fact that we postpone putting on *tefillin* until the afternoon. Apparently, our view is that putting on *tefillin* is obligatory on *Tish'ah be-Av*.)

We all know Rambam's view in *Hilkhot Avel* 1:1 that the first day of *avelut* is biblical in origin, while the rest of *shiv'ah* is rabbinically ordained. Rambam derives a proof from the fact that the *onen*, the mourner on the day of his relative's death, is enjoined from eating sacrificial meat (*kodashim*). But how could Rambam derive *avelut* from this law regarding *kodashim*? Rambam says observance of *avelut* refers to ten prohibitions, such as the wearing of shoes, and so on. The *onen* was enjoined by the Torah from eating sacrificial meat, but it did not say that an *onen* is supposed to take off his shoes, or not wash, or not apply cosmetics or ointment, and so on.

I would explain the matter as follows. There are two *halakhot* in *avelut*, two aspects of the laws of mourning. One pertains to *nihug avelut*—the practical observance of *avelut*, the compliance with Rambam's ten injunctions. Then there is another *halakhah* which applies to the *gavra*, to the person who is called *avel*. Being an *avel* is an attribute of the *gavra*, an adjectival description of the person, and the *gavra* can be an *avel* even without the *nihug avelut*. Rabbenu Tam (cited in *Kesef Mishneh*, ad loc.) disagreed with Rambam and with Rav Alfasi, and thinks that *avelut* has only rabbinic status even on the first day. But Rabbeinu Tam is in disagreement with Rambam only about *nihug avelut* and not about the fact that the personal status of the *gavra* changes into that of an *avel*. About this, Rabbeinu Tam could not disagree.

I will demonstrate this to you. Rambam says, "An *avel* may not send his sacrifices for a full week" (*Hilkhot Bi'at ha-Mikdash* 2:11). This is drawn from a *gemara*: "The *avel* does not send his sacrifices. Rabbi Shimon learned: 'The *shelamim* sacrifices'—when he is *shalem*, complete, and not when he is *haser*, incomplete" (*Mo'ed Katan* 15a). When the *avel* is incomplete, he is not capable of entering the Temple and offering a sacrifice.

Now Rambam, who claimed that the first day's observance is of biblical status, admitted that the rest of *shiv'ah* is rabbinic. Yet he says that the mourner may not send sacrifices for the whole week, an exclusion which is certainly biblical. The explanation is that as far as *nihug* (observance) is concerned, his *avelut* is limited to the first day, but the classification of the *gavra* as an *avel* continues through the whole week. Rambam did not mention the law that an *avel* cannot offer a sacrifice among the ten prohibitions imposed on the *avel* because he deals there with *nihug avelut*, while the prohibition against his sending a sacrifice stems from the person's classification as an *avel*.

As an example of the distinction beween the two laws embodied in mourning, consider the opinion of the Rif (18a in the Alfasi)—it goes back to the Geonim—which Rambam (*Hilkhot Avel* 13:4) and *Shulhan Arukh* (*Yoreh De'ah* 376:3) also quote: If a person who died has no relatives, ten people come and they observe *avelut*. It would be ridiculous to say that the strangers are *avelim*; they are rather engaged in *nihug avelut*.

Now, with reference to *Tish'ah be-Av*, the *baraita* said that "all that is *noheg* during *avelut* is *noheg* on *Tish'ah be-Av*," not that "all Israel become *avelim* on *Tish'ah be-Av*." With regard to historical mourning, *avelut yeshanah*, Jews can observe *avelut*, engage in *nihug avelut* and comply with its laws. But they are not *avelim* wth respect to their *gavra*, their personhood. The prohibition against putting on *tefillin* as a mourner is not part of *nihug avelut*. Rather, the *gavra* as an *avel* is relieved of *tefillin*. A *gavra* who is an *avel* somehow cannot be crowned with *tefillin*, cannot adorn himself with them. Rabbi Akiva Eiger related this to a practical question (*Yoreh De'ah* 388:1). If someone died and was buried during *hol ha-mo'ed*, the intermediate days of a festival, there is no *nihug avelut* until after the holiday because the observance of *avelut* is in conflict with the joy of the holiday. Nevertheless, should a person who usually puts on *tefillin* during *hol ha-mo'ed* put on *tefillin* on what would have been the first day of *avelut*—the day of death and burial?

There is no *nihug avelut*, but the *gavra* is still an *avel*, as witnessed by the fact that *hol ha-mo'ed* counts as part of *sheloshim*. The prohibition against putting on *tefillin* is not part of *nihug avelut* but rather a result of the *gavra* being an *avel*.

But this all has no application to *Tish'ah be-Av*. *Avelut yeshanah*, historical mourning, imposes observance of *avelut*, but it cannot change the *gavra* into an *avel*. Therefore *tefillin* are worn on *Tish'ah be-Av*. The *gavra* is not an *avel* on *Tish'ah be-Av*. Similarly, betrothal is not part of *nihug avelut*. The prohibition of betrothal stems from the individual's reaction to death, as we explained earlier. It depends on the fact that the *gavra* is an *avel*. That is why the prohibition is applicable to *avelut hadashah*, individual mourning, and not to *avelut yeshanah*.

Another distinction between individual and historical mourning is that originally, the mourner would cover his face down to the tip of his nose (*atifat ha-rosh*), but this was never done on *Tish'ah be-Av*. *Atifah* is rooted in the idea of covering a face which has lost its *tzelem*, its Godly image. Another distinction involves the prohibition against the study of Torah. The *Gemara* (*Mo'ed Katan* 15a) derives the prohibition for a mourner from the verse, "Be silent" (Ez. 24:17)—"From here we learn that the mourner may not study Torah." With regard to *Tish'ah be-Av*, however, the *Gemara* explains the prohibition differently: on *Tish'ah be-Av* one should abstain from engaging in any pursuit or in any activity which results in pleasure or comfort, and the study of Torah is linked up with the feeling of joy.

A final distinction between *Tish'ah be-Av* and *avelut* relates to *kefiyyat ha-mittah*, turning the bed upside down, which is not done on *Tish'ah be-Av*. (We no longer do this during *avelut*—something of which the Tosafot [*Mo'ed Katan* 21a, s.v. *elu*] were already aware. Originally, the beds were constructed in such a way that you could turn the bed upside down and still sleep on it. But, our beds cannot be turned upside down, so this was eliminated, and we cover the mirrors as a substitute.) All laws of mourning were derived in *Mo'ed Katan* (15a-b) from two sources: the Divine commandment to Aaron and those to Ezekiel. The exception is *kefiyyat ha-mittah*. As regards this manifestation of *avelut*, the Talmud introduces a strange reason without attempting to derive it from a biblical text: Bar Kapparah taught his disciples, "God says, 'I have set the likeness of My image in them, and through their sins have I upset it. Let your beds be overturned on account of this'" (*Mo'ed Katan* 15a). Enigmatic words. However, the central motif here is that death impinges upon the worth of human dignity and the human divine nature. Man dies deprived of dignity and without his divine humanity. The symbol of humiliated man, of man who goes down in defeat, insult and shame, is an overturned bed. The bed is a metaphor for the moral integrity of the family (*"mittato shelemah"*) or the human personality in general (*"mittato porahat ba-avir"*). This whole manifestation is alien to *avelut de-rabbim*.

Consolation for the Mourning Community

In individual mourning, betrothal is forbidden. Man, vanquished by death, suffers self-degradation. There is no use in continuing the struggle, and he submits himself to his cruel fate. But it is permissible to betroth on *Tish'ah be-Av*. The whole dimension of despair and resignation, the notion of the mourner being unworthy of his own existential experience, sitting like a leper on a heap of ashes, bankrupt and forlorn, is contrary to the very gist of *avelut de-rabbim*. There, the mourner is not the individual but the nation, the covenantal community, which must never lose hope or faith. No matter how difficult times are, no matter how great the loss is, however dreary and bleak the present seems, the future shines with a brilliant glow full of promise. The messianic hope has never vanished; the people have never been enveloped by the dark night of despair.

While the Temple was being consumed by the purple flames of destruction, R. Yohanan ben Zakkai was already planning the future redemption. He introduced *takkanot zekher la-mikdash*, ritual reminders that although we have lost a Temple built by human hands, we will instead find a sanctuary constructed by the Divine hand, ". . . the sanctuary, O Lord, which Thy hands have established" (Ex. 15:17). The more intense the callousness, the drearier the boredom, the more cruel and ruthless were the Roman edicts of religious persecution—the louder Rabbi Akiva used to laugh at the dismal, detestable present and the stronger was his faith in the future (*Makkot* 24b).

Nehamah, consolation, is intertwined in the texture of *avelut de-rabbim*. There the whole method of manifesting despair is out of context and contradicts the very essence of *avelut de-rabbim*, which is a dialectical moving between grief and hope, darkness and a dazzling light, spiritual emptiness and a transcendent vision, bleak autumn and a glowing summer.

ℝ *Abraham Mourns Sarah*

Two Types of Mourning

When Abraham's wife dies, the Bible tells us that "Abraham came *lispod le-Sarah ve-livkotah*" (Gen. 23:2). What is *lispod* and what is *livkot*? The latter refers to *bekhi*, crying, which is indicative of a spontaneous, overwhelming and uncontrollable grief. It is a convulsive and compulsive shriek resulting from pain. The one who weeps does not know why he acts as he does. He could not, if asked, explain his grief in logical terms. The former, *sepod*, refers to eulogizing and is related to another kind of reaction, one rooted in logical judgment. The mourner realizes the extent of the damage inflicted upon him because of the death of a member of his household. It is not the sudden emotional confrontation with disaster which is responsible for *hesped*, the eulogy, but the clear analysis of the disastrous event and its consequences. The mourning at the stage of *bekhi* cannot be verbalized. The grief at the stage of *hesped* lends itself to objectification through words.

The natural order always leads from *bekhi* to *hesped*. The question then arises: Why did the Torah reverse the order, *lis-*

pod le-Sarah ve-livkotah, to eulogize Sarah and cry for her? Sarah's death was a double loss to Abraham. First, he had lost his beloved Sarah, whom he knew and respected since his early youth. Both of them suffered together, praying and waiting for God's promise to come true. Abraham loved Sarah; she lived through all the adventures, all the crises that Abraham had to face. Their life was rich in common experiences; two lives merged into one. Abraham cried: the beloved Sarah was snatched away from him. Her *ohel*, her tent, will be forever empty and forsaken. The blow to Abraham as an individual was almost unbearable. It is not *hesped*, logical interpretation, which describes Abraham's state of mind most precisely in this respect, but *bekhi*, crying, feeling the desolation.

However, Sarah was not only Abraham's mate but his comrade as well. She was a part of Abraham, not only as wife but as disciple and teacher. They exchanged roles from time to time. At times, she used to sit at his feet; at others, he would sit at hers. Sarah was his collaborator and co-participant in all the great plans, hopes and visions. Together they discovered God; together they discovered a new morality; together they joined the covenant. In a word, Sarah and Abraham started the *Masorah*, the Tradition. Not only Abraham taught the people, but Sarah as well. "Abraham would convert the men and Sarah the women" (*Gen. Rabbah* 39:14). Such a life of common suffering and common joy engenders love and deep friendship.

Now the mother is dead and the *Masorah* has a father but no mother. The *Masorah* is incomplete. Abraham mourned Sarah in this respect as a colleague, teacher and co-founder of the *Masorah*. The kind of grief experienced here is therefore classified under *hesped*, not the hysterical *bekhi*; it portrays a different sort of mourning. The rationally endorsed *hesped* describes the state of mind of Abraham who mourned the loss of a teacher-disciple. The Torah tells us that Abraham first mourned the death of the mother of the *Masorah*, and then the death of a lovely wife, without whom his life will be desolate, bleak and dreary.

When Abraham's name was changed from Abram, Sarah's name was also modified by an additional letter *'hei.'* Abraham became teacher-father, Sarah teacher-mother. Moreover, Abraham's historical mission could not have been implemented without Sarah's participation. Both appeared together in Jewish history. When the Torah mentions Abraham, it hastens to tell us that Abraham married Sarah (Gen. 11:26-29). With Sarah's death, Abraham lost his leadership. Together with the tent of Sarah which Rebecca took over, the House of Abraham was passed over to Isaac. Abraham mourned over Sarah but also over the fact that he had to withdraw from the *petah ha-ohel*, the front of the tent, into the shadows of the tent.

Hesped and Bekhi in Halakhah

As a matter of fact, this idea of logical reaction plays an important role in the laws of mourning. The death of a parent is not as devastating psychologically as is the death of a child. Parents who have lost a child will never forget their grief. Their distress is endless; nothing can offer them solace. A son and a daughter, on the other hand, can usually get past the death of a parent. And yet the Halakhah has decreed thirty days mourning for a child and twelve months of mourning for parents.

Apparently, the Halakhah is guided not by psychological, emotional reality but by concerns about the *Masorah*. A parent dies—the mourning is great. Why? The parent was the person who acquainted me with the *Masorah*. My belonging to the covenantal community is his or her accomplishment—no one else taught me. Hence the death of a person who extended the chain of tradition to an individual must precipitate greater formalized mourning than the death of a child, to whom one does not owe any debt of gratitude as far as the *Masorah* is concerned. Abraham's sequence of mourning reflects this philosophy. First *hesped* for a mother of the community of the covenant, then *bekhi* for a beloved mate and wife.

There is no doubt that psychologically Abraham was shattered to the very core of his personality by the death of his beloved wife. Sarah died; Abraham cried. We are not accustomed to seeing tears on our father's face. He was a strong and courageous personality. Weeping and wailing are *prima facie* beneath a great man's dignity. Why did the Torah tell us that Abraham wept? Apparently, it is befitting for a great man to cry like a child. To be insensitive, emotionally unmovable, always cold, neutral and irresponsive is not always the sign of greatness. It is quite often a sign of cruelty, of selfishness and absence of spiritual warmth.

Maimonides writes:

> One should not indulge in excessive grief over one's dead, for it is said, "Weep not for the dead, neither bemoan him" (Jer. 22:10), that is to say, [weep not for him] too much, for that is the way of the world, and he who frets over the way over the way of the world is a fool. . . . [On the other hand,] whoever does not mourn the dead in the manner enjoined by the Rabbis is cruel (*Hilkhot Avel* 13:11-12).

Mourning, if observed with restraint and in compliance with the Halakhah, enhances the status of man. It is an experience of great dignity; it is a sacrificial act enlightening the sufferer as to the meaning of life as well as the destiny of mankind. This axiological critical analysis enriches his personality. It purges him of the ugly and contemptible in life. On the other hand, when man remains emotionally neutral he loses a lot of his *humanitas*. The animal is neutral. Man must not disengage himself from his involvement in the fate of his fellow man. Nevertheless, man must not react hysterically to pain and suffering. He must not surrender to them. He must at a certain moment be capable of rising from the mourner's stool, no matter how difficult it is.

"Abraham Rose Up from Before His Dead"

The great, courageous Abraham did not say a single word when the command to sacrifice Isaac came through to him. He did not collapse and fall on his face in despair and resignation. When coming from a journey, he found his beloved Sarah dead. He mourned the passing of Sarah, cried and wept. Nevertheless, Abraham realized that he could not afford to continue to cry hysterically and wrap himself in the mourner's mantle forever. People watched him; they observed his conduct in his hour of crisis. The future of the covenantal community was dependent upon his behavior. When disaster struck, he had to demonstrate faith in God and act with fortitude and dignity.

"And Abraham rose up from before his dead and spoke to the Hittites" (Gen. 23:3). Abraham rose from the ashes, threw away the sack. He straightened his back, lifted his eyes to heaven and whispered: "Yes, as long as I have You with me I feel strong. I am faithful to You."

Apparently, for some time Abraham was unable to discuss the matter of burial with the Hittites. He could not collect his thoughts. He could not plan or negotiate. He lost his capacity to speak; he lost his personality. The metaphor for *avelut* is falling on one's face, not standing all by oneself. The mourner experiences loss of independence; in other words, the mourner cannot continue to exist alone without the support of somebody else. He has lost the unique ability of man to stand on his feet.

Interesting is the law pertaining to a situation in which one finds himself confronted with the death of a member of the household. The *onen*, the mourner from the time of death until burial, is relieved of all positive *mitzvot*. He is not allowed to say

Shema, to recite benedictions, to don *tefillin* and to perform any of the positive commandments the Torah instructed us to fulfill. Why? Because for a short while, the mourner has lost his freedom, his ability to implement religious norms. When death strikes, it strips the survivor of his human charisma characterized by the posture of standing erect. He falls. There is not much difference between the animal and the mourner. He cannot support himself. The Torah wanted the mourner to be completely involved in grief and despair.

The Torah tells us that "Joseph fell upon his father's face" (Gen. 50:1). This phrase denotes total distress. For a while Joseph lost his human dignity. He kissed his dead father and embraced him. The opposite is true of the phrase, "Abraham rose up from before his dead" (Gen. 23:3). Abraham controlled his emotions, he regained his dignity as a person, his freedom and particularly his inner strength and firmness. Why? Because he had to speak to the Hittites about important matters. He did not want the Hittites to see him low in spirit, completely displaced by endless bleak despair.

No matter how great the suffering, one must not make a public exhibition of his emotional world. The joy is tempered, the grief is limited in the presence of others. Abraham mourned and grieved for Sarah endlessly. However, the grieving and mourning took place in the privacy of his house, in solitude and loneliness, not in public. When he had to negotiate with the Hittites in public, when he had to acquire the field in the presence of the entire community, he got up from his dear Sarah and regained his strength, since the history of a covenant was dependent upon the outcome of his performance.

"*Va-yavo* Avraham, and Abraham came to mourn for Sarah" (Gen. 23:2). What does the word *va-yavo* mean? Of course, we all know the midrash (*Gen. Rabbah* 58:5): Abraham came from Mount Moriah, where he had taken Isaac in response to God's command. In other words, Abraham was not present at Sarah's death. The tragedy of Abraham is heartbreaking. On his return journey he beheld the vision of Sarah receiving both of them with joy and love, of the Sarah who got her son back, of a happy Sarah. He comes home. He begins to wonder why Sarah does not come out to meet them. What happened? An odd stillness prevails. He calls, "Sarah, Sarah"; no answer. This experience was perhaps the most difficult one.

However, the word *va-yavo* also signifies the retreat from a public space into a shelter or house: "Come, my people, enter into your chambers and shut the doors about you" (Isa. 26:20). "The spirit entered into me and set me upon my feet; and He spoke with me and said to me, 'Go shut yourself within your house'" (Ez. 3:24). Abraham mourned for Sarah not in the open but in private; he withdrew from the open in order to cry. When he had to negotiate with the Hittites, he hid his distress and grief. "Abraham rose up from before his dead and spoke to the Hittites" (Gen. 23:3).

Abraham Among the Hittites

Why was his transaction with the Hittites of great importance? Abraham finally disclosed to them his strange identity, his unique way of life, particularly as far as his relationship to other people is concerned. They all respected Abraham; they addressed themselves to him in terms expressing profound reverence: "You are a mighty prince among us" (Gen. 23:6). Yet they knew that he was different. Abraham was a mystery to them. It intrigued them to know: is he one of us or a total stranger? Does he identify himself with us or see himself as somebody different? Abraham had never bothered to reveal his identity.

This time, he knew, he would have to disclose his identity. Otherwise, his request would appear to be nonsensical. What did he ask? He asked for a grave for Sarah. The Hittites responded immediately in the most respectful manner that they were ready to assign any grave, even the choicest of sepulchers, as a resting place for his wife.

They purposely stressed that "You are a mighty prince *among us.*" Are you in our midst, are you ours, do you belong to our society? We respect and revere you as our prince. You lived here; you do business with us. You made your fortunes here. Your son was born here. Hence, when the inevitable happened, the dead should be buried in *our* sepulcher. "The field I give you, and the cave that is therein I give to you; in the presence of the sons of my people I give it to you" (Gen. 23:11).

Baron A. Rothschild told me that when De Gaulle was informed that the Rothschild family was planning to transfer the remains of the *Nadiv*, the Great Philanthropist, to Israel, he became indignant and remarked: "I always thought and asked myself, Is Mr. Rothschild a good Frenchman? Now I realize that I was mistaken. Who is a good Frenchman? One who is reared in France, educated in a French school, whose native tongue is French, who is ready to take up arms to defend France and who is buried in French soil."

The same philosophy was expounded by the Hittites. Since you are a prince in our midst, since you are a Hittite prince, we believe that you will bury your illustrious wife in our graveyard. Listen to us, our master. You are *our* prince. You are *ours.* Bury your wife with *our* princes. She belongs in the choicest of *our* sepulchers.

In reply, Abraham expounded the principle of *kever Yisrael,* Jewish burial. *Kever Yisrael* encompasses two things: first, to be buried among Jews, separating Jewish and non-Jewish sepulchers; and second, that the sepulcher belong to the dead who found its final rest in it. "*Tzaddik kavur ba-kever shelo,* a righteous person is buried in his own grave" (cf. *Bava Batra* 112b). In fact, we write *shitrei harsha'ah* (powers of attorney) which require *kinyan agav* (a tranfer of mobile objects by annexation to a transfer of real estate) even from those who do not possess any real estate, for every Jew has property. Every Jew owns four cubits of land in Israel and four cubits of land where he will at some point in the future be put to eternal rest. That is the reason the Halakhah is strict about exhumation and transfer of the bones of the dead.

The Hittites suggested to Abraham two things: the grave-yards will be integrated and the grave will not belong to Abraham. "In the choicest of our sepulchers shall you bury your dead; none of us shall withhold from you his sepulcher" (Gen. 23:6). The interment will be in the finest of *our* sepulchers; Sarah's grave will be an integral part of *our* cemetery; the place will not belong to you: it will be our property. We will just per-mit you to use "the choicest of *our* sepulchers"; no one will with-hold "*his* sepulcher."

Abraham, the outstanding gracious host and gentle person, appreciated the generosity of the Hittites. He thanked them profusely. "And Abraham bowed to the host people, to the Hittites" (Gen. 23:7). He graciously acknowledged the kindness of the people of the land who were anxious to see that the stranger be assimilated into the general society and who offered leadership to the newcomer. Yet he declined the offer and explained precisely what he had in mind.

"If you indeed want to help me bury my dead from before me, hear what I am going to tell you" (Gen. 23:8). I have asked two things: a separate place "at the end of the field" (Gen. 23:9) and unrestricted ownership of the site. Of course, I am indebt-ed to you for your graciousness. However, you are mistaken about the relationship between us. If you ask me who am I and what is my relationship to you, I will tell you. "I am both *ger ve-toshav*, a stranger and a sojourner with you" (Gen. 23:4). I am a part of the civilized, scientifically trained, and progress-minded society. I work with you in laboratories, study in the same academia. I participate in industry and commerce, help support the poor, pay taxes and am ready to defend the land. However, I am also a stranger, I am different as far as my covenantal relationship with God is concerned. I worship dif-ferently, I celebrate my holidays in a unique fashion, rejoice as well as mourn in a singular way. I share with you the laboratory but not the place of worship. I will attend the same school but will insist upon a separate *ahuzat kever*, a grave-inheritance. Please speak to Ephron, let him sell me the Makhpelah Cave, and it will become not just a grave but an *ahuzat kever* that is exclusively mine, something that I will pass on to my descendants. It will be the symbol of the commitment of my people to the land.

Yet Abraham wanted more than that: the land must not be given to him as a grant. He refused to accept the field *gratis*, as a gift. He demanded that Ephron sell him the land for its full price. "For the payment of its full value in money shall he give it to me as an *ahuzat kever*" (Gen. 23:9).

Ephron argued that he does not want to take money. He wants to give the land as a gift. He agreed with Abraham pertaining to separation of sepulchers and unrestricted ownership. However, he did not want to sell. "No, my lord, hear me: the field give I to you, and the cave that is therein, I give it to you; bury your dead" (Gen. 23:11). Ephron insists that the land be given to Abraham as a grant, that is, *free*. But Abraham declines to accept a gift; he wants to pay. The vendor refuses to take money. A paradoxical situation. Finally, Abraham wins: Ephron sells him the land. Why?

Judaism's View of Property

Judaism has always looked down on the acceptance of gifts. The book of Proverbs says, "Whoever dislikes gifts will live long" (Prov. 15:27). Why? The property rights of an individual are rooted in his basic right to work, to comply with God's verdict, "By the sweat of your brow you will eat bread" (Gen. 3:19). Human labor, human fatigue and exhaustion, justify man's claim to property rights. This belongs to Mr. X because Mr. X worked hard to get it. However, acquisition of goods without investing one's labor, the sweat of the brow, is morally objectionable. In such a case, a property right is not perfect. When I buy goods, I exchange my labor for those goods. Money represents labor, the sweat and fatigue of the worker. Therefore the goods I buy are absolutely mine, while a gift which I received, lacking the catharsis of work and exhaustion, lacks the redemptive quality. That is why Abraham refused to share in the booty of the four kings (Gen. 14:22-24). He certainly did not want Sarah to be put to her eternal rest in a grave which was given to him as a present, a gratuity, a grave which was not hallowed by the sweat and the fright.

There is something else to which we must give attention. The Torah tells us:

> So the field of Ephron, which was in Makhpelah, which was before Mamre, the field, and the cave which was therein, and all the trees that were in the field, that were all in the border thereof round about, were made sure unto Abraham for a possession in the presence of the children of Het, before all that went in the gate of his city. And after this, Abraham buried Sarah his wife in the field of Makhpelah before Mamre—the same is Hebron—in the land of Canaan. And the field and the cave that is therein were made sure unto Abraham for a possession of a burying-place by the children of Het (Gen. 23:17-20).

Why the redundancy? Why tell us again that Abraham indeed buried Sarah in the Makhpelah cave and that the field plus the trees became Abraham's as a burial plot? Once Abraham bought and paid for it, why was it necessary to repeat that the property became an inheritance of burying to Abraham? Why, in describing the boundaries of the field which was sold to Abraham, is the Torah satisfied to say, "So the field of Ephron, which was in Makhpelah, which was before Mamre" (v. 17), while in describing the boundaries of the field which became Abraham's *ahuzat kever*, the Torah added, "before Mamre in the land of Canaan" (v. 19)?

There are two kinds of property, *sedeh ahuzah* and *sedeh mikneh*. *Sedeh mikneh* is property that one buys easily and sells easily. Usually such property is purchased and sold for the sake of gain. There is no emotional attachment. There is also *sedeh ahuzah*, property which one inherits from his ancestors, property with which one gets emotionally involved, to which one is bound inwardly. *Ahoz* conveys to be held, to be kept pristine— the field is inherited from grandfather and forefather, passed on from generation to generation, and can never be given up.

Such a relationship develops not through a legal transaction but through burying somebody dear, through a grave which contains the remains of a beloved one. When Abraham paid money, he acquired legal rights. The relationship remained that of a *sedeh mikneh*, formal-juridic. Once Sarah was put to rest in the Makhpelah Cave, Abraham reacquired not only the field, but the whole land of Canaan as the place of the first Jewish grave, that of Sarah. "And the field and the cave that is therein were made sure unto Abraham for an *ahuzat kever*" (Gen. 23:20).

❧ *The Redemption of Death*

The laws concerning the *parah adumah*—the red heifer which plays an essential part in "purifying" a person who came into contact with a dead body (Numbers, chapter 19)—were classified by our Rabbis as unintelligible and mysterious "*hukkim*"—enigmatic laws which the human mind is incapable of assimilating. The Satan and our foes ridicule and abuse them, yet our Rabbis did not try to rationalize them. They acknowledged the antinomic character of the laws of *parah adumah* and simply said that we must accept all of them as a whole—with their inner contradictions and antithetic motifs—without asking for an explanation, reason or motive. The Sages demanded that man suspend judgment and act in accordance with the inscrutable will of God, even though the logos is perplexed.

However, even though it is forbidden to ask for motivation and reasoning pertaining to God's imperatives and norms, we may inquire as to the meaningfulness of the *hok*, the unintelligible law, for ourselves. It is perfectly legitimate to search for the spiritual message of the *hok*. Nahmanides as well as Maimonides emphasized time and again that the element of *avodah she-ba-lev*—worship of the heart—must be present in every religious act. (See Nahmanides, e.g., comments to *Sefer ha-Mitzvot*, positive commandment no. 5; Maimonides, *Guide* III:51.) The ritual as well as moral actions must be endowed with emotional warmth, love and joy, and the mechanical act converted into a living experience. Of course, all this is unattainable if there is no message to deliver, no idea to suggest, no enriching meaning. In order to offer God my heart and soul, in order to serve Him inwardly, one thing is indispensable—understanding, the involvement of the logos.

Of course, I must never say that the message I detected in the *mitzvah* explains the *mitzvah* and answers the illegitimate question of why the Almighty commanded us to act in such an unintelligible way. However, I am permitted to raise the question of what this *mitzvah* means to me. How am I to understand, not the reason for the *mitzvah*, but the essence of the latter as an integral part of my service of God? Let us therefore see what the *parah adumah* tells us. How do we experience this *hukkat ha-Torah*? What is the central motif of the whole institution? In a word, I am asking not "why *parah adumah*?" but "what is *parah adumah*?" (The distinction between "why," which should not be raised, and "what?" was introduced by Nahmanides in his commentary to Deut. 22:6.)

I believe that we would do well to abandon the popular approach to the topic which identifies the singularities with the strange manner in which the red heifer is offered. Of course, the ceremonial aspect is puzzling: the offering of a sacrifice outside of the Temple and Jerusalem (contrary to the accepted law pertaining to other sacrifices, which are offered in the Sanctuary exclusively), the burning of the heifer and its conversion into ashes and mixing the ashes with spring water. Moreover, the law that the same water that effects purification for the defiled person causes *tum'ah* to the clean person intrigues the mind. However, I believe that the enigma of the *mitzvah* is to be found in the nature of *tum'at met*, the "impurity" that results from contact with the dead and which is basically different from all other forms of *tum'ah*.

Generally, all that is required to remove one's impurity is *tevillah*—immersion in a *mikvah* or the "living water" of a spring, river or ocean. But while this applies to, say, a person who becomes impure by contact with the carcass of a dead animal, it does not apply to the *tamei met*, the individual who became impure by contact with a dead human body. The sprinkling of the "*mei hattat*" (spring water mixed with ashes of the red heifer) is indispensable for the *tamei met* to regain his previous status of *tahor*, pure. *Tevillah* alone does not suffice. The sprinkling is done twice, on the third and the seventh day of the count; otherwise the person remains a *tamei met* and is enjoined from offering in the Sanctuary. The real question, then, is, why did the Torah single out the *tamei met*? Why should not the latter be subject to the universal cleansing through immersion? What lies at the root of that distinction? Reading the Torah section, we are impressed by the emphasis on *haza'ah*, sprinkling, as an inevitable element of cleansing: "If he purify himself with it on the third day and on the seventh day, he shall be clean: but if he does not purify himself on the third day and the seventh day, he shall not be clean" (Num. 19:12). It is as if the Torah warns us not to take the sprinkling lightly. What does the purification process symbolize; what story does it tell us?

I believe that the peculiar method of cleansing the *tamei met* is indicative of the human situation, of the existential metaphysic of man. The basic difference between immersion and sprinkling lies in the fact that the *tevillah* is accomplished by the impure person himself. No one can help the *tamei* to immerse; he must bow his head and bend his knees in order to obtain *taharah*. He plunges into the water and then emerges from the water *tahor*, clean and pure, because of his own effort. Man defiles himself and must cleanse himself. *Tevillah* symbolizes human freedom and creativity. Man has the ability to raise himself to greatness, to take the initiative and reach new heights.

However, as regards sprinkling, the situation is the reverse: the *tamei met* cannot sprinkle the water upon himself; another person must do it. "And the clean person shall sprinkle upon the unclean" (Num. 19:19). The *tamei met* cannot liberate himself from the state of impurity. Someone who is clean, who possesses the strength to redeem others and restore purity after it had been lost, must sprinkle *mei hattat* on him. He cannot attain *taharah* if left completely to himself. Pertaining to other impurities, *taharah* is within the reach of the individual who lost it; but the impurity associated with human death is of a more persistent character and does not lend itself to being washed away with plain water. Another person, a *tahor*, must assist the *tamei*, sprinkle upon him the *mei hattat*. Otherwise the *tamei met* will never free himself from the bondage of *tum'ah*, which holds man in its clutches and does not let him go.

The distinct status which the Torah has granted the *tamei met* is due to the unique experience which man lives through whenever he is confronted with death. Other objects which contaminate a person are experienced as either aesthetically ugly or physically abominable. Any dead organism is a source of filth, squalor; the organism is in a process of decomposition, a scene arousing unpleasant emotions. Disease can also be subsumed under the category of the repulsive; *tzara'at*, biblical leprosy, is an excellent example of the ugliness of the disease. "*Tum'ah*" and "*zohama*," impurity and filth, are synonymous terms.

Tum'at met constitutes a unique category. Of course, a dead person is *ipso facto* a dead organism, and whatever we said of the animal cadaver may be also said of the lifeless human body, which is also exposed to the ugly process of decomposition. However, there is something more horrible to be experienced when one is in contact with human death. As far as the zoological kingdom is concerned, death is not a monstrosity; it simply destroys the functionality of the organism. Human death, however, terminates a personality, an ontological dimension, a spiritual individuality who was self-aware and self-conscious, a personality which was driven by vision and hope, which despaired, rejoiced and grieved, which lived not only in the present moment but in both retrospection and anticipation. In a word, death destroys a world. It is the tragic experience of the human being who is endowed with the time-awareness, and knows that his existence is a mockery. Death contradicts the God-man relationship. How can one imagine love of God in *She'ol*? (See Ps. 30:9, 116:9.)

In the animal world, the death of the individual is not tragic because the existence of the genus is not threatened by the death of an individual; there is no individualistic existence among the animals. The individual exists as the representative of the class. Hence the death of the individual does not count. The class continues to set the tone. Among people the situation is completely different; the individual does not lead a representative but an individualistic existence. Each human is an individuality, a personality, a microcosm. Existential legitimacy is to be found in the individual person himself. Death denies the very worth of human existence. Hence the *tum'ah* is due not to organic but to spiritual destruction. It is the expression of human anxiety and terror, human helplessness in the face of a mocking Satan. *Tum'at met* is the result of the traumatic experience that dislocates man's self, I-awareness and existential security. Death lurks in the shadows. Death defeats everyone, great or small, clever or simple. "All things come alike to all" (Eccl. 9:2).

Hence *tum'at met* represents not just an experience of ugliness, but the human situation, the tragic and absurd human destiny. Its cleansing is therefore a dual one. Man, on one hand, must struggle with death and try to defeat it—the cleansing requires *tevillah*, which is symbolic of the human effort in reducing the power of death and prolonging life. In course of time, Judaism believes, man will succeed in taming the death-monstrosity, in limiting its power. However, Judaism is not so naive as to have unrestricted faith in human capability to eliminate death and raise man to the level of the immortals. The plague of death, it says, will trouble man until the Almighty will save man from the curse of death. "He will swallow up death forever, and the Lord God will wipe off the tears from all faces" (Isa. 25:8).

How can man redeem himself from death, how can he cleanse himself from the fright of death, how can he attain *taharah* from the defilement by death? Through a double procedure. First, through *tevillah*, an organized scientific-medical effort to limit its power as much as possible. Man cleanses himself from *tum'at met* the way every *tamei* person does—all by himself. Second, by *haza'ah*, by placing our trust in the Almighty that at some point in the future He will redeem us "and the clean person shall sprinkle upon the unclean" (Num. 19:19). "The clean person" who will free the unclean from the bondage of defilement is the Almighty, as the prophet says, "Then I will sprinkle water upon you, and you shall be clean" (Ez. 36:25). Only He will heal man from the threat and terror of nihility. Man cannot solve the enigma or mystery of death. Only God will elucidate and explain to us this awesome mystery. Death is the great marvel, the unintelligible experience, the *hok*, the Torah no one can grasp—"This is the Torah: when a man dies in a tent . . ." (Num. 19:14).

🦅 The Essential
Nature of Mourning

The High Priest as Mourner

In the section of his *Mishneh Torah* devoted to the laws of mourning, the Rambam (Maimonides) takes up the question of whether the High Priest must observe those laws. He rules that:

> The High Priest is subject to all the rules of mourning, except that he is forbidden to rend the upper part of his garment, or to grow wild hair, or to escort the bier. All the people come to his home to comfort him, and when they provide him the meal of consolation, they recline on the ground while he reclines on a bench. When they comfort him, they say to him, "We are your atonement," and he responds, "May you be blessed from Heaven" (*Hilkhot Avel* 7:6).

The Rambam's source is a mishnah in tractate *Sanhedrin*:

> If [the High Priest] suffered the death of a relative, he does not escort the bier . . . , and when he is comforted by

---

Notes to this essay appear on p. 85.—Eds.

others, the people say to him, "We are your atonement," and he responds, "May you be blessed from heaven." And when they provide him the meal of consolation, all the people recline on the ground and he reclines on a bench (Mishnah *Sanhedrin* 2:1 at 18a).

The detailed rules to which the Rambam here refers are all found in the mishnah, but not so the novel general point with which he begins, namely, that "the High Priest is subject to the rules of mourning." This *halakhah* is not stated expressly in the mishnah, and Rambam apparently infers it logically, reasoning that the mishnah's references to providing the meal of consolation and comforting the mourner imply that those practices pertain to the High Priest, which would not be so were he exempt from the laws of mourning.

Nevertheless, many *rishonim* (medieval halakhic authorities) disagree with the Rambam and hold that the High Priest is altogether exempt from mourning. In their view, the comforting and meal of consolation referred to in the mishnah do not embody aspects of mourning, for the mishnah (*Mo'ed Katan* 3:7 at 27a) rules that we comfort a mourner—and, according to many authorities (see *Mo'ed Katan* 20a, Tosafot s.v. *she-kevar*) even provide the meal of consolation—on a festival, when, as explained below, mourning generally is not in effect. Thus, the Me'iri (R. Menahem ben Solomon Me'iri), R. Asher ben Yehiel (in his *Tosafot ha-Rosh*), and an anonymous student of R. Yehiel of Paris (all commenting on *Mo'ed Katan* 14b) expressly write that the mourning regime does not apply to a High Priest.

Truth to tell, a talmudic discussion of a related issue, if closely read, seems to require the conclusion that the High Priest is not subject to mourning practices. The discussion pertains to whether the mourning-like practices of a *metzora*, the biblical leper, are followed on a festival. The *sugya* (textual unit in the Talmud) that takes up the issue reads as follows:

Rava said, "Come and hear: The [seemingly unnecessary] word *'ve-ha-tzarua*, the person suffering from biblical leprosy' [in Lev. 13:45] teaches us that the High Priest [is, no less than others, subject to the rules of *tzara'at*, biblical leprosy]. Now, we know that the High Priest's year-round status resembles that held by all Jews on a festival, as was taught, 'The High Priest brings sacrifices [even though] he is an *onen* [a person in a state of *aninut*, the first stage of mourning, during which one's close relative has died but not yet been buried], though he does not eat of them' (Mishnah *Horayot* 3:5 at 12b). From this we infer that the *metzora* follows the requirements associated with his condition on a festival." Indeed, we so infer (*Mo'ed Katan* 14b).

An unstated premise of the *gemara's* reasoning here is that an *onen*, whose state of mourning normally bars him from bringing a sacrifice, may bring one on a festival, when mourning is not permitted. Since a High Priest who has become an *onen* may nevertheless bring a sacrifice at any time throughout the year, it follows that he always has the status that ordinary Jews have on a festival. And, the logic continues, if the High Priest, despite that perpetual status, nevertheless follows all the mourning-like rules of leprosy, it appears that even on an actual festival, any *metzora* would similarly follow the mourning-like rules associated with his condition.

The *sugya's* proof works, of course, only as long as we grant that the High Priest has, by virtue of his office, the status of a Jew celebrating a festival and that, just as Jews of all stripes do not mourn on an actual festival, so, too, the High Priest does not mourn at any time. But its conclusion would be invalid were we to adopt the Rambam's contrary view that the High Priest is subject to the rules of mourning. That position implies a difference between the High Priest's perpetual status and that of all

Jews on a festival and thus precludes the *gemara's* reasoning that his being subject to the rules of leprosy implies that all Jews are subject to them on a festival. Indeed, many prominent *aharonim* (later halakhic authorities) have found difficulty with the Rambam's comments. (See *Keren Orah* on *Mo'ed Katan* 14b and *Minhat Hinukh*, *mitzvah* 264, par. 4.)

Upon close examination, moreover, the *sugya* itself appears difficult to understand. The *gemara* infers laws regarding the festivals from the law authorizing the High Priest to bring sacrifices in a state of *aninut*, but the law validating ritual actions performed by the High Priest as an *onen* is, in fact, unrelated to the law of festivals. It is, rather, a special scriptural ordinance, inferred from the passage in Leviticus recounting the death of Aaron's two sons. Aaron there asks, ". . . and if I had eaten the sin-offering today, would it have been well-pleasing in the sight of the Lord?" (Lev. 10:19); and his asking only about eating the offering but not about sacrificing it is taken to imply the clear acceptability of sacrificing as an *onen*. But if it is that verse from which the law is specially derived, there is no reason to assume, on the basis of that law, that the High Priest's year-round status is the same as that of all Jews on a festival. And if that assumption falls, so does the link between the High Priest's *aninut* and a *metzora's* practices on a festival.

Moreover, we cannot attempt to restore the link by saying that the validation of ritual acts performed by the High Priest as an *onen* implies that the very category of *aninut* is annulled with respect to the High Priest, for the *sugya* quotes the mishnah's statement that the High Priest, when an *onen*, does not eat of the sacrifices. It is thus plain that the High Priest, too, is subject to being an *onen*, even though ritual actions performed when he is in that state remain valid. Given all of this, nothing regarding the festivals can be proven from the High Priest's situation!

Public Rejoicing on a Festival and Private Mourning

Like the *metzora* already referred to, a *menuddeh*, that is, one punished by *niddui*, a form of ostracism or excommunication, also must observe certain mourning-like practices. The *Gemara* considers whether a *menuddeh* and a *metzora* follow their respective regimes on a festival, but the very inquiry seems questionable, for why should their conditions be more resistant than that of a mourner to the festival's countervailing effect? The *Gemara* explains (*Mo'ed Katan* 14b) that the reason a mourner does not follow his mourning practices on a festival is that the community's positive commandment to "rejoice on thy festival" (Deut. 16:14) supersedes the individual's positive commandment to mourn. But if that is so, why not apply the same rationale with respect to the *menuddeh* and the *metzora*; that is, why not say that the positive commandment to rejoice on the festival supersedes the commandments to follow the mourning-like practices of *tzara'at* and *niddui*?

In fact, some *rishonim* had similar difficulties, as we see in the effort by Tosafot (ad loc., s.v. *mahu*) to resolve the issue with respect to the *menuddeh*. And *Tosafot ha-Rosh* includes the following comment:

> It makes sense to me to resolve the matter by reasoning as follows: With respect to a mourner, we can say that the positive commandment to observe the festival, which includes the injunction "you shall rejoice," supersedes the positive commandment addressed to the mourner, which is to refrain from rejoicing. The law of the *menuddeh*, in contrast, is intended to carry out the commandment of not straying [from the rulings of the sages]; and the individual in question has been subjected to the regimen of *niddui* because he disobeyed the sages' rulings.

That regimen, however, does not contradict the commandment to rejoice on the festival, for it entails no commandment to refrain from rejoicing.

The Ritva (R. Yom Tov ben Abraham Ishbili) writes to similar effect:

We can respond that, *mi-de-oraita* [as a matter of biblical, as distinct from rabbinic, law], inasmuch as [the *menuddeh*] has rejoiced through the eating of meat and similar observances, the festival has not been desecrated and 'You shall rejoice on your festival' has been carried out.

But these comments themselves pose serious difficulties. A mourner, no less than a *menuddeh*, may eat meat and drink wine (*Ta'anit* 13a); these activities, though prohibited before the deceased is buried, are permitted thereafter. Since mourning nevertheless is annulled on the festival, it appears that what contradicts the festival joy is not the abstinence from meat and wine but the observance of the specific rites of mourning: removing one's shoes, sitting on the ground, refraining from washing and anointing, and so forth. But if that is the case, the festival joy should be seen as precluded in connection with the *menuddeh* as well; for he, too, is obligated to follow most of the rules that bind the mourner, as the *sugya* later makes clear. Given all that, what could the Rosh have meant in saying that "this regimen of *niddui* entails no commandment to refrain from rejoicing"?

In his commentary on *Mo'ed Katan*, the student of R. Yehiel of Paris previously referred to explains the matter differently. After establishing that a *metzora* is forbidden to wash his clothes and extend greetings (the rules at issue in the *sugya*) only *mi-de-rabbanan*, that is, as a matter of rabbinic law, he goes on to explain:

Accordingly, one can ask whether we [in fact] reason that the community's positive commandment [to rejoice] displaces the individual's commandment [to mourn]. For we might, alternatively, reason from the premise that festival joy cannot be fulfilled in the case of the *metzora*, who is obligated to tear his garment, to allow his hair to grow wild, and to cover his upper lip and who is forbidden to enter the camp and rejoice with his fellows. All of these [restrictions] are biblically ordained, and, with respect to all of them, Scripture speaks in plenary terms, not distinguishing between festival and secular days. Therefore, since festival joy simply cannot be made to prevail in his case, no aspect of his otherwise applicable regimen is canceled.

The explanation of Rabbi Yehiel's student runs counter to those of the Ritva and the Rosh. The latter resolve the problem by reasoning that the *metzora* completely fulfills the commandment to rejoice on the festival even though he follows the mourning-like practices associated with his condition. Rabbi Yehiel's student, in contrast, explains that the *metzora* cannot fulfill the obligation of festival joy because he is forbidden to enter the camp. To account for this contrast, it is necessary to understand how the respective proponents of these conflicting positions regard the nature of the commandment to rejoice.

Public and Private Mourning on Sabbath and Festivals

In commenting on the *sugya's* statement that "the community's positive commandment supersedes the individual's positive commandment," Rashi explains that the individual's positive commandment is "to mourn, as it is written, 'Make yourself mourning, as for an only son (*yahid*)' (Jer. 6:26)." Rashi's comment is perplexing, for there seems to be no need for a special scriptural ruling that mourning is a positive commandment that pertains to an individual. Indeed, how could one even imagine that mourning might become a matter for the community?

[Some insights in this regard may be had by comparing the rules of mourning on Sabbaths and on festivals.] The Halakhah follows the opinion in the *Gemara* (*Mo'ed Katan* 24a) that, even though public mourning practices are suspended on the Sabbath, mourning as a state nevertheless exists, inasmuch as private mourning practices [such as the prohibition on marital relations]—the subject of that *sugya*, according to Tosafot ad loc. and other *rishonim*—are followed. Accordingly, the Sabbath day is counted as part of the prescribed mourning period, in contrast to a festival day, which is not. As the mishnah states: "The Sabbath is counted [as part of the mourning period] but does not terminate [it]; festivals terminate [a mourning period] but are not counted [as part of it]" (*Mo'ed Katan* 19a). (In other words, a festival occurring after a mourning period has begun terminates it, but if the mourning period has not yet begun—if, for example, burial took place on the intermediate days of the festival—the full mourning period must be observed following the festival's conclusion.)

The *rishonim* are divided, however, with regard to whether mourning is practiced on a festival. The Rambam rules that "No aspect of mourning is practiced on the festivals or on Rosh Ha-Shanah and Yom Kippur" (*Hilkhot Avel* 10:3). The Tosafists disagree, taking the view that private mourning practices are followed on festivals, just as on the Sabbath. Their view follows their reading of a *sugya* in tractate *Ketuvot*:

> The teacher said: The statement that "[a groom whose father has died] sleeps among the men and [his bride] sleeps among the women" provides support for Rabbi Yohanan, who said, "Even though it is said that there is

no mourning on a festival, private mourning practices do apply" (*Ketuvot* 4a).

According to the Rambam's view—apparently based on a version of the *sugya* in *Ketuvot* that read "there is no mourning on the Sabbath"—the distinction between Sabbath and festivals is straightforward: the Sabbath, on which private mourning practices are followed, is counted as part of the mourning period, but a festival, on which mourning is not followed in any respect, is not so counted. But the Tosafists' view that private mourning practices are followed on both festivals and Sabbath makes it difficult to account for the difference between the two occasions that is set forth in the mishnah. The Tosafists tried to deal with the issue by explaining:

> Even though the Sabbath is counted [as part of the mourning period], festivals are not; for mourning does not apply at all on festivals, given Scripture's reference to "joy" [as part of the festival observance]. But no such reference to "joy" is made in the context of the Sabbath, which therefore is counted [as part of the mourning period] even though [public] mourning practices are not followed (*Mo'ed Katan* 23b, s.v. *man*).

This very perplexing statement poses a logical dilemma, however. If the very concept of mourning were annulled on the festival, why would private mourning practices be followed? If, on the other hand, some mourning practices were followed, mourning as a category would appear to remain operative, in which case the day should be counted as part of the mourning period!

The *sugya* raises a further uncertainty:

> Abbayei asked of Rava, "If one buried a relative on the festival, does the festival count toward *sheloshim*, the

thirty-day mourning period, or not? I do not ask this question with regard to *shiv'ah* [the initial, more stringent, seven-day mourning period], for the obligation of *shiv'ah* does not apply on the festival. But I do ask it with regard to *sheloshim*, for the obligation of *sheloshim* does apply on the festival" (*Mo'ed Katan* 19b).

Most of the *rishonim* explained that the *sheloshim* practices are obligatory on a festival because pressing clothes and cutting hair, which are forbidden during *sheloshim*, are forbidden on the festival itself as well (albeit as forms of labor rather than as activities inconsistent with mourning). Observing those rules therefore becomes a private matter, for people cannot discern whether the mourner's conduct reflects compliance with the festival's requirements or with those of *sheloshim*. But this *sugya* is perplexing regardless of whether one follows the Tosafists' approach or the Rambam's. Given the Rambam's view that even private mourning practices are not followed on a festival, in what way can the commandment of *sheloshim* be said to apply? It makes no difference that shaving and laundering are forbidden as well by the laws of *hol ha-mo'ed*, the intermediate days of the festival; the mourning prohibitions remain annulled by the festival, and, if so, why should the festival be counted as part of the thirty days? Tosafot's approach, meanwhile, seems unable to account for the distinction between the requirements of *shiv'ah* and of *sheloshim*. In both cases, the mourner observes some of the private mourning practices while the public mourning prohibitions are annulled; if so, why should the festival count as part of *sheloshim* alone and not as part of *shiv'ah* as well? *Sheloshim*, like *shiv'ah*, encompasses some practices that are within the rubric of public mourning (such as refraining from international commercial travel and from participation in weddings and other joyous gatherings); and since the mourning practices of *sheloshim* are only partially fulfilled on a festival, why should the festival count as part of the thirty-day period?

The Source and Nature of the Commandment to Mourn

[The inquiry thus far has disclosed a series of ambiguities and uncertainties affecting the laws of mourning and their relationship to other halakhic areas they intersect. How are public and private mourning practices related? What are the implications for mourning practices and mourning periods of intervening Sabbaths and festivals, and how do Sabbaths and festivals differ in this regard? How does mourning resemble the regimens of the *metzora* and the *menuddeh*? And, the issue with which we started, how do the laws of mourning affect the High Priest, in both theory and practice?]

To resolve these difficulties, we must examine the very foundation and source of the commandment to mourn. The Rambam writes:

> It is a positive commandment to mourn for one's [deceased] relatives, as is written: "And if I had eaten the sin-offering today, would it have been well-pleasing in the sight of the Lord?" (Lev. 10:10.) But mourning is biblically ordained only on the first day, the day of death and burial (*Hilkhot Avel* 1:5).

The dispute over whether mourning is biblically ordained on the first day is well-known, as is the statement of the Ri (R. Isaac b. Samuel of Dampierre), who determined (in disagreement with the Rif [R. Isaac b. Jacob Alfasi] as well as with the Rambam) that "no *avelut* [mourning] at all is biblically ordained; and while *aninut* on the first day is biblical, *aninut* and *avelut* are different matters." (This statement is quoted in the name of the Ri in the comments of the Rosh on *Mo'ed Katan*, 3:3.) However, the statements of the Rambam and of the Rif indeed pose considerable difficulty. For even granting that *avelut* and *aninut* are identical in principle, sharing the same rubric of grief, as a practical matter there is no overlap between them. Biblically ordained *aninut* takes effect immediately upon the relative's death, before burial. *Avelut*, in total contrast, begins only after burial. Before burial, the prohibitions governing a mourner do not yet apply, at least according to the Rambam's view, in contrast to that of Ramban. (See Rambam, *Hilkhot Avel* 1:2; Ramban, *Torat ha-Adam*, "*Inyan Mi she-Meto Muttal Lefanav*" ["Concerning a Bereaved Person Prior to Burial of the Deceased"], *Kitvei Ramban*, ed. C. Chavel, pp. 28-38 [Heb.] and the final passages of "*Inyan Avelut*" ["Concerning Mourning"], ibid., p. 212.) But if that is so, how can *avelut* be analogized to *aninut*?

The Rambam's view indeed appears to be that *avelut* and *aninut*, though parts of the same conceptual complex, nevertheless differ in their essential character. *Aninut* triggers prohibitions regarding participation in the Temple service, the eating of sacrificial meat, etc., but involves no *kiyyum*, that is, no affirmative fulfillment, or realization, of any *mitzvah*. In contrast, biblically ordained *avelut* entails, in its very essence, carrying out the positive commandment to mourn; and it encompasses, in the first instance, not the observance of prohibitions but the affirmative *kiyyum* of mourning as a phenomenon. To be sure, the Rambam writes that the eleven prohibitions associated with *shiv'ah*, such as the bans on cutting hair and washing clothes, apply on the first day as biblically ordained commandments and on the remaining days by rabbinic law (*Hilkhot Avel* 5:1). But these prohibitions are merely the mechanisms for realizing the state of *avelut*, the concrete means by which the commandment to mourn is carried out. Conceptually, mourning remains a *kiyyum*, a positive realization. A mourner who fails to practice the mourning norms violates thereby no particular prohibition; rather, he fails to fulfill the positive commandment to mourn.

In a passage near the one already quoted, the Rambam adds:

How weighty is the commandment to mourn! On its account, [concern about] the impurity [that a priest, who is prohibited to defile himself by contact with a corpse, would incur] from his [deceased] relatives is put aside, so that he might tend to them and mourn for them, as is written, [A priest may not defile himself] "except for his kin that is near unto him, for his mother [and six others], for her shall he defile himself" (Lev. 21:1-3). [This defilement] is a positive commandment, and if the priest does not wish to defile himself [in order to tend to the corpse], he is made to do so against his will (*Hilkhot Avel* 2:6).

It thus appears that when the priests carry out the commandment to defile themselves for their deceased next-of-kin, their action constitutes a *kiyyum* of *avelut*, and that *kiyyum* is the very reason they are permitted to become defiled. To similar effect, the Rambam states, near the beginning of *Hilkhot Avel*, that it is a positive commandment to mourn for one's deceased relatives and that even a priest defiles himself and mourns for his relatives. The two *halakhot*—the requirement to mourn one's deceased relatives and the requirement that a priest become defiled for them in a manner that desecrates his priestliness—constitute a single positive commandment among the enumerated 613 and come under the same rubric. (See Rambam, *Sefer ha-Mitzvot*, positive commandment no. 37.) It thus is clear that the essence of mourning as a phenomenon is in its *kiyyum*, which is expressed through two types of concrete actions: for all people, by following the mourning practices and refraining from the eleven forbidden activities; and, for priests, by the additional step of desecrating their priestliness. According to the Rambam, therefore, the onset of *avelut/aninut* triggers two things: a set of prohibitions, related to sacrifices, and an affirmative *kiyyum*, expressed through the eleven detailed practices.

The Impact of Burial on the Mourner's Obligations

It further appears that the law delaying the onset of mourning practices until after burial refers to the *kiyyum* of mourning; for the mourner is not obligated in that regard until after the deceased is interred. This may be an aspect of the general *halakhah* that one who confronts a corpse that he is obligated to bury is exempt from all positive commandments; alternatively, it may be a separate rule that defers the onset of *avelut* for as long as the bereaved is engaged in burying the deceased. In either event, it appears, the rubric of "mourner" applies to him, though he is unable to effect a *kiyyum* of that status. This is proven by a ruling of Rava, who told the people of Mehoza, "Those of you who do not follow the bier [all the way to the burial site] are to begin reckoning [the mourning period] from the time you turn away from the city gate [to return home]" (*Mo'ed Katan* 22a). The Rambam rules likewise: "Those whose practice it is to send a corpse to another province for burial . . . reckon *shiv'ah* and *sheloshim*, and begin to mourn, from the time they turn away from escorting the deceased" (*Hilkhot Avel* 1:5). If the obligation to mourn were triggered only at burial, and if the concept of "mourner" did not even exist before then, how, in the instances just noted, could *avelut* begin before the deceased was buried? One must conclude, rather, that the obligation to mourn comes into effect at death, not at burial, but that while the bereaved is engaged in burying the deceased, he is unable to engage in the *kiyyum* of *avelut*. In other words, burial constitutes a pre-condition to the *kiyyum* of mourning, but it is not the event that triggers the mourning obligation itself. And the foregoing rulings thus refer to that *kiyyum*: one who sends off a deceased for distant burial begins the *kiyyum* of mourning immediately thereafter, for the obligation to mourn has already been imposed by the death itself, and the deferral of the *kiyyum* on account of the need to tend to burial has been terminated.

We can now understand the distinction between how burial affects *aninut* and how it affects *avelut*. In principle, *aninut* is not distinguishable from *avelut*; indeed, they are identical. The primary distinction to be drawn is between the prohibitions imposed on the mourner and the affirmative *kiyyum* of the mourning. As we have seen, it is not burial that triggers the obligation to mourn. That requirement goes into effect immediately at the time of death, but there can be no *kiyyum* of mourning while the deceased remains unburied and his relative is preoccupied with funeral arrangements. Once that impediment is removed, the bereaved begins to mourn affirmatively, and he does so even if the deceased is not yet buried. It thus appears that the need to attend to burial operates as a postponing factor only with regard to the *kiyyum* of mourning and not at all with respect to the prohibitions imposed on the mourner. When the bereaved is occupied with the deceased, he cannot occupy himself with his *avelut* so as to achieve its *kiyyum*, and he therefore is exempt from the positive commandment to mourn. But that in no way affects the mourning prohibitions of *aninut*, for the bereaved is within the category of "mourner," and there is no reason to exempt him from its prohibitions. *Aninut* therefore begins immediately at the time of death, and its associated prohibitions are not at all deferred until after burial. *Kiyyum* of the commandment to mourn, in contrast, though also an obligation that comes into effect at the time of death, must be delayed until after burial. And that, in turn, is why biblically ordained mourning is envisioned only when death and burial occur on the same day. It must be the day of death so that the obligation to mourn will be triggered (just as *aninut*); but it must also be the day of burial, so the bereaved will have the opportunity to achieve the *kiyyum* of the *avelut*. If the deceased is not buried until the following day, the mourning regime, which begins only after burial, is not biblically ordained, for it is not the day of death.

As proof for the view that the onset of mourning depends not on burial but on death alone and that burial operates as a precondition only to the *kiyyum* of mourning but not to its prohibitions, one may cite the approach of [R. Isaac of Corbeille in his] *Sefer Mitzvot Katan*[1] (in large part adopted as binding by the Rema [R. Moses b. Israel Isserles] *Yoreh De'ah* 341:5). According to that view, a person "whose deceased lies before him" is obligated to follow all the rules of mourning even though the deceased has not yet been buried, yet the time preceding burial is not reckoned as part of the mourning period. This explicitly reflects our observation that it is the death itself that subjects the bereaved person to the practices of mourning.

Sefer Mitzvot Katan also takes the view that the mourner himself is affected by two halakhic concepts: the prohibitions associated with *avelut*, and the *kiyyum* of *avelut* for the specified number of days. The *kiyyum* of *avelut* must await burial, and the intervening time is not reckoned toward the mourning period even though the mourning prohibitions nonetheless remain in effect and must be followed. The Rambam, however, disagrees and takes the view that the mourning prohibitions, other than those specifically associated with *aninut*, were not at all independently imposed and that *avelut* cannot be practiced without a *kiyyum* that involves counting the seven days. Inasmuch as the time before burial is not reckoned toward the seven days, it follows that mourning does not apply at all; for if the mourner does not yet fulfill the commandment to mourn affirmatively, none of the mourning prohibitions apply to him. According to the Rambam, only the prohibition against eating sacrificial meat during *aninut,* which is merely a free-standing prohibition unrelated to the *kiyyum* or practices of mourning, applies to the bereaved immediately at the time of death.

The Source and Nature of the Commandment to Rejoice on a Festival

One must now, however, examine the *sugya* that states, "A mourner does not follow his mourning practices on a festival, for it is written, 'And you shall rejoice in your festival . . .' (Deut. 16:14): the community's positive commandment [of rejoicing] displaces the individual's positive commandment [to mourn]" (*Mo'ed Katan* 14b). Inasmuch as the commandment to rejoice is fulfilled by eating meat and drinking wine (*Pesahim* 109a), and those activities are permitted to a mourner, why should he refrain from following his mourning practices on the festival? Indeed, a mourner could fulfill festival rejoicing even in Temple times, when the commandment to rejoice entailed the eating of sacrificial meat, for a mourner was permitted to eat such meat, and only an *onen* was forbidden to do so. Why, then, did the *sugya* see rejoicing and mourning as inherently opposed?

Notwithstanding the ways in which we have been commanded to fulfill the *mitzvah* of rejoicing on a festival (in Temple times, by eating sacrificial meat; nowadays by other practices such as eating meat and drinking wine), it is plainly-clear that this *mitzvah* in fact entails a joyful heart in the simplest sense, requiring the individual to be joyful on the festival. The specific *halakhot* pertain only to how the commandment is to be carried out in a technical sense, but the essence of the commandment, it is clear, pertains to the person's inner state on the festival. In formualting specific details, the Torah simply directed how the inner joy is to be actively affirmed.

Three proofs may be offered for the foregoing proposition.

First, the Rambam takes the view, contrary to Tosafot (at *Mo'ed Katan* 14b, s.v. *aseh*), that even nowadays our obligation to rejoice on a festival remains a matter of biblical law. He writes: "Even though the rejoicing spoken of [in Scripture] refers to the *shelamim* sacrifice . . . , it encompasses as well the individual's rejoicing together with his children and his household, each as befits him" (*Hilkhot Yom Tov* 6:17). At first blush, it seems perplexing that the biblical obligation to rejoice on the festival can be fulfilled nowadays. We can understand how the eating of sacrificial meat on the festival fulfills the obligation, but how can that purpose by achieved by the mere consumption of meat for pleasure, or the distribution of roasted nuts or the purchase of color-ful clothing—the aspects of rejoicing that Rambam cites for men, children, and women, respectively (see *Hilkhot Yom Tov* 6:18)? One must conclude, rather, that the *kiyyum* of rejoicing consists, in essence, of heartfelt inner rejoicing, which can be expressed in various ways: in Temple times, through the eating of sacrificial meat; nowadays, through bringing about happiness in the vari-ous ways likely to arouse it in the human heart.

Second, consider the following statement by the Rambam: "Even though each of the festivals entails a commandment to rejoice, the festival of Sukkot, in the Temple, included a day of especially intense rejoicing, as is written (Lev. 23:40), '. . . and ye shall rejoice before the Lord your God seven days' (Lev. 23:40)" (*Hilkhot Lulav* 8:12). The Rambam apparently held that the rejoicing at the Temple ceremony of *Simhat Beit ha-Sho'evah* falls under the same rubric as rejoicing on the festival, for the festival of Sukkot encompassed an obligation of especially intense rejoicing in the Temple, i.e., *Simhat Beit ha-Sho'evah*. Similarly, in his *Sefer ha-Mitzvot*, the Rambam writes:

> In stating, "And you shall rejoice in your festival" (Deut. 16:14), [Scripture] encompassed as well the rabbinic directive to rejoice through various joyous activities, including eating meat and drinking wine on the festivals, wearing new clothes and so forth, and making music and dancing [these only in the Temple, i.e., at *Simhat Beit ha-Sho'evah*]. All of these activities are included within the statement "And you shall rejoice in your festival" (*Sefer ha-Mitzvot*, positive commandment no. 54).

Later in the same work, the Rambam writes: "[Scripture] commanded us to take the *lulav* and rejoice with it before God seven day" (ibid., positive commandment no. 169). Taking the *lulav* all seven days of Sukkot in the Temple is, in principle, a *kiyyum* of the commandment to rejoice in the Temple on a festival, as Scripture says, ". . . And you shall rejoice before the Lord your God seven days" (Lev. 23:40); the rejoicing is made concrete through the *lulav*. (The Jerusalem Talmud [*Sukkah* 3:11] reports an amoraic dispute regarding this commandment: "There are some who teach that Scripture refers to rejoicing with the *lulav*; and there are some who teach that Scripture refers to rejoicing through [eating of] the *shelamim* sacrifices.") This proves that, in the Temple, carrying out the commandment to take the *lulav* is identified with fulfilling the obligation to rejoice. Further, it appears that the same commandment to rejoice can itself be fulfilled in various ways through the consumption of sacrificial meat, through various delights, through song in the Temple, and through use of the *lulav*. But each of these actions is an expression of the single commandment to rejoice on the festival, whose essence is inner, heartfelt joy. The techniques may vary, but the concept remains the same.

Third, consider the comments made by the Rosh in assessing how to refer liturgically to Rosh ha-Shanah and Yom Kippur. [Currently, the phrase "set times for joy, festivals and times of happiness" is used in the *Amidah* and *Kiddush* only for the three pilgramage festivals of Pesah, Shavuot and Sukkot.] The Rosh quotes the remarks of the Geonim and other early authorities on the subject:

> A responsum by Mar Sar Shalom states: "At both [Babylonian] *yeshivot*, worshippers on Rosh ha-Shanah would refer, in the *Amidah* and in the *Kiddush*, to [the general remembrance] . . . 'set times for joy, festivals and times for happiness,' [and also the specific] 'this Day of Remembrance. . . . ' The reason is that Scripture states, at the beginning of the [festival] passage, 'These are the appointed seasons of the Lord' (Lev. 23:4) and, at the end of the passage, 'And Moses declared unto the children of Israel the appointed seasons of the Lord' (Lev. 23:44). These [bracketing statements] refer to the entire pas-

sage . . . [including] Rosh ha-Shanah and Yom Kippur, . . . [showing that] all of them are comparable to each other in being considered appointed seasons and holy convocations.' Moreover, Rosh ha-Shanah is described as a memorial proclaimed with the blast of horns, a holy convocation' (Lev. 23:24) (Rosh, at *Rosh ha-Shanah*, chapter 4, par. 14).

The Rosh goes on [regarding the *ve-hasi'enu* passage, which currently is recited only on the three pilgrimage festivals]:

Rabbeinu Isaac bar Judah, in the name of Rabbeinu Eliezer the Great, instituted in Mainz the practice of reciting *ve-hasi'enu* on Rosh ha-Shanah and Yom Kippur, and Rabbi Meshullam, after posing the question to the head of the *yeshivah* in Jerusalem, received the same ruling.

These prominent authorities hold that rejoicing is associated with Rosh ha-Shanah, but their view at first seems difficult to understand. Israel was never commanded to sacrifice *shelamim* joy-offerings on Rosh ha-Shanah, and any realization of joy on Yom Kippur, when eating is forbidden, seems hard to imagine! The answer, of course, is simple: the joy is realized inwardly; and Rosh ha-Shanah and Yom Kippur differ from the other festivals only in the external actions through which the commandment to rejoice is fulfilled. On festivals other than Rosh ha-Shanah and Yom Kippur, the eating of sacrificial meat was the means through which Jews were commanded to concretize their obligation to rejoice. On Rosh ha-Shanah, no specific action was commanded to give expression to the inner joy; but the obligation to effect a *kiyyum* of joy applies then, and on Yom Kippur, nonetheless.

Similar to these geonic statements is the halakhically authoritative comment of Rabban Gamliel in the mishnah:

"Rabban Gamliel says Rosh ha-Shanah and Yom Kippur are as festivals" (Mishnah *Mo'ed Katan* 3:6 at 19a). and they displace mourning. The *sugya* previously discussed (*Mo'ed Katan* 14b) explains that mourning is displaced by the festival because of the commandment to rejoice. Thus one can see that rejoicing applies to Rosh ha-Shanah and Yom Kippur as well, when its *kiyyum* is internal and can be achieved specifically through confession and feelings of penance, although on Rosh ha-Shanah, of course, in contrast to Yom Kippur, the internal affirmation can be expressed through actions as well, albeit not through the eating of sacrificial meat. (The Rosh, ibid., added: "In the Book of Ezra as well we find that the people, on returning from Babylon, wept [on Rosh ha-Shanah] but Ezra admonished them that 'this day is holy unto our Lord' (Neh. 8:10) and told them to eat and drink well so that the ensuing year might be a rich and a sweet one and to send gifts to those in need.")

The Clash between Mourning and Festival

Mourning on a festival thus appears to be contradicted not by the activities that concretize the festival joy, for even a mourner can give treats to his children, purchase colorful clothes for his wife, and eat meat and drink wine. Rather, it is the *kiyyum* of festival joy through heartfelt experience that is incompatible with mourning. Seen in this light, mourning and rejoicing are, indeed, inherently opposites; and since a mourner could not possibly realize the essential commandment of inner joy, it follows that all his gestures on the festival, such as eating meat, would lack real substance. Those actions, after all, are simply means for concretizing the goal of inner joy.

It appears further that mourning too—although in practice realized through the mandated eleven prohibitions—constitutes in its essence and basic *kiyyum* an element of inner experience. In effect, the Torah has required that inward soulful mourning be expressed through observance of the eleven prohibitions, but the central *kiyyum* consists of a psychological state of dejection and sadness. Could one imagine that the obligation to mourn had been fulfilled by a mourner who, though adhering diligently to all the prescribed practices and violating none of the eleven prohibitions, at the same time brought into his home and enjoyed, during the mourning period, all manner of pleasant diversions? There is, in fact, a mishnah to this effect: "[The relatives of an executed transgressor] would not mourn [*lo hayu mit'abbelin*] but, instead, would grieve [*onenin*], for grief lies only in the heart" (Mishnah *Sanhedrin* 6:6 at 46b). That is, they are exempt from active mourning practices, but they mourn their loss inwardly, for the *kiyyum* of mourning is inward. (The term "*aninut*" [here rendered "grief"] as used in the mishnah refers not to the prohibition on eating sacrificial meat but, rather, to the *kiyyum* of mourning. It is referred to as "*aninut*" because it is inward, in contrast to the term "*avelut*" [mourning], which refers to effectuation in practice.)

We see as well that even though the seven days of mourning are not biblically ordained, the personal status of mourner applies throughout the *shiv'ah* period. Thus, the Rambam ruled (in opposition to Rabbi Simeon's view [*Zevahim* 99b] that only an *onen* is barred from sending animals to be sacrificed) that throughout *shiv'ah* a mourner may not send sacrificial animals. From his comments, it appears that Rambam regarded this ruling as biblically ordained and, hence, held as well that a sacrifice sent by a mourner does not discharge the obligation the sacrifice was meant to fulfill. He states: "A mourner does not send sacrifices during the entire *shiv'ah* period. . . . It is uncertain, however, whether a *menuddeh* sends sacrifices; accordingly, if a sacrifice was made on his behalf, it is accepted" (*Hilkhot Bi'at Mikdash* 2:11). Through the tacit contrast he draws, Rambam implies that a sacrifice made on behalf of a mourner is not accepted. Thus, we see, even though the mourner is biblically required to express his mourning through the eleven restrictions on only the first day, the mourning weighs on him all seven days and precludes his sending a sacrificial animal.

At first glance, it is hard to understand the idea of mourning divested of its manifestations in practice, but the matter is actually quite clear. The *kiyyum* of mourning goes on for all seven days, but, as a matter of biblical law, it comprises exclusively inner mourning, not the external, concrete actions through which it is expressed. Only on the first day did the Torah command the use of active mourning practices (that is, the eleven restrictions) to concretize the inner mourning in recognizable ways. Rambam states (*Hilkhot Avel* 1:1) that mourning after the first day is not biblically ordained, despite the Torah's statement that Joseph "made a mourning for his father seven days" (Gen. 50:10); for the Torah, when given, superseded prior practice. The Rambam can be understood to mean that the practices of mourning associated with the eleven prohibitions do not apply beyond the first day, yet inner mourning continues to prevail throughout all seven days.

This, then, is the meaning of the *sugya*'s determination that a mourner does not follow mourning practices on a festival because the community's positive commandment to rejoice on the festival displaces the individual's positive commandment to mourn. Mourning and festival rejoicing are mutually exclusive; the *kiyyum* of one cancels that of the other and the two cannot be achieved simultaneously. The external actions, to be sure, can co-exist, and one could practice outer, concrete expressions of mourning while still eating sacrificial meat. But these actions were intended merely as expressions of psychological states, as means for effecting the *kiyyum* of inner mourning or inner rejoicing, and one commandment is displaced by the other.

It turns out, then, that a festival day is not reckoned as part of *shiv'ah* because the *kiyyum* of mourning, which is grounded in the heart and finds its essence there, is annulled on such a day. And that is why the Rambam holds that even private mourning practices are not followed on a festival; for it is simply impossible for the res (*heftzah*) of mourning to be realized on a festival day. A festival differs in this regard from the Sabbath, which entails honor and delight but not joy. Honor and delight require outer actions, not inner states: one honors the day by wearing clean garments and expresses delight by eating tasty food. The Sabbath, therefore, precludes only acts of public mourning, such as going shoeless and observing the other prohibitions, for those practices would preclude the *kiyyum* of honor and delight. The mourner remains obligated, however, to follow the private mourning practices, which are not sensed by others, for he can honor the Sabbath while still mourning his departed. The inner *kiyyum* of mourning can be embodied in concrete, private actions on the Sabbath, for there is nothing to contradict it. But on a festival, when all possibility of *kiyyum avelut* is annulled, there is no reason to follow even private mourning practices, for nothing would be realized through them.

Moreover, it may be suggested that even the Tosafists, who would enforce private mourning prohibitions on a festival, may acknowledge the annulment on a festival of any trace of a *kiyyum* of mourning. They nevertheless reach their conclusion by following the view of *Sefer Mitzvot Katan* that the prohibitions associated with mourning exist independently of its *kiyyum* (as, for example, prior to burial, when mourning is expressed solely through the observance of prohibitions and the day accordingly is not reckoned as part of *shiv'ah*). Analogously, if mourning prohibitions could be followed without any *kiyyum* of the mourning and without the day being reckoned toward the mourning period, those prohibitions could apply on a festival. The Rambam, however, disputes the view of *Sefer Mitzvot Katan* and holds that mourning prohibitions lack independent existence. He ascribes such existence only to the *kiyyum* of mourning, which the prohibitions concretize. If that *kiyyum* is precluded, it follows that the prohibitions are annulled; and he therefore rules that even private mourning practices are not followed on a festival.

This conceptual framework resolves Tosafot's difficulty regarding why a festival day does not count as part of the mourning period even though the Sabbath does. On a festival, there is no *kiyyum* of the mourning whatsoever, for festive joy precludes and cancels the inner sense of mourning, and it follows that the day is not counted as part of the mourning period. Adherence to the private prohibitions (as required on the festival according to Tosafot, though not according to the Rambam) constitutes merely observance of the mourning through actions, without any positive *kiyyum*. On the Sabbath, in contrast, the mourner can achieve the *kiyyum* of mourning, even though its public embodiments are suspended on account of the requirements to honor and delight in the Sabbath; and the day, accordingly, is reckoned as part of the prescribed period. Tosafot's comments in this regard are illuminating: "The answer is given that the festival is not reckoned toward the mourning period even though the Sabbath is so reckoned because there is no mourning at all [on a festival], in connection with which Scripture refers to 'joy.' 'Joy' is not referred to in connection with the Sabbath, however, and it therefore counts toward the prescribed period even though [public] mourning is not practiced."

Similarly, we can resolve the seeming anomaly in the *sugya* that proved that a festival day counts toward the *sheloshim* because some aspects of mourning are practiced on it. Given the Rambam's view, we asked why private mourning prohibitions should indeed be waived on a festival, as he rules, and why there should be any distinction at all between *sheloshim*, when some prohibitions are said to apply, and *shiv'ah*, when none of them do. Concurrently, given Tosafot's view, we raised the concern that during *shiv'ah*, no less than during *sheloshim*, private mourning prohibitions are observed on a festival day. On either view, accordingly, the distinction between *shiv'ah* and *sheloshim* seemed problematic.

The simple answer is that the mourning of *shiv'ah* differs from the mourning of *sheloshim*. Mourning during *shiv'ah* entails an inner *kiyyum* of mourning, of the sort that is annulled by the festival; in contrast, mourning during the remainder of *sheloshim* entails no such *kiyyum*. Five of the mourning restrictions (such as the bans on haircuts and weddings) continue in force during *sheloshim*, but they do so only as bare prohibitions, without any affirmative *kiyyum*. Accordingly, the mourner on a festival practices those aspects of *sheloshim* that do not negate the honor and delight (as distinct from the joy) associated with the festival; and his practicing of those prohibitions warrants reckoning the day toward the thirty. The mourning of *shiv'ah*, in contrast, is entirely annulled on the festival, for the period is one of *kiyyum avelut*, not merely refraining from prohibited actions; and the festival day therefore is not counted toward the seven.

Similar reasoning easily accounts for the *sugya*'s question and decision regarding how a *menuddeh* and a *metzora* are to behave on a festival. Clearly, there is no inner *kiyyum* of mourning whatsoever in their cases, for nowhere are we taught that they must mourn over their excommunication or their leprosy. Mourning-type prohibitions apply to them; but they follow those practices without any *kiyyum* of mourning. Indeed, it further appears that the legal regimens related to leprosy and excommunication comprise *in toto* only the prohibition of actions. Accordingly, one can follow those regimens on a festival and simultaneously fulfill the commandment to rejoice; for why should one who lets his hair grow wild or wears torn garments or is excommunicated necessarily be unable to fulfill the commandment to be joyful? He can eat meat and drink wine, rejoice inwardly, and discharge his obligation with respect to the festival. Unlike the mourner (whose inner state contradicts the *kiyyum* of rejoicing), his situation entails no negation of joy. The *sugya* therefore determined that all the rules of *niddui* and leprosy are to be followed on a festival.

An Analogy between High Priest and Festival

This analysis can be illuminated and sharpened by a further comparison between the laws pertaining to the High Priest and to a festival. Consider the following statement by the Rambam:

> Just as the priests are admonished to avoid wine only when they enter the Sanctuary, so, too, are they forbidden to grow their hair wild [as a sign of mourning] only when they enter the Sanctuary. To whom does this rule apply? To ordinary priests. The High Priest, however, is barred at all times from growing his hair wild or tearing his clothes, for he is always [considered to have the status of being] in the Sanctuary. In his case, therefore, Scripture says, "[The High Priest] shall not let the hair of his head go loose, nor rend his clothes" (Lev. 21:10) (*Hilkhot Bi'at Mikdash* 1:10).

The Torah, in fact, makes two pronouncements on the subject. One, appearing in the account of the death of Aaron's two eldest sons, pertains to all the priests: "And Moses said unto Aaron and unto Eleazar and unto Ithamar, his sons: 'Let not the hair of your heads go loose, neither rend your clothes, that you die not'" (Lev. 10:6). The other states: "And the priest that is highest among his brethren . . . shall not let the hair of his head go loose nor rend his clothes" (Lev. 21:10). At first glance, there seem to be two distinct prohibitions here. The first admonition pertains to a priest with disheveled hair or with torn garments entering the Sanctuary or participating in the sacrificial service. (Which of the two it is depends on the resolution of a dispute between the Rambam and the Ramban. See the Rambam's

Sefer ha-Mitzvot, negative commandment no. 163 and the Ramban's comment ad loc.; Ramban's *Hilkhot Bi'at Mikdash* 1:14; and Ramban's Commentary on the Torah at Lev. 10:9.) The second admonition bars the High Priest more broadly from tearing his garments or allowing his hair to grow wild even when he is not in the Sanctuary. The Rambam, however, does not list these as separate items in the enumeration of the 613 commandments in his *Sefer ha-Mitzvot*; instead, he includes the admonition to the High Priest in the Torah portion *Emor* (Lev. 21:10) within the more general prohibitions that apply to all priests and that govern entry into the Sanctuary. (See *Sefer ha-Mitzvot*, negative commandments nos. 163 and 164.)

At first glance, it is perplexing that he would merge these two prohibitions, which pertain to wholly distinct matters. But the Rambam explains his view by specifying that "the High Priest, however, is barred at all times from growing his hair wild or tearing his clothes, for he is always in the Sanctuary. In his case, therefore, Scripture says, 'He shall not let the hair of his head loose, nor rend his clothes'" (*Hilkhot Bi'at Mikdash* 1:10). In other words, the verse in *Emor* does not introduce a new prohibition; rather, it identifies a novel application of the existing prohibition in a new context. The prohibition remains the same: a priest is forbidden to be present in the Sanctuary with torn clothes or wildly grown hair and applies as well to the High Priest. But a further law specifies that the High Priest retains at all times the status of being in the Sanctuary. Even when he is physically outside the Temple court, he is considered to be situated within the Sanctuary; and the associated prohibitions against torn garments and wildly grown hair continue to apply to him.

Furthermore, the Rambam writes:

> A priest, whether the High Priest or an ordinary one, who leaves the Sanctuary while serving there is subject to death, as is written, "And you shall not go out from the door of the tent of meeting, lest you die" (Lev. 10:7); that

is, "Do not abandon the service to rush out frantically on account of this [Divine] decree [that imposed the death penalty on Nadav and Avihu]." Similarly, the injunction that the High Priest shall not "go out of the sanctuary" (Lev. 21:12) applies only during the service, forbidding him to abandon his service and leave. But if that is so, why is this admonition repeated in connection with the High Priest? Because an ordinary priest who, while in the midst of serving in the Sanctuary, learns of the death of one for whom he is obligated to mourn does not leave the Sanctuary but neither does he continue his service; for he is an *onen*, and an *onen* according to biblical law who nevertheless serves in the Sanctuary defiles his service [subject to the exception next noted], regardless of whether the service is in connection with an individual sacrifice or a communal one. The High Priest, however, does serve while an *onen*, as is written, "Neither shall he go out of the sanctuary nor profane [the sanctuary of his God]" (Lev. 21:12); that is, he remains and continues the service he was engaged in, and the service is not defiled (*Hilkhot Bi'at Mikdash* 2:5-6).

It appears that the principle established by the Rambam with respect to tearing garments and allowing the hair to grow wild stems from the law that validates service by the High Priest while he is an *onen*. We can infer from this law a special scriptural decree that ties the High Priest to the Sanctuary even when he is outside its precincts. So, too, even when he suffers the death of a close relative, he does not abandon his service and leave. Instead, he remains in the Sanctuary, for the rule that he is constantly there has not been annulled. It follows, then, that the *sugya* establishes the maxim that "the High Priest year-round resembles all Jews on a festival," meaning that the High Priest stands perpetually before God, for he is always in the Sanctuary, and his status is that of all Jews on a festival.

Carrying this reasoning further, one may say that just as mourning is displaced on a festival by the *kiyyum* of rejoicing, so, too, is it displaced year-round for the High Priest (in a view held by all the *rishonim* except the Rambam) because of his perpetual presence in the Sanctuary, a situation that annuls mourning. This also is the premise of the *Gemara*'s reasoning that an afflicted High Priest's adherence to the practices of a *metzora* proves that those practices are to be followed on a festival as well. In addition, the *Gemara* cited the rules of an *onen* to show that mourning practices are annulled in the case of the High Priest because he is perpetually in the Sanctuary, standing before God.

Rejoicing Before God

The broader point here is that the festival's nullification of mourning on account of the joy associated with the day is not at all a free-standing phenomenon. Instead, it is tied up with the fact that, as Scripture states, on a festival all Israel stands before God, and the festival's importance is identified with man's rejoicing before his Creator. The joy is merely an emotional expression of the human's experience of standing before God, and it is this appearance before God that fully annuls the mourning, for mourning and standing before God are mutually exclusive. Indeed, there is no rejoicing except before God, as is written, "You shall rejoice before the Lord your God seven days" (Lev. 23:40); wherever one finds joy, one finds as well a standing before God.

Given, then, that the factor displacing mourning is the individual's presence before God, it follows that the High Priest's year-round situation with respect to mourning will be the same as that of all Jews on a festival. And the fact that an afflicted High Priest follows the *metzora*'s rules shows that leprosy differs from mourning, in that it does annul the High Priest's status as one standing before the Lord. It follows, *ipso facto*, that for all people leprosy annuls the festival status of "before the Lord" and that a *metzora*, even on a festival, follows the practices associated with his condition.

That being the case, moreover, one can easily understand the statement, made by the student of R. Yehiel of Paris, that a *metzora*, because he is unable to enter the camp, cannot effect an affirmative *kiyyum* of the commandment to rejoice. The nullification of mourning grows out of the person's presence before God, and the essence of festival joy is the bonding between the human being and God's *Shekhinah*, the Divine Presence, as explained above. Accordingly, the festival joy of a *menuddeh* or a *metzora* is annulled. The expulsion of the *metzora* from all three concentric camps of priests, Levites, and Israelites (see *Torat Kohanim* on Lev. 13:46); the fulfillment of the injunction that "[the *metzora*] shall dwell alone; without the camp shall his dwelling be" (Lev. 13:46); and the isolation of the *menuddeh* from the "congregation of the captivity" (that being how the excommunication is effectuated, as Scripture states, ". . . whosoever came not within three days, according to the counsel of the princes and the elders, all his substance should be forfeited, and himself separated from the congregation of the captivity" [Ezra 10:8])—all of these serve to create a barrier between the *metzora* or the *menuddeh* and God's *Shekhinah*, and to annul their standing before God on the festival. It follows that even if their mourning-like *niddui* practices were suspended on the festival, the *metzora* and the *menuddeh* would remain unable to fulfill the commandment to rejoice, for they would be forbidden, regardless, to enter any of the three camps.[2] Accordingly, the festival does not annul the leprosy and *niddui* practices.

A related point is made by the student of R. Yehiel of Paris, who raises, in his *Shitah* (on *Mo'ed Katan* 14b; p. 14 of the work itself), the difficult question of why *niddui* is practiced on the festival even though mourning, which at first blush is a weightier matter, is suspended. He answers:

Even though we found, earlier in this discussion, many items that apply to a mourner but do not apply in all their stringency to a *menuddeh,* such as the prohibitions against studying Torah and working and the requirement to rend one's garments, we nevertheless found as well areas in which the *menuddeh's* regime is more severe than the mourner's, such as the requirement that the *menuddeh* dwell "within his own four cubits," not going out in public.

The connection between "dwelling within his own four cubits" and practicing *niddui* on a festival seems perplexing, but the foregoing discussion resolves the difficulty: the prohibition against appearing in public expresses the *menuddeh's* isolation from the "congregation of the captivity," and it follows that he does not stand before God and that his rejoicing is annulled.

It further appears that the force by which festival rejoicing can displace other conditions is its status as a community commandment. A community commandment, in turn, appears to connote not merely a precept that obligates all members of the community, for there is no reason why a commandment's force should be augmented simply because many people are bound by it, but one that entails a communal *kiyyum*. In other words, attaining the *kiyyum* of festival joy requires that the individuals not only rejoice on their own but also cause one another to be joyful as well. Thus, we find, one is obligated to gladden his household as explained in Abbayei's statement, "A woman is made happy by her husband" (*Rosh ha-Shanah* 6b) along with the Levite, the poor, and the unfortunate, as Scripture states, "And you shall rejoice in your festival, you, and your son and your daughter and your man-servant and your maid-servant and the Levite and the stranger and the orphan and the widow, who are within your gates" (Deut. 16:14). Similarly, the Rambam writes:

While one eats and drinks [in celebration of a festival], it is his duty to feed the stranger, the orphan, the widow, and other poor and unfortunate people. For he who locks the gates of his courtyard and eats and drinks with his wife and children, without giving anything to eat and drink to the poor and the bitter in spirit—his meal is not a rejoicing in a Divine commandment but a rejoicing in his stomach (*Hilkhot Yom Tov* 6:18).

(Compare Rashi on Deut. 16:11: "Four of Mine [referred to in the verse, i.e., the Levite, the stranger, the widow and the orphan], corresponding to four of yours [i.e., your son, your daughter, your man-servant and your maid-servant].")

We thus find that a precondition to the *kiyyum* of festival rejoicing is bringing about the rejoicing of others. That is why a *menuddeh* and a *metzora*, who are sent out of the three camps and separated from the community of Israel, are unable to fulfill the commandment to rejoice, for it is, again, a communal commandment. This is reflected as well in the precise wording of R. Yehiel's student, who writes, "He is forbidden to enter the camp and rejoice with the group." Accordingly, the *menuddeh* and the *metzora* follow their regimens on the festival, for the commandment to rejoice is annulled for them.

Mourning as Distancing from God

Developing this thought further (and in anticipation of concluding), let me add that the equation of rejoicing with standing before God implies its inverse, namely, the equation of mourning with distancing from before God. This, indeed, is the "ostracism from before Heaven [*niddui la-Shamayim*]" that the *sugya* (*Mo'ed Katan* 15b) considers. On this basis, we can appreciate the analogy between the mourner and the *menuddeh*: the *menuddeh* follows mourning-like practices because mourning itself amounts, in principle, to ostracism from before God. A *baraita* suggests the same comparison in describing a fast decreed in time of drought: "They cover themselves and sit like *menuddin* and mourners until Heaven takes mercy on them" (*Mo'ed Katan* 15a). It thus implies that when all Israel is afflicted, the court practices *niddui*; for the affliction is identified with the withdrawal and concealment of God's *Shekhinah*, and that, in turn, amounts to *niddui*, the most severe form of which is ostracism from before Heaven. Abbaye suggests as much in the cited passage, where he says, "Perhaps a *menuddeh* from before Heaven differs, in that his situation is more severe." Summing the matter up, to rejoice is to stand before God; to mourn is to be distanced from Him.

Seeing the matter in this light permits us to resolve as well the apparent conflict, identified at the outset, between the *sugya* in *Mo'ed Katan* and the Rambam's view that the High Priest is required to mourn. If, following R. Yehiel's view, we understand the import of the *gemara*'s query (*Mo'ed Katan* 14b) about whether the *metzora*'s regimen is to be followed on a festival to be whether a *metzora's* standing before God is canceled, and its conclusion to be that indeed it is, the conflict with the Rambam's ruling that the High Priest is subject to the rules of mourning is resolved. Meanwhile, following the view of the other *rishonim* that the High Priest is not subject to mourning, one can interpret the *sugya* as determining that an afflicted High Priest practices a *metzora*'s regimen because the leprosy annuls his status as one who stands before God and is bonded to God's *Shekhinah*. And if that is so, then on a festival the leprosy likewise annuls the category of joy and the *metzora*'s standing before God, and the *metzora*'s regimen is practiced.

The distinction between mourning, which is not practiced by the High Priest, and the *metzora*'s regime, which is, rests on the view that the two concepts differ in their nature. The mourning that cancels one's presence before God depends on the practice of mourning. One who is obligated to effect a *kiyyum* of mourning is distanced from before God, for that is the practical effect of mourning; but there is no abstract concept of mourning that *per se* cancels one's presence before God. Indeed, "a mourner" as an abstract concept does not exist at all; there is only the practice of mourning and nothing more. Accordingly, a High Priest who stands before God is not obligated to practice mourning, which entails a distancing from before God. Leprosy, in contrast, is tied up not with the *metzora*'s mourning-like practices but with the abstract concept of being a *metzora* and bearing his impurity. The *metzora*'s expulsion from the three camps is attributable to impurity and not to mourning, and it applies, according to all views (except Rashi's), even on a festival. And, if that is so, the High Priest who becomes afflicted will remain isolated outside the camp, and the commandment to rejoice "before the Lord" will not be fulfilled through him, even though his status as High Priest might displace and exempt him from the mourning-like practices that concretize the *metzora*'s situation, such as letting his hair grow wild and tearing his garments. But since the *metzora*'s separation from the community in itself annuls his bonding with God's *Shekhinah* and his standing before God, there is no reason to exempt him, even if he is the High Priest, from the mourning-like practices associated with leprosy. Mourning itself, however, poses a different situation, for the person's standing before God in that instance is annulled not by reason of the concept of mourning *per se* but by its *kiyyum* and practice. That being so, the High Priest, who is defined as one who stands before God, should not be required to adhere to a mourning regimen that will separate him from before God; on the contrary, he is not to follow those practices or isolate himself.

The Rambam also appears to endorse this line of reasoning, i.e., that the impurity *per se* is what nullifies the *metzora*'s presence before God, but that the nullifying factor for a mourner is his following the mourning practices. Accordingly, a *metzora* follows his regimen on a festival, for he is in any event impure, and his capacity to effectuate a *kiyyum* of rejoicing before the Lord is necessarily annulled. A mourner, on the other hand, does not adhere to his mourning regime, and the mourning is displaced by the advent of festival rejoicing; for if he refrains from effectuating a *kiyyum* of the mourning, and does not separate himself from the community, he will remain one who stands before the Lord. Adherence to the mourning regimen, however, would distance him from God's presence; and the law therefore was determined to be that one effectuates a *kiyyum* of festival rejoicing and, in order to remain "standing before the Lord," does not follow mourning practices.

These considerations apply, however, only with respect to a festival, which entails the community's specific, positive commandment to rejoice and to stand before God. That commandment, as already noted, displaces the individual's positive commandment to mourn. In the case of the High Priest, however, there is no positive commandment to remain perpetually in the Sanctuary and before God; rather, there is only an attribute associated with the person who is characterized as "standing before the Lord." Mourning, meanwhile, remains a positive commandment; and, that being so, why should the High Priest not effectuate a *kiyyum* of the mourning, and why should he necessarily remain bonded to God's presence instead? On the contrary, he should separate himself and devote himself to his mourning! For just as we say the commanded joy of the festival displaces mourning, and the mourner should not distance himself on the festival from before the Lord, we should correspondingly say that the commandment of mourning displaces the High Priest's attribute of being perpetually in the Sanctuary. The festival displaces mourning because of the commandment to rejoice; for if the *kiyyum* of mourning is displaced, the resulting separation from before God is annulled. But with respect to the High Priest, there is no commandment that displaces mourning, and he should follow the mourning practices, allowing his constancy in the Sanctuary to be displaced.

Were the High Priest to be exempted from the *metzora*'s regimen, that would prove that such a regimen could be annulled even without the displacing force of a positive commandment and even if the High Priest's standing before God were not affected by his actions. In that case, neither would he mourn, for we would say that the essence of his status exempts him from it. But since that is not the case, and the High Priest does follow the *metzora*'s regimen (for it is not the regimen that determines his status before God; rather the *metzora* is automatically separated from before God on account of his status, even without adherence to his regimen), it follows that the only reason the High Priest's mourning regime might be negated is that it might affect, or annul, his status before God. But that reason would apply only given a commandment and an obligation to stand before the Lord. Such a commandment exists on a festival, and, accordingly, mourning then is totally canceled. But the High Priest is subject to no such commanded obligation with respect to his status, and the rule properly is that he must mourn.

---

1. See *Haggahot Maimuniyyot, Hilkhot Avel,* chapter 4, note 3: "And *Sefer Mitzvot Katan* reads as follows: 'In any event, [the bereaved before burial] is permitted to wear shoes and leave his home because he is obligated to tend to the needs of the deceased, but the [prohibition on] sexual relations and all other aspects of mourning are to be practiced.'" Our text of *Sefer Mitzvot Katan* (near the end of commandment 97) lacks the concluding passage (from "but"), and it is Rabbeinu Peretz who supplied the correct reading in his editorial comments.

2. But see Rashi (*Mo'ed Katan* 14b, *s.v. she-yanhig tzara'ato*), who explained that the leprosy practices under consideration in that *sugya* in connection with a festival are the ones requiring that the *metzora* "not enter the camp and not shave." This would imply, contrary to the premise in the text, that if the practices were suspended, the leper would be permitted to enter the three camps. The Rambam (*Hilkhot Tum'at Tzara'at* 10:6), however, cites the rules regarding wildly-grown hair, torn garments, and banned greetings; and his comments suggest that even if these practices of the *metzora* were suspended on the festival, the *metzora* still would be barred from entering the three camps. R. Yehiel's student takes this view as well.

❧ A Halakhic Approach to Suffering

Whatever I am going to say today is the result of my own thinking and my religious experience of Jewish values. I do not lay claim to objectivity and philosophic validity. I do not claim that my interpretations or analyses are true. It is hard to pinpoint and define a Jewish philosophy, particularly a Jewish philosophy of man. Whatever I am going to say should be taken as a soliloquy, as a monologue. I am thinking out loud and trying to spell out my own experiences and understand the great transcendental adventure of the Jewish people. If someone will find my experiences and my interpretations commensurate with his own, I shall be amply rewarded. However, if one should not concur with me and should feel that my experiences do not correspond with his own attitudes, I shall not feel hurt.

Two Levels of Halakhic Creativity

Before taking up the subject of suffering and mental health, I would like to offer a brief general description of Halakhah, because it will be very important for our analysis. The gesture of halakhic creativity unfolds at two levels. First, at the level of positivistic thinking, the halakhic logos and ethos (the halakhic mind and the halakhic will) posit unique categorical forms, postulate a set of rules and develop well-defined topics revolving around man and his formal relationship to the ontological orders surrounding him. Basically, the Halakhah is concerned with one problem—that of the relationship of man to the existential orders confronting him. At this level were born the great halakhic conceptual system as well as normative disciplines— what we call in the vernacular, the codes—which lay claim to the human mind and will.

The motto of the halakhic logos and ethos was expressed in the answer that the Jews of old gave Moses when he came down from Mount Sinai: "All that God hath spoken, *na'aseh ve-nishma*" (Ex. 24:7). The Latin Vulgate translated "*na'aseh ve-nishma*" in the sense of obeying: "*faciemus et erimus obedientes*, we will do and we will be obedient." However, the Talmud interprets the word "*ve-nishma*" theologically and semantically. In Hebrew, "*ve-nishma*" has the connotation of understanding instead of obeying. According to the talmudic interpretation, "*na'aseh*" means, "We shall be obedient, we shall obey the laws," and "*ve-nishma*" means, "We shall try to understand the laws" (*Shabbat* 88a-89b). This is quite characteristic of our talmudic approach, which is commensurate with the philosophy of Halakhah. It is not enough to do; it is also important and essential to understand, to know. Basically, the positive Halakhah lays claim to the mind of man and to his will—will translated into action; not just the abstract decision in the Kantian fashion, but the decision which is later translated and transformed into deed.

At the second level at which the halakhic gesture unfolds, axiological experiences (that is, experiences of values) emerge. Halakhah disposes with the services of the logos-ethos and leaps over the barriers of cognitive formalism into the realm of living structural value themes. At this level, "beholding" after a prophetic fashion, rather than "discerning" in the philosophical tradition, is the key word. Meaningful themes, in contrast to conceptual topics—I use the terms topical and thematic in the original Greek sense of surface (*topos*) and root (*theme*) respectively—address themselves not to the discriminating mind, the public *homo theoreticus*, man who has the capacity for understanding something in a scientific or intellectual cognitive gesture. Nor does the axiological Halakhah address itself to the tenacious will, to public *homo magnus*, man capable of acting in accordance with something. Instead, it speaks to the clandestine man, to *homo absconditus*, whether he is a soul or spiritual personality. He does not engage in understanding something, nor does he engage in acting out something, but is always concerned with relating to and sharing in something.

The dominant matter of this second gesture on the part of Halakhah—not the positive conceptual gesture but the axiological gesture—is not *"ve-nishma,"* but *"Ta'amu u-re'u ki tov Hashem*, Taste and see that the Lord is good"* (Ps. 34:9). It is very strange that *"ta'amu"* is translated as "consider" in many English translations. This simply destroys the very meaning of the verb. I would accept here the translation of the Vulgate, *"gustate et videte,* taste and see." It means that God can be be tasted, beheld intuitively, confronted and related to. Man can share in God. The themes, values and axiological motifs of the thematic Halakhah cannot be interpreted, nor can they be understood and analyzed. Rather, they are felt intuitively and beheld. The Halakhah never attempted to evolve cognitive instruments by virtue of which the themes could be interpreted and portrayed. It apparently considered such an undertaking futile, since the themes are intrinsically not subject to articulate determination and verbalization. The themes inhabit a nonloquacious, mute halakhic periphery; they are more or less boundary concepts and ideas for which halakhic man, in his questing for absolute security and rootedness, reaches out. However, they always remain outside of his reach. The more rapidly the

Halakhah or halakhic man moves toward those glowing horizons, the more the themata recede into an endless distance.

In a word, the emergent halakhic gesture manifests its dialectical character or nature. On the one hand, it sets up a reasoned, clearly defined, precise system of thought, finding its application in detached deeds which reach the point of being mechanical actions. The disciplines require only acting in accordance with the understanding, but the acting is normative. It means, we might say, being pressed to act not by some physical outside force, but by the inner norm. On the other hand, it insists upon all-out involvement with a singular, unreasoned order of experiential themes, communicated to us through the medium of notched, indented and lens-shaped metaphors. Basically, the themes, the values, the axiological motives, cannot be interpreted, nor can they be understood and analyzed. They are felt intuitively and beheld.

The Example of Shabbat

Permit me to introduce an example which will elucidate the above analysis. If we should examine all the laws pertaining to the Sabbath, we will discover that within their topical normative context, within the halakhic logos, we deal exclusively with formal concepts such as *melakhah* (work) and *melekhet mahashevet* (intentional performance) and so forth, without relating them to any axiological theme. There is no single axiological theme—or call it variant—to which the positivist halakhist relates his concepts. There is no need to place these concepts within a meaningful coordinate system. All the topical Halakhah is interested in is the cognitive substance, not axiological validity; in formal constructs, like those of physicists or mathematicians, and their logical interrelatedness within the system.

The topical halakhist is not concerned with axiological motifs. At the level of topical Halakhah, Shabbat is just a twenty-four hour stretch or period during which one must abstain from work and discontinue his daily routine; that's all. There is nothing else involved in the topical approach to the Sabbath idea. However, when we shift our attention from halakhic thinking to halakhic feeling, from halakhic topics to axiological themata, we suddenly find ourselves in a new dimension, namely that of *kedushah*, holiness. Suddenly the Sabbath is transmuted or transformed from an abstract norm, from a formal concept, into a "reality," a living essence, a living entity; from a discipline in accordance with which one acts compulsorily into a great experience which one acts out spontaneously.

Of course, we have many passages in the Bible dealing with the Sabbath, but the basic biblical text containing the Sabbath idea within the topical frame of formal-systematic reference is the passage in the Decalogue dealing with the normative aspect of the Sabbath: "Remember the Sabbath day to keep it holy, *le-kaddesho*. Six days shalt thou labor and do all thy work but the seventh day is a Sabbath unto the Lord thy God; in it thou shalt not do any manner of work, thou, nor thy son . . . " (Ex. 20:8-10).

The verb *le-kaddesho*, to keep it holy, if analyzed in the light of positive topical Halakhah, means only abstention from the daily routine or separation from work. In the topical context, the term *le-kaddesho* does not refer to or imply a charismatic quality inherent in the seventh day. It is just set aside as a day in the week on which one must abstain from work; that is all. This is a formal approach to the Sabbath idea.

In contrast to the topical Halakhah, the text which forms the main motto of the thematic Halakhah with regard to Shabbat would be, I believe, the mysterious passage in Genesis which concludes the story of creation: "And God blessed the seventh day and hallowed it, *va-yekaddesh oto*" (Gen. 2:3). A twenty-four-hour period was sanctified and hallowed. It has suddenly become a metaphysical entity upon which the Almighty has bestowed a unique endowment, a very strange endowment, namely, that of blessedness and sanctity.

The Need for a Halakhic Theodicy

Let us now turn to the problem of mental health within the frame of reference of the Halakhah. When we attempt to explore the therapeutic and redemptive qualities of the religious act— and this is exactly what modern religion, cooperating with mental health institutions, is trying to do—it is necessary to examine first the philosophy of suffering which that particular religion has formulated. We cannot come to grips with the remedial or redemptive functionality implied in the religious experience unless we know how this religion managed to accommodate, or at least attempted to accommodate, the human passional experience, the pathos and suffering. Without accomodating somehow the human passional experience, it is impossible to develop a religious technology of mental health. Without a precise investigation of this problem, we shall in vain claim a therapeutic role for the religious performance. We will engage, I would say, either in arbitrary statements or in clichés or platitudes.

If this is universally true of all religion in general, it is also true with regard to Judaism, to Halakhah. Therefore, prior to exploring the remedial redemptive potential of our Judaic religious act, we must spell out in articulate, precise terms the Judaic doctrine of suffering and define clearly our attitude *vis-à-vis* an unfriendly world replete with disorder and disharmony. When a rabbi comes to guide a person in distress, or when he wants to counsel him and advise him particularly with regard to health, he must know exactly what our resources are— resources not in homiletical terms but in philosophical-metaphysical terms. Otherwise, his work will be in vain.

The practical and functional motifs are undergirded by theoretical ones. The metaphysical philosophical doctrine leads in religion. The functional methods do but follow, they do not lead. This is one of the cardinal mistakes which people make about religion in general and Judaism in particular. Religion is basically not a technology. Its essence is hard to define, but it is not a technology. Of course, religion is also concerned about the welfare of man, his happiness, his peace of mind, his tranquility. But those functional aspects must be inferred from theoretical premises.

Hence, our immediate attention must be focused upon halakhic theodicy. (I am using a term which Leibniz coined. "Theodicy" means "justification of God," if taken literally.) As an equivalent for theodicy, we must focus on the halakhic metaphysic of evil or suffering, or the halakhic metaphysic of the pathos, the pathetic or passional experience of man.

How does the Halakhah handle the problem of human despair? It is a very elementary question, but the question has somehow never been raised, inasmuch as despair is inherent in our very existence. It is not just incidental, not just contingent, not just temporary and transient. It is inculcated in the very core of our existence. The Halakhah certainly did grapple with the absurd phenomenon of evil and had to fit it into a frame of sensible reference. No religion can afford the luxury of ignoring the most disturbing of all problems, the problem of suffering. The Jewish religion, as a realistic one, could not simply ignore it. No religion could.

Judaism's Dual Frame of Reference

Since the halakhic gesture operates with two frames of reference, the topical and the thematic, our problem applies to both. Thus our question should be rephrased: what position do the topical as well as the thematic Halakhah assign to the passional experience of suffering within their respective frames of reference? Let us bear in mind that the topical reference exhausts itself in arrangement and classification of formal halakhic constructs within a conceptual continuum, while the thematic reference signifies the relatedness of the same formal constructs and norms to an intuited order which lies outside of a conceptual system. Thematic referring implies transcending the conceptual continuum; only such a leap may fill the formal halakhic schemata with meaningful content within the universe of values.

Translating this characterization of the topical and thematic act of referring into more familiar terms, we would say that the topical frame of reference of the positive Halakhah is confined to the world of whose existence we are assured by our sense experience and which is bounded by time and space. The topical frame of reference is this physical universe, the universe of color and sound, of taste and touch, the universe of becoming and disappearing, of life and death. By contrast, the frame of reference of the thematic Halakhah, of halakhic axiology, of the halakhic universe of values, is not limited merely to this world, but envelops Being in its majestic totality as a whole, beginning with the here and now, the finite existing experience, and concluding with our awareness of eternity. The frame of reference of the thematic Halakhah is not only a this-worldly one, but is transcendental as well.

The topical Halakhah or halakhic gesture thus fashions its interpretive axiological methods in the mold of finiteness and sensibility. It displays extreme modesty and sobriety in its approach to Being. The thematic gesture, however, is by far more bold and possessed by the spirit of adventure. It exceeds the boundaries of our own ontological awareness, which is imprisoned within a scientifically explainable universe, and attempts to relate itself to parts unknown, to link up the orders of things and events with the transcendental order of the ultimate. The thematic Halakhah opened up the closed frame of topical reference and accommodated infinity itself.

Judaism, then, operates with two frames of reference because Judaism is engaged in the dialectical method, in an antithetical approach to reality. One frame of reference is one sector of being, the this-worldly sector, and a second frame of reference is Being in its majestic totality.

As regards the topical, positivistic Halakhah, I may go even a step further and state that the Halakhah is not even interested in the physical universe as a whole. Its attention is focused upon just a single sector of reality, namely, the one into which, if I may use an existential term, man is cast and in which his destiny is either fulfilled or he fails miserably.

The Halakhah, of course, is theocentric, or God-centered, because it is of a religious nature. However, it is still oriented around man. The Halakhah, in spite of its theocentric character, is anthropo-oriented. Its concern envelops certain segments of reality insofar as they are relevant to man and his interests. The Halakhah does not venture outside of the human world, and the human world is a very small world. Whatever is relevant to man, to his interests, to his self-fulfillment and his self-realization is relevant and pertinent to the Halakhah. Whatever is irrelevant to man is irrelevant to the topical Halakhah.

Whatever philosophy of man's nature and his destiny the Halakhah may have formulated, it invariably ends up by referring the whole of Being to man. The story of creation of the physical cosmos, of the physical universe, is but a prelude, if we read the story of Genesis carefully, to the wondrous emergence of man that took place on that mysterious Friday, the sixth day of creation.

Moreover, the Halakhah's concern with man is mainly centered on the individual. Man is neither an idea, like humanity, whose praise Plato and the Greek philosophers sang, nor a supra-individual unity, like society or community, which many philosophical systems, including that of Marxism, have idealized and idolized. They sang the praise of society, which is a supra-individual unity. The Halakhah insists that nothing, not the idea nor the collective, should supplant the single transient and frail individual "who is here today and tomorrow is in the grave" (*Berakhot* 28b), who today is here on the platform and the next day, who knows where he will end up. He occupies a dominant position in the Halakhah, and his role is central and indispensable. Of course the Halakhah has not overlooked the community, particularly the community of the committed and the elected, as the bearer of the Divine eternal message. Yet, the individual constitutes a reality whose ontic legitimacy must not be questioned and whose interests the Halakhah, like a devoted mother, had at heart.

Thematic Halakhah's Metaphysic of Suffering

Returning to our problem, namely, the accommodation of the passional experience by the Halakhah, we must admit that the topical Halakhah would treat this experience in a different manner than the thematic Halakhah.

It is very certain that the thematic Halakhah—the Halakhah related to the outside, to what the Greeks called *hyperteles*, something beyond—even though it was embarrassed to the point of perplexity by the existence of evil, managed somehow to accommodate it within its frame of reference. The best proof that the thematic Halakhah—thematic Judaism, axiological Judaism—was embarrassed and even tormented, was confused and bewildered by evil or by Satan, is the Book of Job. I don't have to refer you to any clandestine passages in our literature. But, somehow, the thematic Halakhah emerged from this and countered evil victoriously, depending on the interpretation of victory, of course.

Because the frame of reference of the thematic Halakhah extends into infinity and eternity, it is possible somehow to accomodate evil and assign to it a very prominent role and position. Within the thematic Halakhah, we find a theodicy or, to be more precise, a metaphysic of suffering. Judaism, at the level of axiology or at the level of transcendental reference, did develop a metaphysic of evil, or, I would rather say, of suffering, of the passional experience.

Let us briefly see how the thematic Halakhah managed somehow to accomodate evil. I would not say that evil was a very pleasant guest, but, somehow, the thematic Halakhah had to put up with it. One sometimes puts up with a guest who is not welcome, but is simply foisted and imposed upon you.

The dominant idea which underlies this metaphysic of evil developed by the thematic Halakhah is basically that suffering as a subjective experience—an emotion, an affect, a feeling—and evil as a reality are not identical. The fact that people in distress, the distraught individuals who find themselves in a crisis, ascribe their misery to some outside agency called "evil" or "Satan"—the name is irrelevant—and identify their subjective experiences with a destructive fiend or enemy of man, does not prove that evil actually exists and that it reveals itself through the pathetic mood or the passional mood. On the contrary, the thematic Halakhah's metaphysic maintained that the passional experience represents the highest good.

This sharp distinction between evil and pathos opened up to the thematic Halakhah new vistas which explained suffering. It did so by denying the reality of evil in a twofold way, by introducing transcendentalism and universalism.

Transcendentalism

Let us take a look at these motifs which the thematic Halakhah utilized in its attempt to prove the incommensurability of suffering and evil. It is self-evident that evil as an entity *per se* vanishes as soon as the threshold of man's ontological consciousness is raised from the order of the sensible, phenomenal and transient to a higher order of the absolute and eternal. Any system of ideas, even one of a purely rational-philosophical strain, such as Platonic philosophy, finds no difficulty in separating the pathos as a subjective experience from evil as an objective entity, and in disposing quickly of the latter.

A passage in the Talmud is indicative of the kind of metaphysic of suffering that the thematic Halakhah formulated:

> To what are the righteous compared in this world? To a tree standing wholly in a place of cleanness, but whose bough overhangs to a place of uncleanness. When the bough is lopped off, it stands entirely in a place of cleanness. Thus the Holy One brings suffering upon the righteous in this world in order that they may inherit the future world . . . (*Kiddushin* 40b).

I believe that this is a very clearcut, unequivocal example of how the thematic Halakhah has handled evil. It is a radical approach, of course, simply disposing of it. Sometimes, if a problem is too embarrassing and too tormenting, one simply puts it in the waste basket and ignores it. This passage is indicative of the kind of metaphysic of suffering that the thematic Halakhah formulated.

The same is illustrated by the dictum regarding the biblical passage, "That it may be well with thee and that thou mayest prolong thy days" (Deut. 5:16). R. Jacob says that this refers to an existence in the world of eternal bliss, "*ba-olam she-kulo arokh . . . le-olam she-kulo tov*" (*Hullin* 142a). Many other aphorisms and sayings with which our talmudic and midrashic literature is replete would fit perfectly into this transcendentalistic framework. In death and in suffering one is born to a new true life. The pathos, the fear of death, is the mysterious link between a shadowy existence and true being.

A quotation from Maimonides' *Guide* would suffice to illustrate the transcendentalists' approach to the most dreadful of all evils, death. Death is identified by Maimonides with deliverance. To die means to gain freedom from captivity, to join the beloved friend for whom the soul has been yearning all along. (Interesting is the parallelism between the Maimonidean philosophy and the Platonic dialogue *Phaedo*.)

The more the forces of his body are weakened and the force of passion quenched, in the same measure does man's intellect increase in strength and in light; his knowledge becomes pure and he is happy with his knowledge. When this perfect man is stricken in age and is near death, his knowledge mightily increases. His joy in that knowledge grows greater, and his love for the object of his knowledge more intense, and it is in this great delight that the soul separates from the body. To this state our Sages referred when, in reference to the death of Moses, Aaron and Miriam, they said that death was in these three cases but a kiss (*Guide* III:51).

I would add: a kiss by eternity impressed upon temporality.

Universalism

The motif of universalism is employed by the thematic Halakhah in a similar fashion. Again, the thematic Halakhah maintains the universal doctrine of suffering that evil as a universal entity does not exist, that it is nothing but a chimera, just a figment of our fantasy. Suffering and misery are due to the accidental and contingent character of our existence, which is confined to a narrow segment of being. Yet, within the scheme of Being as a unitary whole in its boundlessness and majesty, the pathos is an unknown datum. Moreover, the thematic Halakhah maintains that sufferings of the individual are ministerial to a higher good within the universal order, basing this doctrine upon the passage in Genesis, "And God saw all things that He had made and, behold, it was very good" (Gen. 1:31). Evil is not an essential part of being if the latter is placed in the perspective of totality.

Rabbi Meir was a man who knew suffering in his private life. He lost two children, he lost his wife, he lost his father-in-law, and he died a martyr's death. His marginal remark that at twilight of the mysterious Friday, when creation was concluded, God cast a glance and found even death to be good (*Gen. Rabbah* 9:5) attests to the universalistic view of our Sages.

In consonance with this universalistic doctrine, our scholars modified a verse in Isaiah before incorporating it into our liturgy. In Isaiah (45:7) we read, "I form light and create darkness; I make peace and create evil, *ra*." In our morning service we recite, "Blessed are Thou . . . who forms light and creates darkness, who makes peace and creates all things, *ha-kol*." The word "*ra*, evil" was supplanted with "*ha-kol*, all things." Apparently, in the perspective of totality, evil vanishes. (This metaphysic of evil is not confined to Judaism. A similar approach is to be found in Plato's *Phaedo*, where Plato quotes the oration delivered by Socrates on the day of his execution. Death is nothing but deliverance of man from the cave, from the Valley of Shadows. Death is an ascent to the heights from which man may behold the ideas, the true Being, the *ontos on*, the real, true, genuine being.)

Can such a metaphysic bring solace and comfort to modern man who finds himself in crisis, facing the monstrosity of evil, and to whom existence and absurdity appear to be bound up inextricably together? Is there in the transcendental and universal message a potential of remedial energy to be utilized by the rabbi who comes, like Zofar, Bildad and Eliphaz, the three friends of Job, to share the burden and to comfort his congregant in distress? We know that the friends of Job were not that successful in convincing Job about the nonexistence of evil. Can a rabbi be more successful? Can he succeed where the biblical friends of Job failed miserably? I will be frank with you; I do not know.

The question is not an easy one. On the one hand, we know that this metaphysic has worked miracles with our people, whose history is a continuous tale of martyrdom and suffering. The Jewish community found, in this metaphysic of evil, relief, hope and courage. Yet what seemed apodictic and simple to our ancestors, inspired by indomitable faith and a passionate transcendental experience, might prove to be an extremely complicated matter for contemporary egotistic man, who is spiritually uprooted, homeless, and perplexed. I can state with all candor that I personally have not been too successful in my attempts to spell out this metaphysic in terms meaningful to the distraught individual who floats aimlessly in all-encompassing blackness, like a withered leaf on a dark autumnal night tossed by wind and rain. I tried but failed, I think, miserably, like the friends of Job.

Topical Halakhah's Ethic of Suffering

The topical Halakhah could not accept the thematic metaphysic which tends to gloss over the absurdity of evil, and it did not engage in the building of a magnificent philosophical facade to shut out the ugly sights of an inadequate existence. Realism and individualism, ineradicably ingrained in the very essence of the topical Halakhah, prevented it from casting off the burden of the awareness of evil.

The topical Halakhah, which is particularly interested in real man, in his body and soul, in his day-to-day activities, in his transient, carnal perceptions and experiences within his small, narrow world, could not be content with a fine metaphysical distinction between evil and the pathos of being, between Satan and suffering. The topical Halakhah lacked neither the candor nor the courage to admit publicly that evil does exist, and it pleaded ignorance as to its justification and necessity. The topical Halakhah is an open-eyed, tough observer of things and events and, instead of indulging in a speculative metaphysic, acknowledged boldly both the reality of evil and its irrationality, its absurdity.

As a case in point let us examine the topical Halakhah's attitude toward death, which was idealized by the thematic metaphysic.

It is enough to glance at the laws of mourning in order to convince ourselves that the topical Halakhah saw death as a dreadful fiend with whom no pact may be reached, no reconciliation is possible. In the act of mourning for a deceased member of the household, the whole traumatic horror in the face of an insensate and absurd experience asserts itself. Death appears in all its monstrosity and absurdity, and an encounter with it knocks out the bottom of human existence.

If the topical Halakhah concurred with the thematic in its interpretation of death as deliverance, as a victory over nihility, then why mourn and grieve for the departed? Why rend our garments, sit on the floor, and say *"Barukh dayyan emet"*? As a matter of fact, the topical Halakhah reflects the despair and horror and bewilderment of biblical man when he was confronted by death. From Moses, who sought passionately and entreated God to save him from death in the desert (Deut. 3:24-25), to King Hezekiah, who in despair and agony petitioned God with extreme urgency to protect him from *she'ol* (Isa. 38), the grisly fear of death and man's stubborn refusal to surrender to its power winds itself through the Bible like a red thread. The mood of biblical man is permeated with melancholy. In the back of everything, he sees the skull grinning at him, and while feasting he sees the hand of death writing on the wall.

Such an attitude is in sharp conflict with the thematic metaphysic of suffering. In short, the practical topical Halakhah did not and could not evolve a metaphysic of suffering. It simply refused. It was not eager to find the rationale of evil and to convert the negation into an affirmation. It neither justified evil nor denied and hid it. The topical Halakhah always held the view that evil exists and that man must face it in perplexity and embarrassment.

Of course, it could not accommodate evil, but there is a difference between accommodating evil and handling evil. Some guests I am eager to accommodate; some guests I do not want to accommodate. But if somebody knocks at my door, I must answer, responding and handling him, even by taking his lapel and throwing him out. So the question is, "How did the topical Halakhah handle evil?" not "How did it accommodate it?" There was no accommodation for evil within the framework of topical Halakhah. Simply, the framework is a realistic one, and a realistic framework cannot have a place or position within its coordinate system for evil and suffering. Yet, whether or not we are ready to accommodate evil, we must deal with it; and the topical Halakhah could not shirk such an elementary responsibility.

Yes, the topical Halakhah has evolved an *ethic* of suffering instead of a *metaphysic* of suffering. While the metaphysic is out to discover the ontological objective reason of suffering from within, the ethic posits meanings from within and without. It is concerned not so much with pathos as such but with the pathetic mood of the person in distress, with the assimilation of pain into the total I-awareness, with man's response to adversity and disaster. This is the difference between a metaphysic and an ethic of evil. The metaphysic seeks to justify evil or deny its reality. The ethic of suffering seeks the transformation of an alien *factum* which one encounters into an *actus* in which one engages, the succumbing to an overwhelming force into an experience impregnated with directedness and sense.

Three Pillars of the Halakhic Ethic of Suffering

To sum up, I would say that the halakhic ethic of suffering rests upon three propositions. First, evil does exist, and evil is bad. The world in which we live is not free from deformities and inadequacies which result in the perennial discord between the interests of man and the unalterable laws of nature. In other words, the reality of evil is indisputable.

Second, one must never acquiesce in evil, make peace with it, or condone its existence. Defiance of and active opposition to evil, employing all means that God put at man's disposal, is the dominant norm in Halakhah. Scientific intervention on behalf of man in his desperate struggle for control of his environment is fully endorsed and justified. At all levels—physical, moral, etc.—in all situations, man must rise against his archfoe— evil—and reject its sovereignty. As an example, consider the problem of medical cures. Whether one may intervene with illness, with disease, was very disturbing to religion in general. We have denominations within Christianity which have not reached, so to say, a pact, a treaty of peace, with medicine. To the Halakhah, it was obvious, apodictic, simple. *"Ve-rappo yerappe,* he shall surely be healed," says the Torah (Ex. 21:19). From here we learn that the physician should cure and heal (*Berakhot* 60a). Man should actively interfere with evil. Man is summoned by God to combat evil, to fight evil, and to try to eliminate it as much as possible.

That is why, perhaps, God put at our disposal such powerful means as our intellect, our capacity for controlling nature. Not only *can* man interfere, but man *should* interfere and subdue the environment to his interests and needs. Of course, the Halakhah idealized scientific intervention on behalf of man in his desperate struggle for control of his environment, at all levels.

Halakhah always preached active opposition to evil. That is why the Halakhah could not understand—and not only Halakhah but we Jews cannot understand—a philosophy of passive resistance to evil. It simply couldn't assimilate this philosophy preached by Gandhi and then by Nehru, not to combat evil actively, not to fight evil the way Jacob engaged in combat with the mysterious antagonist on a dark night, but simply resist evil passively.

The third proposition is faith. If man loses a battle in a war, the topical Halakhah has always believed, based on an eschatological vision, that at some future date, some distant date, evil will be overcome, evil will disappear; *"Bila ha-mavet la-netzah u-mahah Hashem dim'ah me-al kol panim,* He will swallow up death forever, and the Lord God will wipe off the tears from all faces" (Isa. 25:8). Yes, it is a long war; it is a long struggle. In war, one lose battles. If man loses a battle from time to time and evil triumphs over him, he must bear defeat with dignity and humility, accepting the Divine verdict.

Equanimity vs. Dignity

One might say that this halakhic ethic of suffering differs little from the attitude usually adopted by modern man toward evil. Modern man, scientifically oriented, technologically minded, bold and courageous, is sensitive to the disorder and disharmony with which the universe is packed, and he is far from indulging in a happy-go-lucky contentment. Scientifically minded, he tries to combat evil and is convinced that it can be overcome. Otherwise, he would not work so hard in order to find cures for some incurable diseases. He even questions the inevitability of death.

Yet, modern man loses a few battles in his struggle with evil. He is not always triumphant. If you want to see modern man, if you want to convince yourself that modern man is not always triumphant, just go into a hospital for incurable diseases and see how many patients inflicted with cancer, multiple sclerosis, and so forth, are suffering and gradually dying. Man loses many battles in his engagement with the archfoe or fiend of humanity. But, still, modern man says—and this is basically what mental health work is out to achieve—that when one is confronted by evil, one must face adversity courageously; one must not succumb to hysteria when evil strikes viciously at him.

So modern man has developed a stoic approach to stress and suffering. However, no matter how close the resemblance is between the modern approach to evil and that of the topical Halakhah, there is still an unbridgeable chasm separating them. While modern man resigns himself to an unalterable cosmic occurrence and bears distress with *equanimity*, yet without discovering any meaningfulness, the halakhic man accepts suffering and turns it into a great existential experience, one in which he may find self-fulfillment. He bears distress and accepts suffering with *dignity*.

The difference between the halakhic ethic of suffering and modern mental health technique is as vast as the one which lies between equanimity and dignity. While equanimity implies only the absence of any hysterical disturbances and suggests a habit of mind that disowns unpleasant emotions in the stoic tradition, dignity denotes man's divine personality, a new dimension of greatness in man in which his human distinctness as a spiritual being manifests itself. Equanimity is a state of mind, dignity a form of existence. The former is a psychological descriptive term, the latter an ontological attribute.

A dignified existence means a unique existence. Dignity is an existential dimension, not just a psychological idea or a descriptive attribute pertaining to man's behavior. It is more than that. It somehow reflects man's inner personality, the core of his existential experience. In Hebrew, the equivalent for dignity is *kavod*, and the correlate phrase of dignity of man is *kevod ha-beriyyot*. Man's creation "in the image of God" means that man's existence, in contradistinction to natural existence in the animal kingdom, is a dignified existence. As the psalmist says of man, "Thou hast crowned him with dignity and honor" (Ps. 8:6).

What is man's uniqueness, his individuality? How is he distinct from the natural kingdom of existence? There is only one difference: man's existence is dignified. Whatever a table is, there is nothing dignified in the table's existence. There is no dignified existence to the animal in the jungle. There is no dignified existence to a machine. Man possesses this attribute of dignity, which is basically a Divine attribute. That is why the Bible tells us that man was created in the image of God. He is dignified, of course, being, naturally, in the image of God.

The Quest for God

Let us analyze what Judaism understands by dignity. The constitutive essence of dignity comes to expression *par excellence* in man's aptitude to commune with God. The capability of man to relate himself to God, to search and quest for Him and to experience Him in the deep recesses of his own existential awareness is a unique gift that God bestowed upon man, and in this experience the image—the dignity of man—reveals itself.

Whatever frame of reference we might select—the topical or the thematic—we will unavoidably find that the God-man communion—the God-man relationship which lies at the very root of Judaism, which is itself the root of every civilized religion and faith—is a dialectical performance. Communing with God is antithetic insofar as it consists of two contradictory movements, two movements in opposite directions.

Questing for God is synonymous with surging forward and reaching out eagerly for anchorage and security. The human being who is driven and pressed for creative heroic action—who aims at the enlargement of the self by conquering and subduing whatever sectors of being lie outside of his small world—moves towards God. In Him he finds freedom from insecurity and fear, which is a *conditio sine qua non* for man to conquer the world, to develop his ability, to realize and fulfill himself. He finds self-assertion, boundless self-expansion, and serenity.

What is our scientific adventure if not a human desire for conquest, to conquer the impossible, to invade the distant, to discover the unknown? In other words, finding God, not scientific conquest, is the crowning victory attained by man-conqueror. Man triumphs when he meets his Creator. It suffices to read the Psalms in order to realize that the forward movement of the conquering hero, the perennial pursuit of something, is perhaps the cardinal characteristic of the transcendental adventure, and that by confronting God one gains not only security and serenity but power and self-greatness as well. "I will be glad and rejoice in Thee. I will sing praise to Thy name, O Thou most high, when mine enemies are turned back, they shall fall and perish at Thy presence" (Ps. 9:3-4). "It is God that girdeth me with strength and maketh my way perfect. . . He teaches my hands to war so that a bow of steel is broken by my arms" (Ps. 18:33, 35).

Man finding God, associating with God, is a warrior; man-conqueror, an aggressive, bold, courageous adventurer, yearning and longing for self-vastness, for self-explanation, for the infinite—and man conquers the infinite if he finds God. This is a progressive movement in one direction, a forward direction. This is the forward course of man.

We may formulate the following equation: to be created in the image of God = to be endowed with dignity = to be capable of finding God and communing with Him—and to commune with God is the greatest victory on the part of man. In conclusion: the dignity of man and his divine character assert themselves in triumph and conquest.

Recoil

On the other hand, being confronted by God results in a movement of recoil and in withdrawal. Somehow man, in his quest for opportunities for domination and power in a world that lies endlessly before him, extending boundlessly into the unknown, in his incessant drive for self-enlargement when everything in him stirs his fantasy to reach the endless fringes of reality, suddenly comes to a halt, turns around and begins to fall back and to retreat. When he meets God, he begins to retrace his steps. Hard-won positions are evacuated, points of vantage are deserted, and man who has traveled long distances, piling up on his journey victory upon victory, conquest upon conquest, swings back to the point of departure and is defeated—defeated by nobody but himself. To encounter God means both victory and defeat, self-affirmation and self-negation.

In God, man finds both affirmation of himself as a great being, and a ruthless, inconsiderate negation of himself as nothing. This is the main, the dominant theme of Judaism, of both thematic and topical Halakhah. In the moment of exultation, the great purge occurs, a purge by virtue of which man loses everything. Victory, conquest, abundance, success and security are instantaneously extinguished and lost by man when confronted by God, and man finds himself in retreat. And man, when he finds himself in retreat, finds also greatness. Finding God is, on the one hand, the greatest victory which man may obtain and, on the other hand, the most humiliating, tormenting defeat which the human being experiences.

Let me quote the psalmist, the same psalmist who spoke in such glowing terms of his association with God, the same psalmist who said that God rejoices in man, that God teaches him how to engage in combat, that He trains his hand to war, to break steel weapons. That same psalmist says, "Whither shall I go from Thy spirit, O God? Or, whither shall I flee from thy presence?" (Ps. 139:7). Why flee? It is hard to escape from him: "I ascend up into heaven and Thou art there. If I make my bed in the depth below, behold, Thou art there" (Ps. 139:8). "Thou hast beset me behind and before, and laid Thy hand upon me" (Ps. 139:5). The hand of God, when it is laid upon man, weighs heavily on his frail shoulders. It is a great burden, and man must manage to carry this burden. This is his task in this world.

Maimonides, describing the essence of the love of God, writes:

> And what is the way that will lead to the love of Him and the fear of Him? When a person contemplates His great and wondrous works and creatures and through them obtains a glimpse of His wisdom which is incomparable and infinite, he will straightway love Him, praise Him, glorify Him and long with an exceeding longing to know His great name; and when he ponders these matters, he

will recoil affrighted and realize that he is a small creature, lowly and obscure, endowed with slight and slender
intelligence, standing in the presence of Him who is perfect in knowledge (*Mishneh Torah, Hilkhot Yesodei ha-
Torah* 2:2).

And so David said, on the one hand, "When I consider Thy
heavens, the work of Thy fingers, what is man that Thou art
mindful of him?" and then continues, "Man is a little less than
God; Thou hast surrounded him with glory and honor" (Ps. 8:4-
6). There is both glorification and complete negation in man.
Man is victorious in his communion with God, but he is horribly
defeated.

The basic relationship to God expresses itself in two opposite
motions: forward and backward. The formulations which we
developed above would have to be modified: to be created in the
image of God = to be endowed with dignity = to be capable of
finding God and communing with Him—and in communion with
God, man defeats himself. In conclusion, the dignity of man and
his divine character assert themselves in defeat and failure.

Judaism's Philosophy of Man

The dialectical content of the religious experience stands out
as an archetype after which the Halakhah has fashioned its philosophy of man—and not only its philosophy of man but its
codes, its norms, and its disciplines. If we should introduce the
old prophet Micah's challenge: "It has been told thee, O man,
what is good and what the Lord does require of thee" (Mic. 6:8),
the Halakhah would meet this challenge by stating in paraphrase, "Only to move forward boldly, to triumph over opposition and to conquer nature and to retreat humbly and take
defeat at your own hands when confronted by thy God." In a
word, the dialectical movement of surging forward and falling
back is the way of life ordained by God for the Jew.

At every level of our existential experiences—aesthetic-hedonic (which means the carnal experiences of man in which the element of pleasure is involved or implied), intellectual (which includes man as scientist, metaphysician, theologian and historian), and emotional—one must engage in the dialectical movement of surging forward boldly and swinging back humbly, of making a series of steps outside of the self and immediately reversing the motion and retracing the steps into the self. The onward course, the journeying forward, is the prime task with which man was charged. Both the topical and the thematic Halakhah were aware of the program that God set up for man: "Replenish the earth and subdue it" (Gen. 1:28). He was called upon to defy opposition and march to victory. Biblical man is a conqueror. The desire for vastness and greatness is a legitimate one and was endorsed by the Halakhah in all areas of human endeavor. Halakhic disciplines cover the full gamut of human activity through which man exercises his power over nature. Commerce, agriculture, political community, science, and even the aesthetic-hedonic aspects of our lives constitute the topics of halakhic thinking and legislating. This is indicative of the latter's endorsing man's involvement in this multiple endeavor which leads him to success and conquest, for one does not work in vain. Yet, when conquest is within our reach and the road to fulfillment has been cleared of all hindrances, man begins to retreat and invites defeat—not to expect defeat to be falling on him or to assault him, but to invite defeat—and surrenders what he has been questing for so long.

It is obvious that after man has taken defeat at his own hands, after he has fallen back and withdrawn from a position for which he had fought tenaciously, after he has given up triumph and conquest, the pendulum begins to swing in the opposite direction, to the pole of greatness, vastness, conquest, victory and triumph. Man defeated surges forth and the questing is resumed; the pursuing and longing for self-expansion and self-assertion sets in once more. Again man seeks greatness and vastness, experiments daringly with his liberties, searches feverishly for dominion and mastery and of course, again, when he finds himself near his destination he retreats. In a word, the Halakhah teaches man how to conquer, to seize initiative and succeed, and also to give up and disengage and invite defeat.

The Dialectical Principle in the Hedonic Realm

This dialectical principle manifests itself in all halakhic norms pertaining to man as a natural and transcendental being. But nowhere does the doctrine of dialectical movement appear in its full glory and splendor as at the aesthetic-hedonic level. Judaism again operates with an antithetic principle. On the one hand, it considered the carnal drives in man, his biological pressures, as legitimate and worthwhile. On the other hand, it demanded that man redeem reality and himself. The act of redeeming one's natural desires consists in the dialectical movement of withdrawal, of disengagement at the moment when the passion reaches its peak. The stronger the grip and impact of natural desire is felt by man, the more intoxicating and bewitching the vision of hedonic conquest is, the greater is the redemptive capacity of the dialectical movement when man, spellbound by his passion, coming close to victory, suddenly steps backward and accepts defeat.

I will read for you a midrash (*Midrash Rabbah* to *Shir ha-Shirim* 7:3, "Thy belly is like a heap of wheat set about with lilies"), and I believe it speaks for itself. The midrash explains Jewish ritual law pertaining to sexuality. Judaism developed a very strange attitude towards sexual life. On the one hand, it endorsed it, completely rejecting the Aristotelian negative approach which Maimonides had somehow accepted. Sex can be a sacred performance if treated properly, if placed in a worthwhile, dignified perspective. In one's sexual life, the dignity of man is the most important factor. It determines the whole character of the sexual life, whether it is low, primitive, hypnotic and orgiastic, or dignified and sacred.

The Halakhah developed a very strange, paradoxical law pertaining to the periods of withdrawal and association. But the strangest of all laws in the code pertaining to sex is one norm which borders almost on the inconsiderate. A young man meets a young woman and falls in love, marries her, and consummates the marriage—the norm is that it is then that a period of withdrawal of almost twelve days begins.

"It often happens that a man takes a wife when he is thirty or forty years old and after going to great expense"—expense is not meant in terms of money, but it means he proposed a few times and she rejected him. He was in love and kept on insisting, and finally he won out. "After going to great expense, he wants to associate with her." His heart is overflowing with love and passion. "Yet, if she says to him, 'I have seen a rose red speck,' he immediately recoils. What made him retreat and keep away from her? Was there a wall of iron between them? Did a serpent bite him? Did a scorpion sting him? . . . It was the words of Torah, which are soft as a lily."

The Midrash gives another example. "A dish of meat is laid before a man and he is told that some forbidden fat has fallen into it; he leaves it alone and will not take it." Hungry as he is, however strong his desire for food, he will not taste it. "Who stops him from tasting it? Did a serpent bite him? . . . Did a scorpion sting him? . . . It was the words of the Torah, which are soft as a lily . . . " Bride and bridegroom are young, physically strong and passionately in love with each other; both have patiently awaited this rendezvous, and they met and the bridegroom stepped backward. Like a knight, he gallantly exhibited superhuman heroism, not in a spectacular but in a quite humble fashion, in the privacy of their home, in the stillness of the night. And what happened? He defeated himself at the height of his triumphant conquest, when all he had to do was to reach out and take possession. The young man overcame himself, the conqueror in his orgiastic hypnotic mood retreated, performed a movement of recoil. He displayed heroism by accepting defeat. And in this act of self-defeat one finds the real dignity of man.

Dignity in Defeat

If man knows how to take defeat at his own hands in a variety of ways as the Halakhah tries to teach us, then he may preserve his dignity even when defeat was not summoned by him, when he faces adversity and disaster and is dislodged from his castles and fortresses.

What is the leitmotif of the strange drama that was enacted by Abraham on the top of a mountain when, responding to a paradoxical Divine summons to take his son, his only son, whom he loved, and offer him in a distant land called Moriah, he surrendered his son to God (Gen. 22)? It was more than a test of loyalty that Abraham had to pass. God, the Omniscient, knew Abraham's heart. It was rather an exercise in the performing of the dialectical movement, in the art of reversing one's course and withdrawing from something which gave meaning and worth to Abraham's life and work, something which Abraham yearned and prayed for on the lonely days and dreary nights while he kept vigil and waited for the paradoxical, impossible to happen. And when the miraculous event occurred and Abraham emerged as a conqueror, triumphed over nature itself, the command came through: Surrender Isaac to Me, give him up, withdraw from your new position of victory and strength to your old humble tent, all enveloped in despair and anxiety, loneliness and gloom. Abraham, take defeat at your own hands, give up heroically what you acquired heroically; be a hero in defeat as you were in victory.

Abraham obeyed. He realized that through this dialectical movement a man attains redemption and self-elevation. And the improbable happened; as soon as he recoiled, as soon as he gave Isaac up, the forward movement, the march to victory was resumed again. He received Isaac from the angel and the pendulum began to swing to the pole of conquest.

This drama is reenacted continually by the man of Halakhah, who is dignified in victory and defeat. The Halakhah taught man not *contemptus saeculi*, but *catharsis saeculi*.

Halakhah wants man to be conqueror and also to be defeated—not defeated by somebody else, not defeated by a friend, not defeated by an outside power, for there is no heroism involved in such a defeat; such a defeat, on the contrary, demonstrates cowardice and weakness. Halakhah wants man to be defeated by himself, to take defeat at his own hands and then reverse the course and start surging forward again and again. This directional movement, like a perennial pendulum, swinging back and forth, gives exhaustive expression to man's life and to Halakhah.

Is this important for mental health? I believe so. Of course, I cannot spell out here how this doctrine could be developed into a technology of mental health, but I believe this doctrine contains the potential out of which a great discipline of the Judaic philosophy of suffering, an ethic of suffering, and a technology of mental health might emerge.

What I have developed is more a philosophy of the Halakhah. How this philosophy could be interpreted in terms of mental health is a separate problem, one that is quite complicated. But I believe that the trouble with modern man and his problems is what the existentialists keep on emphasizing: anxiety, *angst*. Man is attuned to success. Modern man is a conqueror, but he does not want to see himself defeated. This is the main trouble. Of course, when he encounters evil and the latter triumphs over him and he is defeated, he cannot "take it"; he does not understand it.

However, if man is trained gradually, day by day, to take defeat at his own hands in small matters, in his daily routine, in his habits of eating, in his sex life, in his public life—as a matter of fact, I have developed how this directional movement is applicable to all levels—then, I believe, when faced with evil and adversity and when he finds himself in crisis, he will manage to bear his problem with dignity.

❧ *Out of the Whirlwind*

The Cosmic and Apocalyptic Orders

Faith is fraught with absurdities; otherwise, it would not be an act of faith but one of logic. Absurdity means the nonconformity to either formal logical criteria or the rules we infer from experience. However, is there only one logical discipline or perhaps several? Is there only one kind of experience or more than one? Perhaps faith is in full conformity with that different kind of logic and experience.

Let me spell out clearly what I mean. The image of man in Judaism is reflected in two experiences: the cosmic and the covenantal. At first, man emerges in the Bible out of the depths of nature; he belongs to the cosmic continuum; he is involved in the great drama which follows an unalterable order and sequence. His methods of thinking and experiencing were born out of these patterns in the unfolding of the cosmic process. He attuned himself to the great occurrence of which he is a part and tries to accommodate, through his intellectual gesture, his sense-awareness of creation. In a word, there is a *Bereishit*-logic which reflects the wisdom of God embedded in nature.

However, the Bible also sees man in a different role. Man, in his encounter with God who addresses Himself to him not from within but from without the cosmic continuum, is exposed to an experience wholly other from the cosmic encounter. This apocalyptic dialogue which takes place between man and God consists of entirely different categories and a singular vocabulary. A new awareness dawns upon man, one that is not rooted in the cosmic logic and regularities. Human existence is interpreted differently in cosmic and covenantal terms, since God's kerygma [messages] revealed to man through these two media—nature and prophecy—are not commensurate, at least as far as the structural patterns are concerned. The logos which rules cosmic events and which expresses itself in the system of ideas is not identical with the *devar Hashem*, the word which was disclosed to man in his meeting with God.

Hence, when we say the act of faith belongs to the absurd, we mean that faith cannot be understood in terms of the cosmic context. Faithful man is burdened with a new message that is not comprehensible in the terms of natural logic. There is a very strange logic of the word as such, and only in this perspective must faith be understood. Any attempt to rationalize religious concepts overlooks this unbridgeable gulf which separates the cosmic from the covenantal experience, the logos of creation from the logos of the revealed message.

When I speak of the conflict between religion and science, I have in mind not the discrepancy between dogma and scientific dicta but the incongruity of the experiences, which can be traced back to the duality of the addresses God delivers to man, the natural and the apocalyptic. For instance, man himself is experienced differently in cosmic-natural and apocalyptic-covenantal terms. His position in the world, his existence, his worth and destiny, his duties and prerogatives can all be seen in two perspectives—either in light of the event of creation or in relation to the event of the God-man confrontation. Neither experience must be rejected. The severance of man from the cosmic would result in an unmitigated asceticism and monasticism. Denial of the apocalyptic experience would lead man to egotism and crude materialism.

Can a complete harmony be achieved? Certainly not, since the natural and the covenantal belong to different and incommensurate orders! They must engender in man conflict and strife. Man must wrestle with himself, or, cosmic man is engaged in combat with covenantal man. Man oscillates between the cosmic and covenantal experience like a pendulum swinging back and forth between two poles. Yet this schism in the personality is indicative not of a sick soul but of a great one that sees God in both the flames of a rising sun and the fire of the Sinai apocalypse. The religious teacher is charged with the task of teaching the apocalyptic experience to cosmic man. It is a difficult but great task.

The dichotomy between the covenantal and cosmic within man comes to its fullest expression with regard to the problem of evil or suffering—theodicy.

Suffering and the Covenant

Faith is a passional experience, an experience of suffering. From the very dawn of our history, with the emergence of Abraham, suffering was considered both the main challenge which the covenantal community was expected to meet heroically and the great means of realizing the metahistorical destiny of this community. Abraham, as the incarnation of the knighthood of faith, was a great sufferer, a martyr. His greatness is manifested through his superhuman capacity for endurance and acceptance of sorrow. As a matter of fact, the election of his seed as a covenantal community was to be realized through suffering. The birth of the charismatic community was accompanied by affliction and pain. When we read the chapter in Genesis dealing with the covenant and God's pledge to Abraham respecting His involvement with Abraham's clan, we are impressed by the weird scene full of undefined dread and grisly uneasiness.

> And when the sun was going down, a deep sleep fell upon Abram; and lo, a horror of great darkness fell upon him. And He said to Abram, "Know of a surety that your seed shall be a stranger in a land that is not theirs and shall serve them; and they shall afflict them four hundred years" (Gen. 15:12-13).

The realization of the covenant is possible only if the people is tested in the crucible of affliction. The historical occurrence which is the realizer of God's covenant within His elected community is strange and enigmatic, containing the element of absurdity. It cannot be interpreted in simple human psychological and historical categories such as pleasure, happiness, etc., for these ideas were disclosed to man not through the apocalyptic-transcendental but through the immanent-natural revelation.

The basic tendency in man to avoid the painful and search for the pleasant belongs to the original scheme of creation and is implanted in man and animal alike. The Bible felt that to rank man as a pleasure-seeking and happiness-questing being, prone only to the natural order of things, would amount to a kind of denial to man of his transcendental-covenantal nature. What has revelation given man that his creatureliness (as a natural being) did not disclose to him? Why is a natural ethic not sufficient to regulate man's existence and to realize his destiny? Why do we feel that the philosophico-ethical norms are neither meaningful enough nor binding upon us? Why have all attempts since ancient Greece to reduce morality to a convention, to a construction of the human mind and experience without involving any outside intervention, failed in impressing and impelling society to accept it unconditionally?

The answer is a simple one. Most natural ethical codes seek human happiness and utility. They tell man to behave in accordance with certain norms in order to improve his condition, to better his lot. Revelation has opened up to man a new existential dimension, the one of suffering. It has endowed man with the capacity for sacrificial action—sorrow. The word handed down to man by God from His transcendent recesses enlightens him about a new mission which he is called to perform, a new role he is summoned to play as an actor in the great covenantal drama—the sacrifice through the passional experience.

The covenant is born through the dialectic of suffering, through the contradiction implied in a shattered existence, in the mystery of a torn and desolate being. The person receiving the covenant must rise above his naturalness, above the order of creation, and ascend to a new event, to a new experience, namely, revelation. This departure from the natural-historical to the covenantal-metahistorical is possible only if the covenantal personality learns the mystery of *consummatio mundi* [consuming his natural world] by the fire of suffering, if he is experienced in affliction and toil. In order to confront God, man must purge himself and pass through a catharsis.

Cosmic man, whose world is replete with orderliness and beauty, serenity and peace, who has fulfilled all his ambitions and desires, who is satisfied with himself and his destiny, must forfeit, at least for a while, his neatly arranged world in order to discover God. The mere meeting with God is, according to Judaism, not only a great and blissful but also a shuddering and horror-filling experience. Not only does a bright sun rise upon the horizon of human existence, but also a darkness of a grisly night, full of strange echoes and visions, envelops the finite being. Chancing suddenly upon God, man becomes aware of his evanescence and the absurdity of a conditioned and relative existence. Infinity swallows up finitude. What importance can we ascribe to the flickering candle-flame when the latter comes close to the great all-consuming fire? Little man forfeits his identity when he is confronted by all-inclusive Divinity. Finitude is sucked in by infinity; a bounded being disappears in the eternal boundlessness. Temporality submerges in eternity.

Two Moments of the Revelational Experience

In describing the revelational experience, we have isolated two antithetic moments. First, there is the moment of shock, when finite man, upon being confronted with infinity, becomes aware of the ontic void, of the inner contradiction within his existential experience, and suddenly realizes that the very foundation of his existence has collapsed. In other words, man in his rendezvous with God is confronted by non-being, by nihility, since God, addressing Himself through apocalypse, negates any other existence.

Second, there is the moment of ecstasy and rapture which rehabilitates and reconstructs man to heights unattainable at a cosmic level. Meeting God is a glorious and the most blessed event; it helps man transcend himself and make him greater than he really is. Man becomes transported out of himself and suddenly awakens to new dimensions of reality that were alien to him before. Communion with God elevates the spirit, cleanses the heart and spurs on the mind to absurd greatness. At the cosmic level, the fellowship with the God whose image is reflected in the great drama of creation, in natural law and mechanical regularity, affords man a consummated and fulfilled existence. The rendezvous with the God dwelling within being brings the ideal of self-realization within his reach. The God of the cosmos is the well of the existential experience; to come close to this well is tantamount to the finding of one's self. Yet no act of rising above oneself is involved in the God-man relationship within the cosmos. However, the apocalyptic experience of God expresses itself in a leap outside of oneself, in a journey from a here-and-now reality to the numinous.

In recapitulation, let me state that the apocalyptic experience is paradoxical insofar as it manifests itself in an ambivalent state of mind. On the one hand, there is shock and violence which leave behind considerable mental anguish and horror. "And when the sun was going down, a deep sleep fell upon Abram; and lo, a horror of great darkness fell upon him" (Gen. 15:12). On the other hand, there is a feeling of endless grace that remakes man in the image of God, who is enveloped in mystery and transcendence. Man passes over the boundary of selfhood and becomes greater than he really was destined to be in the cosmic scheme of things. While the confrontation of cosmic man with God is fundamentally an intellectual achievement via the "idea," via knowledge—the greatness of cosmic man manifests itself in his being the bearer of the idea, or in his cognitive genius—the encounter of covenantal man with *Deus Revelatus* is an experiential performance in which the total personality is involved. It is more a "sense-experience" than a noetic, intellectual act. It is an ultimate reality rather than an "idea." It is a frightening and fascinating vision that is real, powerful and overwhelming. As R. Yehudah Halevi writes,

> The Kuzari said, Now the difference between the names "E-lokim" and "Hashem," the Tetragrammaton, has become clear to me, and I comprehend how broad is the distance between the God of Abraham and the God of Aristotle. For Hashem is the object of yearning of those who have perceived Him with the senses and on the basis of visual evidence, while E-lokim is the object of logical inference (*Kuzari* IV:16).

Suffering and Nihility

Let us understand this a little deeper. We stated above that there is no place for suffering within the system of a cosmic existence. Only through revelation, when man becomes involved with God, does the former encounter sorrow. We must distinguish between pain and suffering. While pain is a physico-psychical sensation and is proper not only to humans but even to the animals, suffering is a spiritual experience which is characteristic of man alone. A mother in labor who fervently beseeches God to give her a child cannot forego the sensation of excruciating pain. But she is not a woman of sorrow; on the contrary, she is a happy woman whose most cherished dream comes true. On the other hand, one who suddenly discovers that he is afflicted with a fatal disease and is doomed, even though he is free from pain, is a man of suffering and his distress is overwhelming.

What, basically, is suffering? It belongs to the realm of the spiritual personality, in other words, man's existential awareness. He realizes his uniqueness and otherness as a being who, while possessing a complex structure and a highly delicate nervous system that provides him with certain capabilities which were denied to other animals, is not just part of the physico-chemical world. The existential experience of man is the experience of man alone, of man who rises above the natural form of existence and discovers a new existential dimension. This experience denotes an existence which is not just a successful offshoot of the animal family forming another link in the endless chain of biological emergence, one whose existence has not begun and will not end with himself. It is rather a lonely, closed-in being, whose existence is limited to the narrow confines of an I. This strange being who ran away from the natural order is a man of sorrow and passion. Sorrow is fundamentally the encounter with non-being.

This meeting with nihility may take place in two ways. First, it occurs when the individual existence is threatened with extinction. The anticipation and fear of death is a singular trait of man alone, who was endowed with a strange time consciousness which runs out bit by bit, driving him gradually to his destiny—nihility. Second, it takes place at the axiological level. The existential experience is an awareness of something which not only is but is worthy of its unique form of existence. In other words, man not only exists as a spiritual being but also values his existence as precious. His existence is not a static factum but an actus committed to something which fascinstes him.

Plato, who expounded the doctrine of man as a bearer of ideas, was right in the sense that man stands in relationship to something beyond himself. Yet he did not emphasize the dynamic, creative character of this idea. (Hellas did not know much about creativity.) Man is charged with a task; this feeling of responsibility is part of his existential awareness. Of course, the objectives of his responsible questing and the ways in which he tries to attain them vary. Yet man is a being committed to an idea, even though quite often this idea may be false, absurd and perverted—and the means of achievement degrading. Whenever man realizes that he has failed to fulfill his commitment or responsibility, thus forfeiting the worth of his existence, he turns into a man of affliction. In short, either the anticipated loss of our existential awareness or the forfeiture of its valuableness is the source of suffering. Suddenly man sees himself confronted with nihility at either a factual or axiological level.

To behold the "nothing," the "empty," the non-being, is to suffer. Man as the child of nature, carried by the biological tide and submerged in a senseless existence, is not subject to suffering. There is no commitment and hence no frustration of failure within the *Bereishit* scheme of things. As a matter of fact, before emerging from the fluid continuum of natural life and taking up a position of selfhood, man is unacquainted with the existential experience, both as a heroic creative gesture of unqualified commitment and bold realization, on the one hand, and in its tragic aspect as an encounter with the void and nothingness, on the other. He does not share the joys of a great existence and he is spared the anguish and the tragedy of the existential bankruptcy of man who has met with God—with the Being *per se* who both bolsters and negates other beings, whose existence is all-inclusive and at the same time all-exclusive, who raises man to the pinnacle of exultation and also lets him sink in the abyss of nonsense, who gives man endless joy, tranquility of mind, inner peace and contentment, but also arouses in him fear and anxiety; the One for whom man is questing, searching and longing, and from whom he flees. With this encounter man discovers himself and his existence, and out of this discovery the passional experience is born.

The Metaphysic of Pain

Was Judaism preoccupied with the problem of suffering? Of course! Let us not forget that in Judaism suffering poses a more pointed and complicated question than in any other system of thought. Polytheistic religions had a very convenient solution to the problem of suffering; they divided responsibility among a multitude of deities. Hence the God of light and day was not to blame for the darkness and the night, and the God of life and fruition could not be indicted for death and destruction. Even Greek philosophy (in the Platonic-Aristotelian tradition) availed itself of a dualism of form and matter, granting the latter a share in the endless process of becoming and emerging, finding in it the source of suffering which is due to its instability, transience and amorphous character. Judaism, with its strict monotheistic philosophy, could not tolerate such answers, and thus the problem of suffering became more poignant and perplexing. Christianity faced a similar situation.

The general answer to this question runs as follows. God's works are good; there is no evil element involved in the order of things and events. For goodness is being, and whatever exists is good. However, Being is not a monolithic, uniform system. There are various degrees of being—higher and lower. However, even the lowest level of being is good, since the equation of being and goodness is irrefutable. Since every form of existence, even the simplest one, is good, suffering is only an illusion, a mirage, produced by comparing a low form of being with a higher one. Whatever contains less being is considered evil. The inequality in the natural order engenders in us sorrow.

This optimistic doctrine denying evil was advanced by Maimonides and the medieval scholars of the Christian world.

> After these propositions, it must be admitted as a fact that it cannot be said of God that He directly created evil, or has the direct intention to produce evil; this is impossible. His works are all perfectly good. He only produces existence, and all existence is good; whilst evil can only be attributed to Him in the way we have mentioned. He creates evil only insofar as He produces the corporeal element . . . consequently the true work of God is all good since it is existence. The book which enlightened the darkness of the world says therefore, "And God saw everything that He had made and, behold, it was very good" (Gen. 1:31). Even the existence of this corporeal element, low as it is in reality, . . . is likewise good for the permanence of the universe and the continuation of the order of things, so that one thing departs and the other succeeds. Rabbi Meir therefore explains the words "and, behold, it was very good" to imply that even death was good (*Gen. Rabbah*, 9), in accordance with what we have observed in this chapter (*Guide* III:10).

Maimonides gives the paradoxical answer to the question, "Why evil?" There is no evil; the lesser good appears to us by comparison as evil. Evil, seen in the perspective of the whole, turns into good. Only if we segregate phenomena from each other and observe them in their particularity do we think that they are absurd. Death, for instance, is an evil experience if viewed from the level of individual existence. However, if seen under the aspect of the total destiny of man as such, the elimination of the old and obsolete or the departure of people who belong mentally to a different age is the greatest of blessings. In a word, within the range of totality, all evils disappear.

Interesting is a strange substitution which our liturgists of old introduced into a prophetic text and which conveys the same idea. We read, "I form light and create darkness, I make peace and create evil. I the Lord do all these things" (Isa. 45:7). This sentence was incorporated in our daily liturgy preceding the recital of *Shema*. Yet our sages changed a word in this sentence and supplanted "evil" with "all things." In our prayers, we say, "Blessed art Thou . . . who forms light and creates darkness, who makes peace and creates all things." Instead of stating that God creates evil, we circumscribe it and say He creates all things. Apparently, in the expression "all things," evil is converted into good.

Physical Sensation and Spiritual Existence

All this, however, is fine if we consider evil within the frame of reference of creation, in the form of pain and corruption. Then we may say that evil is only a privation of the true good, but as privation of the true good it is still good. It is perhaps better for the natural primitive man to live a short period of time than for him not to live at all. Yet when we shift the perspective from creation to revelation, from pain to suffering, from a physical sensation to a spiritual experience, I do not believe that the metaphysical approach is applicable. For here the question is not "Why suffering?" and we are not trying to formulate a dialectic of sorrow, but rather "How should we handle suffering?" and our inquiry aims at a halakhah of suffering.

Revelation itself is a paradoxical experience which is not interpretable in terms of our natural reason. The encounter of man and God does not lend itself to rationalization and categorization at a cognitive level. It is a numinous awareness which is very little concerned with dialectics and the "why" question. The cognitive trend is typical of cosmic man, created on that

Friday afternoon as a part of the general order, but not of covenantal apocalyptic man, for whom reason is not a guide and who accepts the numinous and mysterious as superior to the familiar and comprehensible. Cosmic man asks "Why?" and is concerned with harmony in being; covenantal man inquires "What does it mean to me?" and is interested in the paradox in being. Cosmic man is interested in the causa and rationale, covenantal man in the norm, the kerygma, the message. Hence, suffering as a singular experience of covenantal man is subjected not to metaphysical but halakhic inquiry.

To the Halakhah, suffering is the great medium through which God, of the all-consuming fire of Mount Sinai, discloses Himself to man. "And the sight of the Glory of the Lord was like a devouring fire on the top of the Mount" (Ex. 24:17). He reveals Himself through the whirlwind, through the sharp pain and sorrow, and appears to man through the violent shock of encountering infinity. We have explained before that the apocalyptic trauma of revelation is due to the fact that finite-conditioned man, confronted suddenly by God, the numinous, all-powerful and all-negating, becomes aware of the suspension of his own selfhood. Man is tossed back from his existential position into the darkness of nihility. However, as is the case in mathematics, an equation works both ways. Not only is the apocalyptic experience catastrophic, but the converse is also true. Whenever there is a catastrophic experience, there is disclosure—man is confronted by God. Sorrow delivers a message to the man of sorrow; God addresses the sufferer through his suffering. God speaks to him through every trauma, every swing-back of peaceful man from his position, every sharp pain. Suffering is the whirlwind out of which God addressed Himself to Job. Whenever the sun sets and man feels the horror of darkness, he comes face to face with God. The apocalyptic revelation, in contrast to the cosmic, is not an ontic-eudaemonic but a nihilitic-passional experience. Whenever man catches a glimpse of the nothing—an agonizing experience—he meets God.

In this respect Judaism has sharply disagreed with the classical tradition. Plato and Aristotle identified deity with the harmonious and lawful, with the orderly, intelligible component in the world; they were completely perplexed when they came across the incidentally ugly, absurd and catastrophic in nature. Judaism, with its monistic rigidity, revolutionized the doctrine of divinity by introducing a new experience—that of revelation through the catastrophic. Judaism found God in the violent outbursts of a negating energy in the universe. The anxiety of the lonely, the sorrow of the man facing nihility and the dark night of an exhausted and despairing man are media of the great revelation. In short, pain is always kerygmatic; it bears a message.

A Halakhah of Suffering

This is, of course, not a dialectic or metaphysic of, but a halakhah of suffering. While the explanation of sorrow is not of much help to the afflicted person, a halakhic ethic of pain, the discovery and deciphering of its message, is very relevant— since suffering is not only a traumatic but also a redemptive experience. As a matter of fact, a redeemed personal existence is possible only if man set his foot upon the way of purgation and purification which suffering paves for him. Catharsis can be attained only through sacrificial action, which is nothing else but the experience of crisis, of failure and complete despair on the part of man. If man is capable of passing courageously through the valley of sorrow, he will emerge into bright sunshine rejuvenated and redeemed.

Judaism disagrees with all mental health doctrines which claim that the sooner man dismisses from his mind the catastrophic, the happier he will feel. On the contrary, it must sink into man's memory and be integrated into his existential awareness. To be means not only to enjoy or to rejoice but also to suffer and to carry the load, to experience great desolation and the dark night of affliction. The redemptive power which is inherent in endurance and perseverance is effectual only when the experience is not dismissed from one's mind.

Of course, we must discriminate between the various components of the passional experience. There the shock transports man out of his usual self. This shock is a result of one's encounter with non-being, of his peeping into the abyss of nihility. Man suddenly realizes that his existence is not secure and self-evident to the extent that the opposite, non-existence, is unthinkable. The man of sorrow begins to understand that the existential experience is an antithetic one. It contains its own contradiction—the awareness of non-existence. To exist means to know that this particular existence will at some future date be extinguished. However, this paradoxical awareness is of a metaphysical nature, without involving man in the fright and fear of death. It is more a metaphysico-axiological than a psychological shock. Metaphysical man suffers. There is no pain in the body, nor mental torment involved in this awareness. What occurs is a re-evaluation and reexamination of one's ontic consciousness.

Let me explain in psychological terms what transpires at the metaphysico-axiological level. We all know that we are mortal. Yet this bit of knowledge does not impress our existential consciousness. We simply do not experience our finitude. We speak of death, of the time when we all will be gone, we make out our wills, even buy cemetery plots; yet all this does not represent a real awareness of our limited existence, of nihility. Our experience, paradoxically enough, exhausts itself in categories of exclusive existence. Tolstoy writes in *The Death of Ivan Illich* that although everybody knows the Aristotelian syllogism: "All men are mortal; Socrates is a man; hence Socrates is mortal"—yet we do not apply this syllogistic inference to ourselves. Application as used in this context means *experiencing* the negation, not mere knowledge. To us, death is a conception but not a human experience. Only sickness somehow transforms the conception into a living reality and makes us encounter death in all its ugliness and sharpness, and this rendezvous with nihility leaves a mark upon our existential consciousness. No more do we experience ourselves in terms of immortality. This shock, which has awakened us to a new vision of non-being, must never be forgotten. The heart engages in a dialogue with nihility, and this dialogue should never be terminated. Recollection of our finite destiny is a part of the message of suffering.

A Personal Example

Let me illustrate this in terms of my own experience. My existential awareness was an absolute one. Non-being did not enter into it. I would not sustain my gaze upon nihility. Whenever I started to think of death, my thoughts were dashed back and they returned to their ordinary objective, to life. When I looked upon my grandson, I always tried to think of him as if he were my contemporary. I believed that we would always do things and play together. Then sickness initiated me into the secret of non-being. I suddenly ceased to be immortal; I became a mortal being.

The night preceding my operation I prayed to God and beseeched Him to spare me. I did not ask for too much. All I wanted was that He should make it possible for me to attend my daughter's wedding, which was postponed on account of my illness—a very modest wish in comparison with my insane claims to life prior to my sickness. The fantastic flights of human foolishness and egocentrism were distant from me that night.

However, this "fall" from the heights of an illusory immortality into the valley of finitude was the greatest achievement of the long hours of anxiety and uncertainty. Fundamentally, this change was not an act of falling but one of rising toward a new existential awareness which embraces both man's tragedy and his glory, in all its ambivalence and paradoxality. I stopped perceiving myself in categories of eternity. When I recite my prayers, I ask God to grant me life in very modest terms. A more logical self substitutes himself for a self who was intoxicated to the extent of insanity with the vision of being. I do not have to tell you that modesty is perhaps the most relevant element in prayer, both as to the efficacy and dignity of the latter.

When one's perspective is shifted from the illusion of eternity to the reality of temporality, one finds peace of mind and relief from other worries, from his petty fears and from absurd stresses and nonsensical nightmares. At the level of the antithetic existential experience, man extracts himself from the throng of ghosts which keep on haunting him. At the root of our restlessness lies a distorted conception of ourselves as immortal beings. Hence, everything that causes pain or annoyance is placed in the wrong frame of reference. We foolishly imagine eternity to be affected by a particular event which disturbed us; we magnify the significance of incidents because we exaggerate our own worth. Man sees himself in the mirror of immortality. Hence his desires, dreams, ambitions and visions assume absolute significance, and any frustrating experience may break man. When one frees himself from this obsession, his perspective becomes coherent and his suffering bearable. He learns to take defeat courageously. His frustrations and disillusions are balanced by the keen sense of a here-and-now existence in which he is submerged, and he understands that no pain lasts forever.

Suffering and Loneliness

In addition to bringing man to confront nihility, the shock of suffering opens up to man another dimension of being: loneliness. In this respect, the apocalyptic revelation and suffering display a common motif. The trauma is caused by the surprise of being singled out. When God revealed Himself to Moses, the latter argued with Him. "Who am I, *mi anokhi*, that You should send me?" (Ex. 3:11). The individual who was elected by the

Almighty out of the crowd with which he identified until the last instant finds himself suddenly different from others. In his dialogue with God he is lonely, since no one joined him in this paradoxical venture, no one shares the burden which was foisted upon his shoulders. He is even impotent to communicate to others the indescribable content of the great message which was delivered to him; it can never be told and explained. The elected remains a solitary figure, and the question which troubles his mind is a short one: *Mi anokhi,* Who am I, or to paraphrase, Why me? Why did You, great God, lift me to new heights while You left the multitude behind? Why should I be unique, different; why should I be the elected one? The pointing out of one in the crowd is a traumatic experience.

The same is true of the man of sorrow. When the blow strikes, the first question which pops up upon the lips of the sufferer is: Why me? Why should I be different from others? Why was I selected to explore the valley of sorrow? A feeling of envy fills out the heart of the afflicted. He envies everybody, pauper and prince, young and old. They were spared, while I was picked out.

When I eulogized my uncle, R. Velvel Soloveitchik, *zt"l,* in the auditorium of Yeshiva University while knowing of my affliction, one nagging thought assailed my mind. All these thousands of people are healthy and expect to live a long and happy life, whereas I am not certain that I will be able to accompany my daughter to the wedding canopy. While these thoughts are passing through one's mind with the speed of lightning, one feels forsaken, forlorn and lonely. I am different; I have met with a strange destiny. No one else is like me.

Gradually this feeling of loneliness pervades one's whole being with ever-increasing predominance; the whole self becomes immersed in solitude and the awareness of being taken away from the community. The man who is bound to others by countless invisible threads is torn loose from his social bearings. He makes his exit from the community and retreats into himself because he was singled out. Elisha, upon being elected, abandoned his father and mother. The elected retreats even from his closest friends and beloved ones, not excluding wife and children.

The night before my operation, when my family said good-bye to me, I understood the words of the psalmist, *"Ki avi ve-immi azavuni, va-Hashem ya'asfeni,* When my father and my mother forsake me, the Lord will take me up"* (Ps. 27:10). I had never understood this verse. Did ever a parent abandon his child? Of course not! Yet in certain situations, one is cut off even from his parents or his beloved wife and children. Community life, togetherness, is always imbued with the spirit of coopera-tion, of mutual help and protection. Suddenly one realizes that there is no help which his loved ones are able to extend to him. They are onlookers who watch a drama unfolding itself with unalterable speed. They are not involved in it. This realization brings to an abrupt end the feeling of togetherness. I stand before God; no one else is beside me. A lonely being meeting the loneliest Being in utter seclusion is a traumatic but also a great experience. These two experiences, that of non-being and that of loneliness, must not be forgotten.

Cosmic and Jobian Revelation

Let us return to our discussion of how God discloses Himself to man through suffering. Of course, we accept metahistorical revelation as a transcendental occurrence. Judaism originated in the revelation-experience, and to dismiss this event would mean to undermine the very foundation upon which Judaism rests. It is useless to rationalize it. It is a paradoxical event fraught with strangeness, horror and unknowability. Yet we believe that there is another revelational experience, one which is not associated with a metahistoric event.

This latter experience is revelational in the sense that it contains the element of the catastrophic. Disclosure and the catastrophic (the act of instantaneous overturning or shattering of existential patterns) are identical concepts in Judaism. Any form of suffering, any sharing in the travail of the world implies a movement of recoil, turning away from the old and familiar, from viewpoints so ingrained that they have become part of the personality, from attitudes so clear that they assumed apodictic significance, from activities so frequent that they turned into routine. In a word, the passional experience is traumatic and as such it acts with catastrophic force—it tears man loose from his fixed attachments to himself and to others and shakes him out of involvement with his well-known environment. Wherever the catastrophic emerges, the great disclosure is made: man is confronted with God.

We know very well that Judaism distinguished between the natural and the visional revelation. Man may encounter God in His works, either in the external or in the spiritual order of creation. It is a commonplace in the Bible that the works of God attest to His existence, omnipotence and wisdom. Anyone who comes in contact with creation at all levels is *ipso facto* confronted with God. "The heavens declare the glory of God, and the fimament proclaims His handiwork" (Ps. 19:2). Both through the cosmic occurrence and through the spiritual drama of man, God makes His wisdom and will known. This revelation to which cosmic man is receptive is attained only in the rapturous experience of Being in all its glory and grandeur. Creation, abounding in orderliness, architectural magnificence and overpowering beauty, is the medium which is employed by God for disclosing Himself to man. In a word, God reveals Himself through the ontic experience, the experience of being, which abolishes the barriers of finitude and goes out toward the absolute. This cosmic experience of God is portrayed in Psalm 104: "Bless the Lord, O my soul. O Lord my God, Thou art very great; Thou art clothed with honor and majesty. Who covers Himself with light as a garment; Who stretches out the heavens like a curtain . . . " *Majestas Dei* represents the revelation of

God at a cosmic level. The Greeks were not immune to the majestic-ontic experience of God even though they did not know anything about creation.

Yet Judaism introduced another form of revelation: the Jobian catastrophic one, when God addresses Himself to man through the whirlwind. This doctrine of the catastrophic is most unique in the history of the philosophy of suffering: God's revelation in the dark night of existence, or—to phrase this idea in paradoxical terms—the revelation of God through His alleged abandonment and absenting Himself from man who finds himself suddenly *tête-à-tête* with nothingness. This motif was spelled out in the halakhic categories of repentance and prayer. The experience of the catastrophic in a variety of ways—and this occurs whenever one relapses to lower existential levels—must find its response in soul searching and prayer. Both *teshuvah* and *tefillah* are the outcry of man who has met catastrophe, whose joy and peace of mind are gone. There is no prayer and there is no soul-searching if man does not experience the "great desolation" (as the mystics called it).

> When you are in tribulation and all these things are come upon you, even in the latter days, if you turn to the Lord your God . . . (Deut. 4:30).
> And it shall come to pass, when all these things are come upon you, the blessing and the curse, which I have set before you, and you shall call them to mind among all the nations where the Lord your God has driven you, *asher hidihakha*, you shall return to the Lord your God and hearken to His voice (Deut. 30:1).

The term *hidihakha* is of interest. *Hidiah* means to drive one away, in a physical sense, from home, or, as a metaphor, to make him abandon a belief, an opinion, an idea. "Certain men, wicked fellows, are gone out from your midst, *vayadihu*, and have thrust out of the way the inhabitants of their city, saying, 'Let us go and serve other gods,' to drive you away from the path" (Deut. 13:14). *Dahoh* signifies moving something from its proper place, or turning over. In a word, it is the equivalent of the Greek "*katasthrophein*," to turn down or turn over.

In the dedication address by King Solomon, prayer is defined as the response of man to suffering. "Whatever prayer and whatever supplication is made by any man or by all Thy people Israel, who shall know every man the affliction of his own heart, and he spread forth his hands towards this place . . ." (I Kings 8:38).

"The affliction of his own heart" translates itself into prayer. What is prayer? The dialogue between man and God; they both address themselves to each other. And what is a dialogue if not the mutual revelation of those engaged in it? Through the catastrophic God reveals Himself to man, and the latter, out of the depths and darkness, calls out and discloses his heart to God who spoke to him through the whirlwind of distress. The whole idea of prayer rests upon the premise that God meets man through the latter's encounter with non-being. The nihilitic revelation calls for a response on the part of man. Man oscillates between the natural revelation, which is experienced by the cosmic man's illuminated, joyous ontic consciousness, and the catastrophic revelation, which addresses itself to the tormented nihilitic consciousness. The ontic revelation employs the medium of order, stability and knowability, the nihilitic—the *tohu va-vohu,* the formless void. God's spirit hovers over the *tohu va-vohu.*

In other words, the cosmic revelation implies an affirmation of man's existence, while the catastrophic expresses itself in pure negation. The paradoxical alternation between these two revelations is, as a matter of fact, a basic motif within our existential consciousness. Since the latter manifests itself in a finite experience, it is *ipso facto* a bounded-in consciousness and, as such, antithetic. Moreover, our existential consciousness is interwoven in a time-texture, which, as the old Greeks pointed out already, is an anticipation or a remembrance of the opposite, of the contradiction of the factum upon which my consciousness at present is focused.

In a word, with the temporal-existential experience, the thesis and the antithesis coexist. Each joyous emotion reflecting God, the Creator and Sustainer of Being, contains its own contradiction, the painful realization that God negates the very order of creation. The blessed ecstasy enveloping man while viewing the great cosmic drama entails its own negation, the catastrophic ecstasy of confronting nihility. Never must one succumb to the temptation of absolutizing human experiences, of letting himself be swept away by the intoxicating awareness of "I am," forgetting the great contradiction involved in this very awareness. One's existence is a dialectical experience of positing and negating. The Psalms (2:11) speak of rejoicing while trembling, and Isaiah declares, "Then you shall see and be brightened up, and your heart shall stand in fear and be enlarged" (60:5). If man at the cosmic level of existence is not mindful of the dialectics of being, if he is prone to absolutization and hypostatization of experiences (which is an idolatrous performance) and does not identify God who called for him out of the ontic consciousness, then the great cosmic experience is supplanted by the nihilitic catastrophic. Many people have paid in this way, by the receiving of catastrophic communication of God's word, for the naivete they displayed while this word was waiting for them in the great affirmation at a cosmic level. The shocking experience of the apocalypse follows a period of grace, during which God had attempted to reach man through his ontic consciousness and man refused to receive the great communication. *Hesed* wasted, a Divine offer rejected, a message misunderstood: all these call for atonement—in other words, they call for the nihilitic revelation, which is out to accomplish what the ontic disclosure failed to do.

Job

Job, while he enjoyed the Divine blessings, rich, influential, respected by all, did not avail himself of this outpouring of Divine kindness in the interests of a great destiny which he was called to fulfill. The kerygma of the ontic revelation was not accepted by him. Power, riches and influence are given to an individual or to a community for the sake of utilization for a worthy cause. Each gift presented to man by God entails a summons. If the latter is ignored, the great swing back from ontic to nihilitic revelation takes place. This is exactly what happened to Job.

Interesting is the aggadic approach to Job. The aggadah (*Bava Batra* 15a-b) tried to have the chronology of the events narrated in the book of Job coincide with the most outstanding periods in the biblical history of our people. One aggadic scholar maintained that Job was a contemporary with our Patriarchs; another advanced the guess that Job lived at the time of the Exodus; a third one identified him as living during the period of Ezra. (There are other opinions as well.) The aggadah was emphasizing the relevance of events which transpired during Job's life, the destiny-charged moments in our emergence as a people. Job could have contributed greatly to them, accelerating the historic tempo of realization and relieving the heroic figures who were involved in these dramatic developments of the great burden they carried. He could have, had he wanted, used his influence and spared Jacob, Moses or Ezra agonizing moments of frustration, impotence and mental distress. He had the means to alleviate their suffering, to promote the cause to which they were dedicated, to help them realize the covenantal vision.

God addressed Himself to Job through abundance and wealth, through the ecstasy of joy. Job missed the message. The pendulum swung toward the catastrophic revelation, to the dialogue not via the universal harmony of the ontic consciousness but through the whirlwind whose fury is perceived in horror by the nihilitic consciousness. "And behold, there came a great wind from across the wilderness and it smote the four corners of the house and it fell upon the young men, and they are dead; I only am escaped alone to tell you" (Job 1:19). The cosmic address was supplanted by the apocalyptic address. When Job complained and questioned the intelligibility of the dark night of the apocalypse, the absence of God, the Creator, he suddenly was confronted by God, again appearing in the whirlwind, in the catastrophic. "Then the Lord answered Job out of the whirlwind" (38:1).

And what was the gist of the answer which Job received from the whirlwind? "Where were you when I laid the foundations of the earth? Declare if you have understanding. Who has laid the measures thereof, if you know? . . . Know you the time when the wild goats of the rock bring forth?" (38:4, 39:1).

In short, Job did not grasp the meaningfulness of the cosmic drama to man; he did not encounter God in creation, nor did he comprehend His summons which was communicated to Job through the magnificent order of cosmic grandeur and might. He failed at the level of the ontic experience. Hence God addressed Himself to him through the cataclysm.

The Message of Suffering

What is the kerygma which suffering delivers to man? I believe that the essence of the passional message consists in a simple sentence: Do not disown the passional encounter with God. Instead of rejecting it, assimilate the remembrance of suffering into the all-embracing existential awareness. Let the catastrophic experience be placed in the framework of your spiritual personality. Assign to it a position within your inner world. For the risk is great that man, driven by his innate tendency to immerse in spiritual joys, to keep away from himself the memory of any unpleasant sensation, to repress disturbing thoughts and to escape from a past that abounds in sorrow, will let the catastrophic event drift aimlessly in a vacuum without finding anchorage in the total personal experience. This would amount to wasting the catastrophic disclosure, to an admission that God was absent from the whirlwind that thwarts man's drives and dreams. In consequence, man would, after meeting God in the whirlwind, return to his routine which operates exclusively at the level of affirmation, refusing stubbornly to relate itself to the negation. The antithetic character of our existential experience would be lost if the sufferer reverts to old practices. Hence the fundamental norm inscribed in pain is: Forget not. Let the passional experience always be the other pole towards which the experiential pendulum swings from time to time.

The Halakhah formulated several *mitzvot* pertaining to remembrance. Two of them emphasize the passional experience: "You shall remember that you were a servant in the land of Egypt . . . " (Deut. 5:15 and elsewhere). "Remember what Amalek did to you by the way . . . How he met you by the way, and smote the hindmost of you, even all that were feeble behind you, when you were faint and weary" (Deut. 25:17-18). As a matter of fact, the event of our affliction in Egypt forms the foundation of the Jewish ethos: our deep understanding for the trials and tribulations of the stranger; our keen sense of justice and fairness; our dislike for brutality; our demand for equality. Quite often, in conveying to us an ethical norm the Bible refers us to our historical experience in Egypt. Apparently, the ethical gesture is born out of the assimilated passional experience.

Isaiah and Ezekiel

There are two narratives in the Bible in which Isaiah and Ezekiel respectively describe the apocalypse which they beheld. The theme, the vision of God, is almost identical; but the presentations vary in their basic features. Isaiah was confronted by a simple vision; Ezekiel encountered a very complex and mysterious image. Isaiah's narrative is short and terse; Ezekiel's is long and abounding in details which, instead of clarifying, make the narrative more enigmatic and awesome.

> In the year that King Uzziah died I saw the Lord sitting upon a throne, high and lifted up, and His train filled the temple. Above Him stood the seraphim; each one had six wings; with twain he covered his face, and with twain he covered his feet, and with twain he did fly. And one cried to the other and said: "*Kadosh, kadosh, kadosh*, Holy, holy, holy, is the Lord of Hosts; the whole earth is full of His glory." And the posts of the door moved at the voice of him that cried and the house was filled with smoke . . . (Isa. 6:1-4).

The historical setting for Isaiah's vision was one of relative peace and serenity. The kingdom of Judah still enjoyed freedom and prosperity. The Temple, abounding in magnificence and beauty, stood firmly atop the fair mount. The Jewish historical drama was not yet interrupted by any cataclysmic events. Exile, the disaster, defeat and national humiliation were yet unknown to the Jewish people rooted in their soil and leading a normal life. Isaiah and his people were at home and he beheld a vision of God abiding in His home in circumstances similar to those which accompany the cosmic revelation—through the display of God's might and glory. In a word, Isaiah saw *majestas Dei* reflected in the historic drama as well as in the cosmos. "The whole earth is full of His glory, *kevodo*" (6:3). Let us not forget that *kavod* signifies weight, impact. His power is universally felt. His will guides the cosmic occurrence and the historical events. *Kavod* in Hebrew denotes also light, radiation. "God's *kavod* was revealed in the cloud" (Ex. 16:10). God's majesty-light-beauty penetrates the whole earth. The skirts of God fill the temple. He is ubiquitous, and not even a single aspect of creation can afford to free itself from His might and control. He is the Lord of the Hosts. He is the king; His dominion is the whole of reality.

Of course, as an apocalyptic experience, the encounter with God was not lacking some numinous aspects. We face here a dichotomy. While the confrontation of Isaiah with God is apocalyptic, transcendental and numinous, his response was this-worldly. Isaiah saw God outside creation—high and exalted—and he rediscovered Him within creation. Isaiah saw God's skirts filling every phase of Being. Even the *seraphim*, transcendental intelligences, in the second half of their cry announced the cosmic majesty of God. As we pointed out before, the encounter was not completely devoid of the numinous. The mere attributes of *kadosh, kadosh, kadosh* denote distance, separation and distinction. Moreover, not only was the vision itself mysterious and awe-inspiring, but it also contained a traumatic element. The vision of God filled Isaiah with fear. The doorposts trembled and the house was filled with smoke, representing of the wholly other character of an event that evokes a dramatic response. Isaiah continued, "Then said I, 'Woe is me! For I am undone, because I am a man of unclean lips; . . . for my eyes have seen the King, the Lord of Hosts'" (6:5).

Yet neither the numen nor the trauma have succeeded in stripping the experience of its ontically affirmative motif. The vision in all its strangeness and otherworldliness focused Isaiah's glance upon the here-and-now reality and he began to explore not the beyond but the various dimensions of the cosmos, searching for God who addresses Himself to man not through the apocalyptic trauma but through the joyous cosmic experience. During the first commonwealth, the prophets did not hear God speaking to them from the whirlwind, since the cataclysmic or catastrophic events were unknown to the nation as a whole. God spoke to His servants and His message was an encouraging one and became immediately related to a stable order of creation. When we proclaim in *Kedushah,* "Holy, holy, holy is the Lord of Hosts; the whole earth is full of His glory," we discover God in our ontic awareness. *"Sum ergo Deus est"*—since we exist, we find at the very root of our existence God, who is Being *par excellence.* Of course, God is also distant, He is holy, and yet this remoteness does not somehow negate our existential experience. Rendezvous with God enhances our own existence. The ontic cosmic awareness emerges out of the apocalyptic confrontation.

Ezekiel was the first prophet who encountered God in the whirlwind. He experienced the catastrophic revelation; God addressed Himself to Ezekiel through the fire of disaster and the hurricane of the north. "And I looked, and, behold, a whirlwind came out of the north, a great cloud and a fire unfolding itself and a brightness was about, and out of the midst thereof as the color of amber out of the midst of the fire" (Ez. 1:4).

God revealed Himself out of the storm-wind, the destructive hurricane that left in its wake ruins and debris in the hills and plain of Judea and uprooted an entire people from its native soil, converting free, proud men into slaves and prisoners. Out of this cataclysmic whirlwind that wiped out Judea, the sanctuary, the glory and pride of Israel, out of the fire that caused havoc, out of the cloud of a dark, gloomy, lonely night, God addressed Himself to Ezekiel. Where did the prophet behold the great apocalyptic vision? In the temple, in the courtyard, surrounded by the pomp and glory of an independent people like his predecessor Isaiah? No! He met God in a prison camp, in the land of the Chaldeans by the river Kevar. And the vision he saw lacked the simplicity of the Isaiah encounter, the direct apprehension of God's glory and the majesty of God's skirt filling the temple. He sees first not God but holy creatures whose visage is like burning coal, and like the appearance of torches; he notices wheels which went with the creatures—a strange apocalypse, filling the viewer with grisly fear. The whole vision is weird and frightening.

At the outset, Ezekiel missed God; he was confronted by mechanical forces in action. He perceived the tremendous energy potential entailed in this heavenly mechanism which is engaged in perpetual motion. "It went up and down among the living creatures, and the fire was bright and out of the fire went forth lightning" (1:13). Yet he did not see God in these heavens which were wide open to his searching glance and exploring mind. The creatures ruled; they set the wheels in motion, "for the spirit of the living creatures was in the wheels." And yet there was no vision of God. He heard the noise of the wings, like the noise of the great waters, as the noise of a host—but was there something behind all this activity, drive and movement, or was there nothing in the background? The creatures, the wheels, the fire, the lightning, the torches, the roar and tumult originate and end in a great void. They are born out of nothingness and move on to their own doom.

For the fraction of a second, Ezekiel beheld a weird vision: "And the likeness of the firmament was over the heads of the living creatures like the color of the terrible ice crystal stretched forth over their heads above" (1:22). It seemed for a short moment that the terrifying vision beheld by Ezekiel was projected against an icy, cruel, insensitive and insensate reality. All prayers bounced back, all petitions echoed through the empty black spaces. The warm human voice which rose out of the depths of a yearning soul questing for God was chilled upon reaching the icy heavens. Man with his aspirations, dreams, petitions and supplications seemed a nonsensical, displaced being drifting along bleak uncharted lands, lonely and abandoned. Above his head spread forth an icy heaven, indifferent and irresponsive.

When catastrophe strikes man, when the whirlwind sweeps across his private world leaving wreckage behind—he first hears the tumult of the *hayot* and *ofanim*, the noise of mechanical, nonsensical forces ruling the universe. Beyond this insensate, unalterable, causal nexus he sees the cold indifference of empty, bleak heavens. Satan's laughter can be heard out of the roar of the whirlwind. Yet Ezekiel suddenly perceived something new, a strange sound coming from afar, from a remote corner of Being, from above the icy firmament, penetrating this terrible icy spread which shut everything out of sight. This voice was not drowned out by the tumult of the wheels, the noise of the living creatures, the host of the great waters. It prevailed in spite of the roar of the tempest.

"And there was a voice from above the firmament that was over their heads; when they stood still, they let down their wings" (1:25). Everything suddenly came to a standstill. Ezekiel saw a new vision, reminiscent of Isaiah's encounter.

> And above the firmament that was over their heads was the likeness of a throne, in appearance like a sapphire stone; and upon the likeness of the throne was a likeness . . . As the appearance of a bow that is in the cloud in the day of rain, so is the appearance of the brightness round about. This was the appearance of the likeness of the glory of the Lord (1:26, 28).

God disclosed Himself suddenly to Ezekiel. After an allegedly futile search for God in the heavens, after vainly exploring creation for Him, at least for a trace of His glory and might, wisdom and beauty, after encountering living creatures, wheels, automatic senseless movement, a tumult and noise, after confronting a cold, indifferent heaven, after resigning himself to an absurd existence in a prison camp, after plunging into the abyss of black despair, the scenery changed suddenly. He heard a voice of one that spoke, a meaningful voice and not an absurd noise, not the tumult of mighty waters. He saw God in the likeness of a man; the questing I met a lonely Thou, not in the temple, but in the camp of downtrodden, homeless prisoners. The words were addressed out of the whirlwind, and the likeness of the glory of the Lord emerged out of the frightening fire. God spoke out of the catastrophic event, out of the distressing encounter with nihility, out of the seeming void and emptiness, from above the icy firmament, from nowhere. It took Ezekiel a long time to make the great leap from an insane existence to the throne of God that stands above the ice crystal firmament, from the absurdity of a historical cataclysm to the great dialogue with the hidden, numinous, mysterious God, abiding behind the heavens. Suddenly a new light was shed over everything he beheld before. The weird creatures, the wheels, the great noise, the host, the mighty waters—these did not fill him with grisly fear any more; a spirit lifted him and he heard the voice (not the noise) of a great rushing, "Blessed be the glory of the Lord from His place" (Ez. 3:12), from His transcendence. Blessed be the Lord who speaks to man out of the whirlwind and horrible fire. In our *Kedushah* we profess our faith in the cosmic and also in the catastrophic revelation of God. We are always confronted through our ontic and nihilitic experiences.

> We shall sanctify Your Name in the world as it is sanctified on High, as it is written by Your prophets: "And they call one to another and say: 'Holy, holy, holy is the Lord of Hosts; the whole earth is full of His glory'" (Isa. 6:3), while opposite them they proclaim, "Blessed be the glory of the Lord from His place" (Ez. 3:12).

God's Summons to Service

When we experience the swing back from an illusory eternity to a temporal reality, a new category is discovered, namely, that of service. God summons us to His service; we are called upon to serve Him. We are appointed as the servants of God. "Hallelujah, praise O you servants of the Lord" (Ps. 113:1), "O Lord, truly I am Thy servant; I am Thy servant the son of Thy handmaid" (Ps. 116:16). There can be no religious experience if it does not entail the element of service. Our existence is not just a coincidence, a mechanical fact, a meaningless caprice on the part of nature or providence, but a meaningful assignment which abounds in responsibility and commitment.

The aggadic literature considered man as a day laborer who is paid for his creative time, for the utilization of his days to their fullest extent. "Is there not a time of service to man upon earth? Are not his days like the days of a hireling?" (Job 7:1). Existence equals one's service to God or creative action.

Judaism believes that every individual is capable of qualifying himself for Divine service. Rich and poor, genius and simpleton, master and slave—they are all fit to serve God in some capacity. Every person possesses something unique, by virtue of which he differs from the thou, making him or her irreplaceable and indispensable—the inner worth of a one-timely, unique, never-to-be-duplicated existence, which can and must serve God by self-involvement in the drama of redemption at all levels. This is Judaic humanism, or Judaic democracy. All men are equally worthy as God's servants. The great intellectual may discover new rules guiding the cosmic occurrence and thus serve God by explicating unknown aspects of His primordial will imbedded in creation. The dull mind serves God by trying to learn about elementary truths, by displaying humility, perseverance and patience, by receiving instruction from others better informed, by improving his mind as much as possible and widening his knowledge. In a word, the call is issued to all. God calls: Abraham, Abraham, Moses, Moses; you are elected. And the individual must answer: *Hineni*; here I am!

If one lives in an illusory eternity, he may miss the call; he may not hear the voice which addresses itself to him; he may not realize that God Himself turns to him and summons him to His service. For in eternity nothing passes, nothing is lost; there is no time which lies behind us; everything persists and endures. There is eternal repetition. Yet if the time awareness is awakened in me, if I suddenly become cognizant of an existence which has been withdrawn from the realm of my influence, where I convert the present moment into creative performance, potentiality into an event and time into service, I realize that I have missed the call, that I am late for the execution of my task, for the fulfillment of my mission. I also begin to comprehend the responsibility which my time-experience entails, the norm of vigilance and alertness every moment, since the call comes through often, at very short intervals. I anticipate the future with trepidation and anxiety, because it is the time in which I may act and serve. Every fraction of the infinite stream of time becomes precious. For this moment I am alive and capable of action; what will happen the next minute I do not know.

Judaism was always very sensitive to the flux of time. God's rendezvous with man occurred at an appointed time. "And Moses said, 'Thus says the Lord: About midnight will I go out to into the midst of Egypt . . .'" (Ex. 11:4). "And the Lord said unto Moses: Go unto the people, and sanctify them today and tomorrow . . . and be ready by the third day, for on the third day the Lord will come down" (Ex. 19:10-11). Be ready!—this is the command of Judaism. Each moment of a conscious existence is a Divine gift out of which the summons to the service of God emerges. Judaism believes that each person has a fixed place in creation. If I find myself thrust in here and now, it is because God thinks that I can act here and now efficiently. If I had been born a hundred years ago or if I would come into this world a century later, my contribution as a servant would be nil. God wills me to act right here and now.

On Yom Kippur, we pray, "My Lord, before I was created I was of no worth, and now that I have been created it is as if I have not been created." Before I was created there was no need for my service, I had no place in the order of things and events and I could not serve God. My creation implies a twofold message: my service is required and I have the ability to act here and now. With the birth of every person, a situation is formed within which he can serve God; otherwise he would not be born. However, I misunderstood the call rising out of my existence and did not accomplish anything. Hence the miracle of birth was wasted—"and now that I have been created, it is as if I have not been created."

If man comprehends the role of a servant of God, then his life is one long service, and death is the conclusion of this hallowed service. However, if the Divine call is ignored, he lives in vain and dies in a very absurd manner. "Dust am I in life, and all the more so in death." There is a great capacity in me; yet it is filled with vanity. "Before Thee, I am like a utensil filled with shame and disgrace." In a word, every man has a fixed place in space and in time where he can serve best. He must not misread the kerygma.

❧ The Crisis of Human Finitude

The Philistine Personality

Judaism has always insisted that man recognize not only his great God-given abilities and his capacity for self-transcendence, but also the tragic fact of his own finitude and the consequent incompleteness of his existential experience. Not everyone, however, is willing to confront these truths. For example, the philistine personality (so common in *bourgeois* society) leads a narrow, shut-in existence, focusing all his efforts on a single object: self-preservation. He recognizes no value beyond this, and is animated by the belief that, with sufficient effort, the attainment of this goal is within his grasp. When faced with evidence of his own inadequacy and vulnerability, instead of revising his philosophy, he is driven to invent new means of safeguarding and protecting himself against defeat (v. Emil Brunner, *The Divine Imperative*, pp. 22-23). The philistine must always be successful, the first to attain and the last to lose, or, better yet, the one who need not relinquish anything at all. This drive for conquest and security is the motivating force of our civilized effort.

I must add that it does not matter what methods the philistine employs in order to succeed in both the acquisition and the protection of his privileges. He may utilize his intellect to this end, as scientific society recommends, constructing intelligent means of attainment and preservation; or he may turn to God for help. He worships the Almighty, prays to Him and complies with His commands because, by so doing, the religious philistine hopes to appease his Creator and thus secure success and safety for himself and his family. He expects God to do for him what the agnostic anticipates science will accomplish—to promote self-survival in the most comfortable way. Seeking security and conquest, he takes in God as a partner. Whatever he gives to God, he expects to receive back with a considerable dividend. This religious egotist cannot sacrifice anything to God, since he is incapable of sharing anything with anybody—not even with his Creator. Whatever he brings to the altar is a capital investment rather than an offering. Fundamentally, the religious act of the egotist is an expression of a utilitarian, economy-minded individual. He never feels the unique, redeeming and uplifting power of man's transcendent adventure, nor has he the capacity to transcend his self-centered life.

Job, the Religious Philistine

The religious egotist and philistine is represented by Job. The Bible portrays him as a very limited personality, a law-abiding citizen who "fears God and turns away from evil" (1:8). He did not engage in evil, but did not commit himself to God. His efforts were directed toward a circumscribed goal: maintaining the *status quo* of his family. He served the Lord sincerely and conscientiously, not because the service itself conveyed to him a singular meaning, but for egotistic reasons, as a way to preserve his sense of security.

It was the custom of his sons to hold feasts, each on his set day in his own home; and they used to send and call for their three sisters to eat and drink with them. And when a round of feast days had ended, Job sent word to them to sanctify themselves, and he rose up early in the morning, and offered burnt offerings according to the number of them all: for Job said, "It may be that my sons have sinned, and despised God in their hearts" (1:4-5).

This passage portrays a close-knit family, egotistic and self-centered. Community existence was alien to them, the act of giving and relinquishing—unknown. They lived bounded in, distant from others, in retreat, happy and complacent as an independent entity—a Robinson Crusoe life, without responsibilities and bonds, without the fellowship and love which manifest themselves in giving. Of course, Job brought offerings to God. But this ritual was not a natural manifestation of the religious experience, expressing itself in the dignified act of giving away one's own self, his precious possession, of deliberately losing the battle which he has won at so high a cost. It was, rather, a business venture, a pragmatic affair of *quid pro quo*. The burnt offerings were supposed to enhance the safety of his children.

This kind of life went on until Satan struck. Instead of Job giving voluntarily, uncontrolled forces wrested everything from him. He had enjoyed conquest, triumph and continuous acquisition, without going through the agony of defeat, failure and loss. The tragedy was bound to happen; it was inevitable. Tenuously holding on to oneself, continually triumphing over opposition without being defeated even once, steadily clinging to a definitive pattern of existence without manifesting readiness for change, surrender and deviation—this mode of existence must end in catastrophe. Job lacked the dignity and majesty of being which can be attained only through the dialectical experience of victory and voluntary defeat.

At the conclusion of the story, we are told that a new Job emerged out of the cataclysm which had so mercilessly punished him; a heroic personality appeared instead of the old philistine. The tempest that swept him out of his complacency and egotism raised him to a new level of dialectical existence, where triumph is interwoven with defeat, success with failure, and receiving serves a higher end—relinquishing. The Job who was isolated and shut in, living for himself and concentrated into himself, descending deeply into the abyss of his own being, is replaced by a Job who has opened up to and is bound up with others, who has stepped out of his hidden recesses, moved toward the outside and plunged into a community existence. The second Job has abandoned his self-containment, self-sufficiency and self-absorption, and has awakened to a new existence which is not only for itself but also for something or somebody else. Job learned the art of dialectical living. "And the Lord returned the fortunes of Job, *when he prayed for his friends*; and the Lord gave Job twice as much as he had before" (42:10).

The turning point was the prayer. What is prayer, if not returning to God whatever man has received? The successful Job, who could not imagine failure, did not understand the significance of prayer. The latter shatters man's security and self-satisfaction, since it concedes defeat and admits bankruptcy and a frustrated existence. Job certainly did not grasp the meaning of friendship. At this phase, even communal and social relations served the purpose of utility and safety. Real friendship is possible only when man rises to the height of an open existence, in which he is capable of prayer and communication. In such living, the personality fulfills itself.

Kohelet, the Daemonic Personality

While Job represents the limited existence of the egotist and philistine, Kohelet (Ecclesiastes) characterizes another form of living, namely, the daemonic (to use the term coined by Emil

Brunner in *The Divine Imperative*, pp. 23-24). The daemonic existence is graced with beauty and fantastic sweep, while the philistine way of living is dull and unimaginative. The daemonic personality indulges in adventures, risks and spectacular things; he dreams of vastness and unlimited expanses. In contradistinction to the philistine, he is never satisfied with his accomplishments. His imagination is stimulated and inspired by success, and his appetite is never stilled. Regardless of the territory over which he roams in his incessant quest for daring projects, conquest and triumph—be it warfare (Alexander the Great, Napoleon, Communist Russia), be it finance (the robber barons, the financial wizards and manipulators), be it science (man's technological aspirations, his unquenchable thirst for knowledge, his insatiable curiosity, e.g. Faust), be it hedonic pursuits (Don Juan, Cleopatra)—the driving force is the same: self-glorification, reaching out for the impossible, the desire for an endless existence, for infinity. When he sinned, paradisiacal man became involved with the serpent, the daemon. There is a daemonic origin to his arrogant quest to equal God, to be greater and bigger than He is, to transcend finitude and plunge into infinity. "And you shall be as gods, knowing good and evil" (Gen. 3:5).

Kohelet also leads a closed existence of repose within himself. He is interested only in his own greatness and his own pleasures, even when he engages in charitable deeds on a grand scale (whatever Kohelet does is flamboyant and spectacular). In helping others, he asserts his own power and genius.

That Kohelet did not fulfill his destiny is a truism, and this is the lesson which this strange book seeks to impart to us— "This also is vanity and a striving after wind" (Eccl. 2:26). Why was Kohelet disappointed in his glorious career and his stupendous exploits, why did he lament the vanity of all efforts, why this pessimistic note which reverberates throughout the whole book? Why the skeptical mood which, because of failure, doubts everything? The answer is simple. The human existential experience is intrinsically incomplete; finitude means the absence of wholeness and fullness. The existential thesis is always bounded in by the antithesis, by the negation.

For example, the ontic awareness ("*ergo sum*, therefore I am") contains the moment of nihility, nothingness; life is encompassed by death and is always beheld as if it were running to its own doom. Similarly, the cognitive gesture points towards the unknown, towards the *mysterium magnum* which escapes our comprehension. Man's knowledge rests upon substitution of the known for the unknown, the comprehensible quantity for the qualitative phenomenon; the immediate sense experience will remain an eternal enigma. The wider the areas our intellect explores, the greater and more challenging becomes the mystery of Being as a whole. Science explores reality only within; it never tries to explain it from without. The intellectual adventure inspires man with awe before the great unknown Being as such. God's response to Job is, "*Ha-yadata*, Do you know?"

The moralist's performance, too, is incomplete. One can never realize his moral destiny. The greater the moral power of the person, the more distant is the goal, the promise. Moses could not enter the promised land. Likewise, aesthetic enjoyment always ends in the encounter with satanic gluttony, ugliness and vulgarity, as in the cases of Samson and Delilah, Amnon and Tamar, and so forth. The ontic experience is never complete; it is fraught with its own negation. The awareness of being is absurd, since it contains a *contradictio in objecto*, or, in Hebrew, *shenei hafakhim be-nosei ehad*, two opposites in one subject.

The Humanistic and Religious Solutions to Human Finitude

Man, facing this problem, has at his disposal two solutions.

1) *The humanistic answer*: He may deny the very truth and try to convince himself that everything is perfect and full, that he moves toward his ultimate end along a straight road, with-

out having to detour or retreat. Fundamentally, this solution underlies all humanistic secular utopias, including that of Communism—an unshakable faith in the perfectibility of man, in his gradual emergence as an omniscient and omnipotent being. Disappointments, handicaps and failures must be expected, since the evolutionary process of emergence is a long one and we have not yet reached the final stages. However, the term "progress" is the shibboleth of these humanistic creeds, and gradually our experience will expand and become more and more consistent and complete.

Of course, it is hard to foresee future developments, but, judging by past experiences, we are impelled to assume that the humanistic approach is wrong and self-deceiving. It is a fraudulent solution. The problem posed by Kohelet has lost nothing of its poignancy and acuteness, notwithstanding the fact that civilization has covered such an endless distance since the days of that skeptic. Apparently, cultural ascent and scientific achievement do not relieve man of the curse of vanity and incompleteness which presses on his frail shoulders. The restlessness which drove Kohelet to his bold adventures rushes with us in the same direction.

2) *The religious-metaphysical answer*: The incompleteness of our existential experience at all levels is rooted in the nature and destiny of man. He is a creature and, as such, a part of a finite reality—and finitude is incomplete, deficient and impregnated with paradoxes and absurdities. Death is an integral part of the biological process. The "x" cannot be separated from the equation—there is always an unknown quantity involved in the cognitive performance. Beauty is somehow projected against the dark background of ugliness, and absolute goodness is engaged in an eternal contest with Satan. Maimonides and Leibniz termed the incompleteness of our being *malum metaphysicum*, a metaphysical evil, from which man can never free himself. Intoxication with our given existence is accompanied by disillusionment.

Yet we can somehow relieve ourselves of this burden of despair brought on by the tantalizingly full existence which recedes into vast distances like a mirage as soon as we think that we have found our destination. We can accomplish this by consecrating this incompleteness as an offering to God, giving up our illusions of grandeur and glory, of success and conquest—not like Kohelet, forcibly, because we have tried all recipes for happiness and found them ineffectual, but on account of our craving for dignity and majesty: for fulfillment not through accomplishment without, but through ascent within. We find dignity and majesty not in the madness of "draining" one conquest "to the dregs" in order pass on to another, but in self-conquest and self-giving; in the quest for catharsis, for redemption by returning my existence to its Owner; in the heroic sacrifice.

If this singular being called man is caught in the incessant pursuit of the intellectual mirage, he must finally admit defeat. He must turn to God and say, "He who increases knowledge, increases sorrow" (Eccl. 1:18). The more knowledge I accumulate, the more the mystery deepens, the more complex is the problem, the more fascinating is the unknown. I shall restlessly explore, investigate, search and try to comprehend, but I know that the radius of the scientifically charted sectors will grow one-dimensionally, while the area of the problem will expand two-dimensionally. I am not regretting my search for knowledge, but I am renouncing my arrogant desire for a complete cognitive experience, for conquest which is not followed by defeat.

If he happens to be a *homo religiosus*, the person should say: God Almighty, the closer I try to come to You, the greater is the distance that separates me from You; the more troublesome becomes my conscience; the less worthy of communicating with You I find myself. I shall never stop seeking You and clinging to You. However, I must dispel the illusion of possessing You. Is not the drama in the Song of Songs a portrayal of the disturbed depths of the God-intoxicated person, of the fugitive satisfaction of meeting God for a while and then losing Him forever?

If he is an ethicist, a moralist in quest of the full realization of the good, let him confess his frailty and helplessness as far as the moral act is concerned. Let him declare: God, I shall never cease striving for the realization of the ethical goal, the *summum bonum* (highest good). However, I know that I will never attain the peace of mind and tranquility which comes with the most cherished and yet most transient of all desires—the full ethical life. I am ready to forego this great experience; accept it, Lord, as my offering.

Actually, when Judaism demands a sacrifice from man in fulfillment of his charisma, it wants him to give away something which he has never received, something for which he stretches out his hand, something he aspires to attain yet which will always remain outside of his reach. In a word, he must relinquish an illusion, a dream, a vain hope. By renouncing an unfulfilled wish to God, man finds self-actualization.

This paradoxical, dialectical act of winning and losing may be realized in a twofold way: first, at the subjective experiential level, as a crisis-awareness spelled out in prayer; second, at the objective level, as a sacrificial decision.

Prayer and the Crisis Awareness

Let us analyze the dialectics in our inward experience in terms of a crisis consciousness and prayer offering. Interesting is a halakhic thesis which expresses a basic biblical motif: *tefillah* (prayer) is closely knit with *tzarah* (distress). A person should engage in prayer only when he finds himself in trouble, in a predicament or in need. The act of praying is the religious response to the experience of *tzarah*, distressing existential narrowness, the awareness of being shut in and sealed off, of being trapped and defeated. Many passages in the Bible confirm this conjunction of *tefillah* and *tzarah*:

When you are in distress, and all these things come upon you, in the latter days, you will return to the Lord your God . . . (Deut. 4:30).

And it shall come to pass, when all these things are come upon you, the blessing and the curse which I have set before you, you shall take them to heart among all the nations into which the Lord your God has driven you (Deut. 30:1).

If you go to war in your land against the enemy who oppresses you, then you shall blow an alarm with the trumpets; and you shall be remembered before the Lord your God (Num. 10:9).

Solomon defines prayer as the outcry of a person in dire need, overcome by anguish:

When Thy people Israel are smitten down before the enemy, because they have sinned against Thee, they shall turn again to Thee, and confess Thy name, and pray, and make supplication to Thee in this house (I Kings 8:33).

When heaven is shut up, and there is no rain, because they have sinned against Thee; if they pray towards this place . . . (I Kings 8:35).

If there be famine in the land, if there be pestilence, blight, mildew, locust, or if there be caterpillar; if their enemy besiege them in the land of their cities; whatever affliction, whatever sickness there may be: whatever prayer and whatever supplication is made by any man or by all Thy people Israel, who shall know every man the affliction of his own heart, and he spread forth his hands towards this place . . . (I Kings 8:37-38).

David, in his Psalms, identifies prayer with the feeling of anxiety and despair:

You did call in trouble, and I delivered you (Ps. 81:8).
Out of the straits, I called upon the Lord (Ps. 118:5).
Out of the depths, I have called to Thee, O Lord (Ps. 130:1).
A prayer of the pauper, when he faints, and pours out his complaint before the Lord (Ps. 102:1).
My God, my God, why have Thou forsaken me? Why art Thou so far from helping me, from the words of my loud complaint? (Ps. 22:2).

Prayer is warranted and meaningful only when one realizes that all hope is gone, that there is no other friend besides God from whom one may expect assistance and comfort, when the soul feels its bleak despair, loneliness and helplessness. However, if one is not haunted by anxiety and brute fear, if one does not look upon his existence as a heap of debris, if his self-confidence and arrogance have not been undermined, if neither doubt nor anguish assails his mind—then prayer is alien to him and any recital of a fixed prayer-text is meaningless. Success and prayer, impudence and prayer, are mutually exclusive.

Prayer as a personal experience, as a creative gesture, is possible only if and when man discovers himself in crisis or in need. That is why the Jewish idea of prayer differs from the mystical idea, insofar as we have emphasized the centrality of the petition, while the mystics have stressed the relevance of the hymn. Since prayer flows from a personality which finds itself in need, despondent and hopeless, its main theme is not praise or adoration, but rather request, demand, supplication. True prayer comes to expression in the act of begging and interceding. However, we must always keep in mind that the concept of crisis has a twofold aspect. We must discriminate between the external crisis and the inner crisis, or, in other words, between the surface experience of *tzarah* and the depth experience.

Surface Crisis

The surface experience of *tzarah* applies to an external or accidental crisis which develops automatically, independently of man. This sort of crisis is engendered mostly by environmental forces, which are not always friendly to man's interests and desires. Many a time, nature proves to be uncooperative and hostile; it attacks man and crushes him under its stupendous mechanical impact. Man is hungry, toils his plot of land and expects a bountiful harvest; the drought or the hurricane destroys his crop. "When heaven is shut up, and there is no rain . . . if there be pestilence, blight, mildew, locust, or if there be caterpillar . . . " (I Kings 8:35, 37).

A man earns a living and supports his family; a cruel malignant disease strikes and cripples him. This type of crisis comes suddenly, with the speed of lightning, uninvited by the individual who succumbs to its destructive might and overwhelming power. This kind of disaster strikes man with the force of a hurricane and destroys him ruthlessly.

This *tzarah*-crisis feeling is a community experience. As an emotion, it is a public response to stress and suffering. First, the experience can be shared by many at the same time. Illness, famine, war, poverty and death may strike the many and expose them to common suffering and torture. The external crisis at times overwhelms the multitude. Its experience is universal in essence and character. There is nothing in the encounter of the individual with antagonistic and cruel forces of nature which would lend it a quality of peculiarity, of being unparalleled. There may be some characteristic properties attached to these experiences which differ in the various individuals who live through an external crisis. However, these differences pertain to concomitants of the crisis awareness, to the attendant reactions, but not to the essence of the experience itself.

Second, the plight of the afflicted person is obvious, exposed to the public eye. Its apprehension is as natural as the perception caused by thunder or lightning. One does not need to be very sensitive nor to be extremely skilled and observant in order to realize that the other fellow is in distress, that his very existence is menaced and his chances of survival are very slim. Therefore, the misery or misfortune of others excites our sorrow and brings forth the conjunctive, inclusive feeling of sympathy. We share, to some degree, the emotional responses of our fellow men who are wronged and ill-treated by the unalterable law of nature. Quite often, we imagine ourselves tormented and grieved by similar circumstances, and our sympathy reflects some foreboding with regard to ourselves.

The prayer associated with this kind of crisis is intercessory in character, seeking answers which are supposed to take place in the outside world. We petition God to effect changes in the objective order of things.

Depth Crisis

In contradistinction to the public experience of a surface crisis, there is the private experience of a depth crisis. This experience deals with unknown, undefined and clandestine distress, a crisis which is not encountered at random and of which man is not at all aware unless he wills to acquaint himself with it. Children do not come across this crisis at all. Only the adult, the mature personality who has outgrown childhood with all its characteristics—substitution of fantasy for reality, cowardice in admitting errors, emotional shallowness, moodiness and whimsicality—may discover this dilemma and problem. The crisis is not brought about by extraneous factors, by coincidental entanglement in precarious and distressingly complex situations, nor is it imposed upon man by elemental forces which are unleashed by Satan (as in the case of Job [1:19]—"And behold, there came a great wind from across the wilderness, and it smote the four corners of the house"). It is found and accepted freely by man.

The crisis is the result of a great heroic adventure on the part of the man who discovers himself. This experience is not something against which man tries to protect himself, nor is it something into which he is dragged compulsorily because of his stupidity—such as war, illness or famine. (If mankind possessed more knowledge, it would be able to control these destructive forces.) Rather, it is an experience of a man of independent thought and deed, self-reliant and emancipated from the trammels of superstition and self-deceit, who has developed all of the competencies and magnificent abilities which God has bestowed upon him. This experience of the depth crisis stems from the most crucial encounter of man—as a spiritual personality—with his destiny. Man is not cast into the crisis, but rather finds it within himself. It belongs to his very existential experience.

This crisis eludes our conceptual grasp in terms of social, economic or environmental forces. It can be experienced only within our existential-transcendental awareness. Human existence exhausts itself in the experience of the perennial crisis which comes to an end with the termination of human self-consciousness, in the continuous discovery of a distressed and tormented self, in the steady awareness of an incomplete existence and an unfulfilled destiny, in experiencing defeat, despair and failure. This depth crisis is woven into man's ontic consciousness. The Cartesian dictum of *cogito ergo sum*, "I think therefore I am," does not convey the full truth. It is an incomplete sentence. We must always qualify it by adding two words at the end: "I think therefore I am *in distress*."

Judaism wants man to be fully cognizant of this tragic aspect of his existence, to explicate and spell out the deep-seated crisis in his very existence. On the one hand, Judaism has recommended an activist philosophy with regard to man's environment. Man must try to combat evil and entrenched wrong at all levels—social, political and natural. God, according to our viewpoint, has charged man with the great mission of completing and supplementing the Divine act of creation by improving nature and himself, by organizing a defense system against disease, poverty and other disasters. Our outlook is optimistic, summoning man to resist the onslaught of an inimical environment and to deliver himself from his bondage to mechanical coincidence. However, on the other hand, man was told not to try to disengage himself from his involvement in the depth crisis. To the contrary, he was commanded to deepen his involvement and to confront the crisis courageously and intelligently. Man must know that there is no escape mechanism which may help him rid himself of this inner feeling of distress. He should condone and accept it voluntarily. Any attempt to flee this experience must end in real disaster.

Job and Kohelet sinned in this respect. Job tried to escape from reality and drugged himself into an illusory sense of serenity and security. He did not understand that the genuine existential experience is fraught with incompleteness and the feeling of distress. He mistook a fantasy for a fact, a mirage for a reality. Although he thought that he had attained the very ultimate and final end, he lived in an unreal world, since there can be no reality-awareness without experiencing the very antithesis of this awareness. What worried Job was not his inner distressed personality, but rather external dangers: Satan's malice, foreign enemies, the natural elements, hurricanes, diseases, death and so forth. His fear was unpurged of its primitive terrors, and this ominous blood-chilling dread of forthcoming disaster moved him to bring burnt offerings every week in order to placate the wrath of the Creator. To Job, crisis meant only external catastrophe. Inwardly, he was contented and happy. Then Satan struck. The external crisis which he had feared became a reality. When man adopts a false sense of happiness and perfection, when he is complacent and lacks self-understanding, when he is too proud to admit failure because he can live only at the plane of majesty, in triumph and victory, refusing to acknowledge inner defeat—this attitude must end in external failure and a holocaust.

Kohelet realized the absurdity of being, the incompleteness of his life and the inner contradictions implied in his total effort of self-activation and self-actualization. However, he too lived in a dream world. He thought that it is possible to overcome this crisis by adopting an aggressive policy. The incompleteness may be superseded by the fullness and perfectedness of the existential experience if man—mature in wisdom and knowledge, and wielding great power—decides to do so. In his pride, Kohelet wanted to reassert himself and to deny the idea of defeat. Arrogantly, he attempted to conquer the invincible, to achieve the unattainable and to realize the impossible. He enjoyed the adventurous for the risk it involved, the daring experiment, the quest for the distant, for the sake of the performance itself. He sought fulfillment not so much in the achieving of his object but in the attempt to realize his desire. Fundamentally, Kohelet did not grasp the essence of the depth crisis, since he believed in complete self-realization and in the possibility of resolving the existential crisis.

The depth crisis is a private affair. It is a unique feeling that cannot be shared by others. Each individual suffers in a way peculiar to himself. The experiences of various individuals are incommensurate; every individual is a shut-in entity. Each person is plagued by something else; each is engaged in a crisis which the other does not experience. Since this crisis is an integral part of the ego-awareness, it necessarily must contain all the singular traits which make a person an individuality, a one-timely strange existence, inaccessible and incomprehensible to others. Each individual, in his own peculiar way, meets his antagonist, who emerges not from the uncharted spaces of the external world, but from within; each individual grapples with the paradox hidden in his own existence. The individual alone comes to grips with the antithesis that is born out of the thesis, and only he himself can feel the sharp pain caused by the conflict between the acts of positing and negating.

Prayer flowing from a heart filled with the inner misery and despair of this contradictory experience is not intercessory petition, which is intended to relieve one of his trouble, but rather has more of a subjective character. It does not ask for help, nor does it try to resolve the crisis. The prayer consecrates the defeat, redeems the misery and elevates it to the level of sacrifice. Prayer flowing *mi-ma'amakim*, from the depths, is a sacrificial service. The supplication imparts meaning and directedness to the crisis experience. The majestic personality of a while ago (at the hour of triumph) acquires dignity, and, of course, greatness through prayer, during which the free surrender is brought about or the defeat accepted. What this prayer accomplishes is remarkable.

Mood vs. Experience

I wish to emphasize that when I speak of the depth crisis from which man is unable to disengage himself, a crisis which expresses the very gist of the human existential awareness, I am not referring to a mood of defeat and forlornness, but to an experience in which the affirmation is indissolubly bound up with the negation, the thesis with the antithesis. The difference between a mood and an experience is basic.

A mood—in its connotation as a frame or cast of mind, an emotional behavioral pattern, or a specific state of mind—is confined to the surface of the mind, without striking roots in the innermost recesses of the human personality. Usually, a mood is an uncontemplative and unrestrained emotional reaction to some external factor, a response to environmental events whose significance and meaning the person has not understood or assimilated into his total existential experience. This sort of reaction may give a person unlimited joy or boundless misery. However, it is transient; sometimes it comes like a hurricane, but blows over quickly, not leaving any trail behind. The moody person reacts easily and quickly; yet, in most cases, such an unrestrained emotional response is degrading. It lacks intellectual insight, intuition of higher values and direction of spiritual energy into the right channels.

One enters the cemetery and is overcome by a melancholy mood. All the aspirations, hopes and dreams of the living seem to lose their worth and to evaporate into thin air. The next moment, one finds himself back in his office, and all the gloomy thoughts about the nihility of man and the vanity of his undertakings are gone; one is again engaged in the feverish pursuit of his daily routine and is completely unaware of death. The shouts of joy on a hilarious occasion or the tear of a sad eye at the bier of a friend do not necessarily reflect a sincerely joyous or grieving soul. Rather, they express a passing mood, an unworthy, alas degrading, emotion, motivated by selfish fear.

Judaism disapproves of all unrestrained affective responses, and instead tries to discipline emotion and convert it into an experience which, in contrast with the mood, is assimilated into one's character and possesses personal value. The very essence of the personality manifests itself in the experience, which is not a detached emotion but an I-feeling, an existence awareness in all its uniqueness and strangeness. When in the sphere of the mood, we are bondsmen, enslaved to our own compulsory responses to a variety of phenomena. When emotion is raised to the level of experience, we gain the upper hand or control over our own emotions. We acquire the freedom to integrate feelings or to disown them, putting them at a distance from us (to use Adler's term). We gather up in our experience those emotions whose worth is meaningful to us, and we reject the feelings which are disjunctive and negating as far as our existential adventure is concerned. We accept or detach ourselves from fleeting moods and over-expanded, void emotions. Freedom of will, according to Judaism, is not limited to external action. Its application extends to the inner life of man. Man freely forms his living experience by selecting ennobling and worthwhile emotions out of a pile of unorganized and amorphous moods, and molds them into a great experience, endowed with constancy and directedness.

Moodiness in Religion

Judaism resents moodiness even in the field of religion. We have never attributed much significance to the impulsive religious emotion, to the impetuous onrush of piety, the sudden conversion, the headlong emotional leap from the mundane and profane into the sacred and heavenly; we are reluctant to accept all kinds of precipitate moods as genuine expressions of God-intoxications of the soul. Judaism is interested in a religious experience which mirrors the genuine personality, the most profound movements of the soul, an experience which is the result of true involvement in the transcendental gesture, of slow, painstaking self-reckoning and self-actualization, of deep intuition of eternal values and comprehension of human destiny and paradox, of miserable sleepless nights of dreary doubt and skepticism and of glorious days of inspiration, of being torn by opposing forces and winning freedom.

Therefore, Judaism has always avoided bringing man to God by alluring him with some external magnetic power or charm. It does not try to gain entrance to his soul by creating around it a soft, gentle and serene atmosphere, full of quieting beauty and tender charm, in which it should almost spontaneously feel relieved of all its worries; nor by suggesting the idea of the numinous and mysterious through different artistic means, in order to render the soul docile and submissive; nor by a display of majestic glory and splendor. Man, according to Judaism, must meet God on realistic terms, not in an enraptured romantic mood, when the activity of the intellect and the free exercise of the willpower are affected by hypnotic influences.

That is why the Jewish service distinguishes itself by its utter simplicity and by the absence of any cultic-ceremonial elements. It lacks the solemnity and magnificence of the Byzantine Greek Orthodox service, the moment of awe-struck wonder of the Roman Catholic Mass of transubstantiation, and the rhythm and streamlined quality of the Protestant church ceremony. It is nothing but a dialogue between God and man, a conversation—ordinary in its beginning, simple in its unfolding and unceremoniously organized at its conclusion. There was never an attempt to use architectural designs (like vaulted halls, half-dark spaces, and lofty gothic sweep), decorative effects (such as the stained glass through which light filters, losing its living brightness and mingling with a magical darkness), or tonal effects (from the hardly perceptible soft *pianissimo* to triumphant hymn singing), in order to suggest to the worshipper on the one hand the great mystery, and on the other hand the heavenly bliss, of the God-man encounter.

Judaism sees in all these esthetic motifs, which are designed to intimate the greatness and ineffability of God, merely extraneous means of creating a fugitive mood which will disappear with the departure of the worshipper from the cathedral into the fresh air and sunshine. Instead, Judaism concentrates on feelings which flow not from the outside, but from within the personality, on emotions which are exponents of much more deep-seated experiences, enhanced not by external stimuli but by the inner existence awareness.

When Judaism portrays pagan worship, it projects it against a specific landscape: high verdant hills, under the shade of green foliage, and blossoming gardens.

> You shall utterly destroy all the places in which the nations, whom you are to dispossess, served their gods, upon the high mountains, and upon the hills, and under every leafy tree (Deut. 12:2).

They who sanctify themselves, and purify themselves in the gardens. . . (Isa. 66:17).

. . . when upon every high hill and under every green tree you did sprawl, playing the harlot (Jer. 2:20).

This type of worship avails itself of the ecstatic moment in the aesthetic mood; beauty may produce a state of exaltation and an overflow of emotion. By encountering a fair landscape and lovely scenes, one feels attracted to the object of adoration—a deity. This technique has been rejected by Judaism. Either the religious experience flows from a heart filled to the brim with love of God, and from a soul stirred to its inmost roots, or it is nonexistent and artificially produced.

The way of every Jew to God must not differ from the trail along which Abraham moved toward his destiny, which had to be blazed through the wilderness of a brute and nonsensical existence. The experience is attained at the cost of doubts and a restless life, searching and examining, striving and pursuing—and not finding; of frustrating efforts and almost hopeless waiting; of grappling with oneself and with everybody else; of exploring a starlit and moonlit sky and watching the majesty of sunsets and sunrises, the beauty of birth and also the ugliness of death and destruction; of trying to penetrate behind the mechanical surface of the cosmic occurrence and failing to discover any intelligible order in this drama; of winning and losing and yet surging forward again; of conquering, giving up and reaching out again; of being able to put on a repeat performance of something which I had and lost; of asking questions and not finding answers; of ascending the high mount like Moses and falling back into the abyss, shattering everything one has received, and yet pulling oneself out of the depths of misery and trying to climb up the mountain again with two new stone tablets.

The Polarity of Existential Awareness

Moods, as detached emotions, are subject to the principle of contradiction—for instance, exultation is irreconcilable with a depressive mood, and fear with serenity. However, when properly chosen and freely accepted by the individual into his total life awareness, emotions may all merge into one experience, interpenetrating and crossing like the weaving of warp and woof in a piece of cloth. This experience is fraught with dichotomies. There is no dialectical mood; a mood is homogeneous and simple. However, there is a dialectical experience, which consists of heterogeneous and even contradictory elements. The joy of victory may somehow be combined with the melancholy of defeat, the pride and majesty of conquest with the humility of surrender.

For the sake of illustration, let me introduce two examples—one halakhic, one aggadic.

We know that the Halakhah requires that the worshipper bow at the beginning and conclusion of the thanksgiving benediction of the *Amidah*—"*Modim tehilah va-sof.*" (In the silent prayer, one must bow five times: twice at the first blessing, *Avot*, twice at the *Modim* benediction, and once when he concludes the *Shemoneh Esrei* and takes leave of his Maker.) We also recite a thanksgiving benediction whenever we say Grace After Meals. In the second benediction of Grace, we express gratitude to God for all the benevolence and mercy He has bestowed upon us. We say a similar passage in *Hallel*, which is centered around the keynote of praise and thanksgiving. Yet the Halakhah, which recommended the practice of genuflecting during the thanksgiving benediction within the silent prayer, has strictly forbidden the same performance during the recital of *Hallel* and Grace.

One *baraita* says that whoever genuflects at the saying of the thanksgiving benediction is to be commended. In another *baraita* we find that he should be reprimanded!

. . . [The answer is that] the *baraita* approving of genuflecting refers to the *Modim* in the silent prayer, while
the other *baraita* [containing a reproach for any kind of
bowing at the recital of praise and thanksgiving] speaks
of Grace and *Hallel* (*Berakhot* 34b).

This dictum reflects the halakhic philosophy of prayer and
its understanding of other forms of worship, such as Grace and
the *Hallel* hymnal service.

Prayer is inseparably bound with crisis. Prayer is supplication and begging; it means admitting complete failure, vain
hopes and dissipated aspirations. In it, the feeling of absolute
dependence (which Schleiermacher considered the fountain-
head of the religious experience) comes to full expression:

A song of ascents. To Thee, I lift up my eyes, Dweller of the
heavens. Behold, as the eyes of servants look to the hand
of their masters, and as the eyes of a maidservant to the
hand of her mistress, so our eyes wait upon the Lord our
God, until He shall be gracious unto us (Ps. 123:1-2) .

It also highlights the creature feeling (to use Rudolf Otto's
term), an awareness of destitution and impotence, a sense of
worthlessness and insufficiency. Abraham, who according to
Jewish tradition instituted prayer, said in the introduction to
his plea on behalf of Sodom: "Behold now, I have taken upon
myself to speak unto the Lord, though I am but dust and ashes"
(Gen. 18:27). Complete self-deprecation is the most important
moment in the prayer experience. Of course, this frame of mind
is symbolized by genuflection, which is, in an abbreviated form,
identical with prostration—an act demonstrating humility and
submission, full surrender and dependence:

And his brothers went and fell down before him; and
they said: Behold, we are your servants (Gen. 50:18).

> A prayer of the pauper, when he faints, and pours out his complaint before the Lord (Ps. 102:1).

However, the emotional backdrop of Grace After Meals and *Hallel* is completely different. Grace is recited on the occasion of full satiety and satisfaction, and *Hallel* on the occasion of a great event which has saved the people from disaster. Instead of feeling that existence is desolate, one is aware of a full and blessed life. The dominant motif is one of abundance. The creature consciousness, "I am but dust and ashes," is superseded by a sense of importance, since God has brought about the great redemption. Apparently, the community is under special Divine care and guidance. Worthlessness turns into a feeling of centrality, self-esteem and self-respect.

The terms in which the Torah describes the idea of Grace are characteristic of a happy emotional climate; they refer to a sovereign people leading a life of security and abundance on the rich soil of a land flowing with milk and honey.

> For the Lord your God brings you into a good land, a land of water courses, of fountains and depths that spring out of valleys and hills; a land of wheat and barley and vines and figs and pomegranates; a land of olive oil and date honey; a land in which you shall eat bread without scarceness, you shall not lack anything in it; a land the stones of which are iron, and out of whose hills you can mine copper. When you have eaten and are replete, then you shall bless the Lord your God for the good land which He has given you (Deut. 8:7-10).

The benediction of *Nodeh lekha* in the Grace After Meals reflects courage and joy, hope and contentment. Man knows that God is with him; he is confident as to his destiny and his future, and is aware of the significance the Creator attributes to him. He is not a pauper any more, but rather a king and a magnificent being who is indebted to the King of Kings, his Creator. According to the Halakhah, therefore, genuflection—representing utter humbleness, self-negation, the feeling of a shattered and bankrupt life—is out of place. In the Grace, man in his full majesty appears before his Creator, while in prayer the supplicant beggar, abject and lost, cast down in spirit and hope, rejected by everybody and exiled from everywhere, comes crawling before God.

Experiential polarity is thus a principle which expresses itself in halakhic externals. In conjunction with the dialectical quality of our self-awareness, I would like to introduce a passage from the *Midrash Tehillim* (102:1) which raises the problem of the paradoxical antithetical experience in a very picturesque manner.

> Rabbi Reuben stated: I cannot grasp the personality of David. Sometimes he calls himself a king—"Lord, the king rejoices in Thy strength" (Ps. 21:2)—and sometimes he calls himself a pauper—"A prayer of the pauper, when he faints" (Ps. 102:1). [The explanation of this is that] when David peered and foresaw with Divine inspiration righteous men coming forth from him, such as Hezekiah and Josiah, he called himself a king, and when he saw evil people coming forth from him, such as Absalom and Manasseh, he called himself a pauper.

The midrashic scholar Rabbi Reuben said that he could not comprehend David: he exhibited contrasting moods, opposite aspects of self-appraisal. At times, he spoke of hope and joy, of himself being a king, successful and triumphant; yet frequently, he looked upon himself as a pauper, destitute and totally wanting. The answer Rabbi Reuben gave does not solve the problem of polarity in the existential experience. Rabbi Reuben only pointed out that David's self-appraisal changed from time to time because his historical experience and the emergent destiny were not monolithic or unalterable. He experienced both triumph and defeat, victory and downfall, Divine grace and wrath; he indeed was both a ruler who commands and a beggar who entreats others for support. The experience of life is ambivalent because existence itself abounds in dichotomies and contradictions. No one can change the dialectical fate and destiny of man. The existential awareness must not mirror ideal conditions, but everyday realities. Therefore, it should not reflect only one or two of the multiple aspects, but the total adventure of man, which contains both affirmation and negation, triumph and loss.

Job lacked the dialectical experience. He did not understand the possibility of emotional polarity, when contrasting states of mind, contradictory value judgments, incongruous awarenesses of the innermost I, are interwoven into one fabric, against which one sees in his own reflection the conflict between the king and the pauper. The absence of the dialectical moment in his existence brought disaster on Job's household.

Job was contented with himself. He thought that his ritualistic performances would somehow protect him against external disaster and appease a wrathful adversary who menaces his well-being. The philistine in him sought security, safety, external peace. He never attained them. In his aloofness and isolation, he always was haunted by the foreboding of doom, by the prescience of something dreadful threatening him from the outside. He was always conscious of Satan lurking behind every bush. He never found happiness and peace. This is the price that the philistine pays for not understanding himself, for covering up his inner crisis, for not experiencing the dialectical tension of affirmation versus negation, for centering his personality around the external event and not the inward experience.

Finally, Job's outside world collapsed. However, if a person recenters his personality about a new experience, namely, that of self-related, inward, dialectical existence, when the I becomes aware of the intrinsic negation that is involved in reality and renders all our acts incomplete, all our wishes unfulfilled and all strivings, however noble, unconsummated, when he discovers the richness of the antithetic and antinomic, the creativity fostered by conflict—then a new wisdom wrought in the deep recesses of his personality may come to the surface: the wisdom of losing everything I attained by the sweat of my brow in order to gain everything, of accepting defeat voluntarily for the sake of triumphing over failure, of inviting distress in order to eliminate disaster, the mystery of living in continuous tension, in perennial crisis, in the *ma'amakim*, the depths of inner contradiction and negation, and, by so doing, finding oneself buttressed and strengthened by the contradiction itself. In your self-denial, you find life:

> And when I passed by you, and saw you weltering in your blood, I said to you: "In your blood live!" Yea, I said to you: "In your blood live!" (Ez. 16:6).

Let me add an observation regarding the anxiety so characteristic of modern man. If, in treating neurotic anxiety, modern psychiatry holds the view that what makes us fearful is not a particular threat to one's physical existence but rather a threat to a certain value with which one identifies himself and to which one is unconditionally committed, it has hit upon a central truth. Modern man is axiologically minded. He can live as long as he thinks that he is in the service of a value or system of values, that he makes a substantial contribution toward the realization of some axiological order. The objective worth of this axiological order is irrelevant, since it represents to him the finest in life. Whether he is dedicated to the political, social, intellectual or even the materialistic-hedonic order is not essential. It is important only that he bases his life upon some set of values, and when he feels that the latter is about to collapse, he becomes anxious and frightened.

If you ask me what is the educational preventative of such a form of anxiety, I will tell you: the dialectical experience of the reality of finitude. The value, however deeply rooted in one's mentality, must not exhaust the very content of one's life. One should know that, regardless of the courage and strength he may draw from a particular value, his existence may and can go on after this good has been lost, as long as the God-man fellowship is maintained. The soul has befriended some value, yet the bond must always be considered dissoluble. There is only one in whom man finds his salvation—God. "When my father and my mother forsake me, the Lord will take me up" (Ps. 27:10).

❧ A Theory
of Emotions

Criteria for Judging Emotions

The Halakhah has used this theory of the polarity of existential awareness [discussed in the previous chapter] for practical purposes. According to this theory, each of us, like King David of old, must be able to see in his own reflection the conflict between the king and the pauper (II Samuel 12). According to the Halakhah, two major advantages accrue from the dialectical nature of our experience of living.

In the first place, the dialectical character of our existence and our total experience manifests itself in the halakhic principle of the *totality of our emotional life*. Judaism has insisted upon the integrity and wholeness of the table of emotions, leading like a spectrum from joy, sympathy and humility (the conjunctive feelings) to anger, sadness and anguish (the disjunctive emotions). Absolutization of one feeling at the expense of others, or the granting of unconditioned centrality to certain emotions while demoting others to a peripheral status, may have damaging complications for the religious development of the personality.

The second principle derived from the dialectical nature of our awareness is that of the *continuity of our emotional experience*. No emotional experience may emerge *ex nihilo*, nor can it cease to exist and disappear into nihility. Moreover, each emotional experience is bounded in by its own negation. In order to comprehend these two principles, i.e., the totality and continuity of emotions, we must first explicate the nature and significance of the cognitive element contained in our emotional gesture.

The affective act [i.e., feeling an emotion] is an intentional experience, having reference to an object; in other words, it is correlated with something. Not only is the logical proposition object-centered—it is directed upon something of which it predicates some quality, property relation or existence in general—but so too is the emotional gesture. The affective attitude is taken *toward* something and it implies an awareness of this something which we posit as an objective that commands our emotional attention and commitment. The same challenge to which the intellect responds with a noetic performance, is also encountered by the feeling-consciousness. The latter, in meeting this challenge, naturally employs intentional acts of feeling that are directed upon the challenging realia.

The relationship between the feeling subject and the felt object is similar to that prevailing in the logical sphere between the knowing subject and the known object. The objective order finds its echo in the subjective order, both at the noetic level, in the form of knowledge, and at the affective level, in the form of feeling-attitudes, pleasure and pain. However, all inward activity has object-relevance and object-attachment. One fears *something*, irrespective of the fact that this objective reference might be imaginary, as in many cases of neurotic anxiety. Even the intellect is frequently preoccupied with non-existent objects. How many books were written about the devil and all kinds of fantastic beings? The logic of a predication is independent of the problem of its correspondence to reality. The former is determined solely by formal-structural criteria, while the truth or untruth of a statement is dependent on external material conditions. The same holds true of the affective experience. Formally, it must always be related to something. Whether this something is real or not depends upon the sanity of the person. The moment of intentionality [or object-directedness] may be discovered in every emotion, such as love, hatred, anger, sadness, joy, etc. Otherwise, one would lose his place within the order of things, since his affective life would neither respond nor attach itself to the concrete existential arrangement.

The objective reference inherent in the affective experience is of a twofold nature: theoretical cognitive predication and axiological assessment. When I say, for instance, "I love my neighbor," there is a double objective stratum to be isolated: there is someone whom I call "neighbor," and this person is worthy of my love. In other words, I have appraised the character, nature and life of my fellow, and have found him deserving and worthy of my friendship and love. Only then may we assert that such a relationship prevails. Most frequently, the upper affective stratum completely covers the two basic layers, the cognitive and axiological [i.e., that of knowing and that of evaluating], and this leads to misinterpretation of the emotional activity. In every emotional act, one intuits something as real and as valuable. Emotions are the media through which the value-universe opens up to us.

In view of the underlying noesis [intellectual apprehension] and valuation of our affective life, feelings may be classified as meaningful or degrading, depending upon the correctness and truthfulness of the noetico-axiological judgments which form the base of these attitudes. A dignified, elevating sentiment expresses a genuine intellectual insight and true value-apprehension, while a detached and unworthy emotion would be the consequence of fallacious cognition or value judgment. An axiological error which results in unwarranted emotional activity, in an outflow of sentiments directed upon an objective or a person whose worth does not justify this particular behavior, is often very harmful to the dignity of the person caught in such a dilemma.

From the premise regarding the objective reference of our emotional life, we can infer a new principle, namely, that the axiology of our emotional experience is heteronomous. It is subject to universal valuation within the objective realm. The worth of a particular emotion must not be measured by some intrinsic quality it possesses, but rather by the relevance and significance of its correlate object. There are neither bad nor good emotions; instead, there are bad or good emotional objective references. The relational aspect can be assessed in accents of moral valuation. However, the emotions themselves remain outside of axiological purview.

The appraisal of the worth of an emotion must not be a performance detached from the external experience to which a person reacts emotionally. Each feeling must be seen as a response to a message received from an external reality, which, battering upon the self continuously, keeps on stimulating and tantalizing him. The value judgment about the worth of a particular affect depends not upon an isolated emotional attitude, or a "feeling-in-itself" (to play on Kantian terminology), but rather on the feeling-event relatedness, on the commensurability or incommensurability of the objective content of the message and its inward decoding, on the correspondence between impressions pouring in from the outside and the interpretations the person gives to these impressions. If this balance is lacking, then the emotion is unworthy. If Judaism has construed ethical norms with regard to the emotional life, the basic moral criterion by which Judaism has been guided in the formulation of a normative system consists in the need for a relationship of congruity between reality and emotional attitudes.

Totality of Emotional Life:
The Rejection of Emotional Exclusivity

This is the reason for our acceptance of the total emotional experience, our rejection of the split table of emotions, of the hypostatization or absolutization of select emotions and the exclusion of others. Christianity, for instance, has absolutized the emotion of love and elevated it to an almost mythical level. It does not realize that a one-sided reduction of the emotional activity of man contributes both toward the impoverishment of human creative abilities and aptitudes, and also toward a distortion of our existential awareness and world-picture—which has, in turn, led to false conclusions and hypocritical practices. Human existence extends over a vast area; it is not a monotonous but a variegated affair. The events with which man must reckon are many, and they require diverse action, flexibility of attitude and mutability of emotional reaction. If life could be reduced to just the uniform occurrence, then a sameness of response would suffice. However, we deal with a multitude of occurrences, whose meanings and impact upon us are incompatible and whose appearances and structural designs are diverse. Our responses must be as multifarious as the happenings themselves.

How can we speak of a variety of responses if the richness of emotional life is dispensed with for the sake of the deity of love? Of course, love is a great and noble emotion, fostering the social spirit and elevating man, but not always is the loving person capable of meeting the challenge of harsh realities. In certain situations, a disjunctive emotion, such as anger or indignation, may become the motivating force for noble and valuable action. George Sand said that the indignation over evil and injustice is the mightiest expression of love. Nietzsche proclaimed: He who cannot hate, also cannot love. It is not always possible to fight entrenched wrong, corruption and abuse if only love and all the attendant emotions, such as humility, meekness and tolerance, are in control of human action. To pray for the sinner is a very fine gesture, but prayer alone would not eradicate crime and depravity. There is need for active opposition, which can be initiated only through righteous anger, hate and detestation of everything that is base and ugly.

While the New Testament has completely forsaken the richness and multiplicity of emotional life and has universalized love as the only worthwhile engagement on the part of man, the Bible abounds in a rich variety of human affective responses and sees emotional life in its fullness. It does not reject any human feelings as unworthy and destructive. Each emotion is the Kingdom of God, which is both "near and far" (Meister Eckhardt). The Torah wants us to run the gamut of emotional expression, from love, humility and meekness to justified pride, desire, contentment and joy. We sometimes wonder at the ease with which the Bible changes its emotional-moral perspective. The transition from norms based on sympathy and love to laws calling for stern, sometimes ruthless, action, is almost imperceptible. One must know how to love, but also must understand the art of hating, resisting and opposing. We must not condone patently flagrant behavior or excuse rampant injustices.

As a result of the exclusivity ascribed by Christianity to love, a schism developed between practice and theory. Christian society has divorced itself completely from the ideal of meekness and non-resistance to evil, and has organized a penal code which, in many cases, has displayed inhuman cruelty. Love, as a dominant attitude in their program of activities, could not cope with reality, and the other extreme was adopted in the arrangement of state and society. On the other hand, certain practices which were associated in the minds of the people with love clearly indicate a paranoid tendency in Christian morality. Institutions such as the Inquisition, Crusades, etc., which utilized the norm of love in order to justify the burning and slaughtering of humans because they refused to conform to Christian orthodoxy, is very characteristic of a sick soul and mental perversion. *Agape* is a very sublime emotion. However, one-sidedness within the emotional realm is destructive.

As a rule, Judaism has always tried to maintain a balance between conflicting emotions and to accept the totality of the human emotional experience. We must not say that love is an absolutely noble feeling, while anger is always a base emotion. Their worth and ethical connotation depend upon the object at which these intentional acts aim and upon historic circumstances. Sometimes a profound hatred is as noble an experience as a great love. With regard to a movement such as Nazism or certain aspects of Communism, the absence of a hatred that dictates action is just as mean and despicable as an unwarranted hatred. The fight against evil must be suffused with disjunctive emotions.

Since selectivity within the emotional realm depends upon the objective reference, upon the occasion or event with which one's emotional attitude is connected, the Halakhah speaks normatively of mourning and joy—feelings of guilt and despair, on the one hand, and unlimited confidence and faith in oneself, on the other. That is also why even the feeling of pride has not been fully condemned as a base and depraved attitude and as the source of all evil. The awareness of the human charisma, revealing itself through the colorful spectrum of our total emotional gesture, must never be suspended.

In his famous third chapter, Kohelet (3:2-8) gave expression to the steady transition of our emotional attitudes, reflecting the kaleidoscopic change of events:

> To everything there is a season, and a time to every purpose under the heaven: a time to be born, and a time to die; a time to plant, and a time to uproot; . . . a time to weep, and a time to laugh; a time to mourn, and a time to dance; . . . a time to seek, and a time to lose; . . . a time to love, and a time to hate; a time of war, and a time of peace.

A changing destiny cannot be appreciated by an unalterable emotional activity.

Continuity of Emotional Life: The Antithetic Experience

Besides the principle of the integrity of the table of emotions, which forbids us from absolutizing certain emotions and excluding others, Judaism has also insisted upon the continuity of the iridescent emotional life. Emotions must not be seen as discrete and isolated phenomena, separated from each other by gaps or affective voids, but rather as a continuum within which each emotion passes into its opposite, covering the full range of intermediate variations. An emotion neither begins *ex nihilo* nor disappears into nihility. Rather, an emotion undergoes uninterrupted change and slowly turns into another, or quite often into a rival emotion. The continuous spectrum in physics illustrates our viewpoint quite clearly. The arrangement of the colors or the wavelengths of some radiant energy is a continuous one. There are no distinct and isolated groups; all wavelengths in the intervals are represented. The gradual change within this range of colors covers an infinite number of gradations, and only by employing the differential calculus may one determine the rate of transition.

However, when we state that emotions form a continuum, we understand this in a twofold manner, as temporal succession and an antithetic experience awareness.

Temporal succession: Under the aspect of the stream of the feeling consciousness (since emotions are a part of the total existential awareness), we shall state that every emotion prevailing at the present moment, even if it be an instantaneous response to an unexpected event, is born out of a previous emotional experience and points toward a new experience into which it will gradually pass. In other words, there is a law of conservation of emotional energy. The manifold of transformations of that hyletic energy (i.e., the immediate, direct, not-yet-analyzed experience of emotions) is an uninterrupted process of self-expression of the personality.

An antithetic experience awareness: Each emotional experience is provided with an implicit reference to its opposite, in either a past or a future experience. The streams of emotional awareness flowing through a succession of time units or a continuum of durations, through emotional contrasts and conflicting meanings, converge into every emotional experience at the present moment.

The integrity and unity of the spectrum of emotions manifest themselves not only in a succession of various emotions which supersede each other in response to the various events which one encounters, but in a single all-embracing experience. The whole range of the emotional table is present in each emotional experience, not only as something unintentionally apprehended as a fringe experience, vague and undefined, but as a deliberately chosen, clear and unequivocally circumscribed experience. Of course, in each emotional experience there is the center-directed glance and the peripheral look. These two forms of attention differ not in clarity or distinctness, but in emphasis. In each emotional response, there is the focus and also the surrounding field of mental reaction; and while emphasis is placed upon the central theme of one's experience, the attendant peripheral motifs are nevertheless relevant and meaningful.

Thus, we may state that each emotional experience is a multifarious affair extending to the antithetic state of mind. Each feeling-awareness embraces both the central emotion and its gradual passing off into the opposite by which it is bounded in. The "pauper" and "king" frames of mind are not just two alternating emotional states, but an all-inclusive experience stretching from feeling the utter wretchedness and helplessness of a beggar to the self-assurance and confidence of a king.

Let me state here in no uncertain terms that the dialectical emotional experience has nothing in common with the Freudian concept of ambivalence, the interpenetration of love and hate. When Freud speaks of ambivalence, he has in mind the immediate, primordial, direct, unanalyzed emotional response to some event, before the person has had a chance to cast a reflective glance upon it. In the very essence of the feeling of love, there is hidden resentment and hate, and in his tempestuous emotional outbursts, one loves and hates at the same time. This running to two opposite poles of feeling is unknown to Judaism. The primeval emotion, which comes uninvited and strikes us with its full elemental power, is not antithetic or dialectical. When one is aflame with love, there is no swinging toward hate; neither must joy be marred by its rival feelings, such as grief. Sincerity and honesty in emotional life is a basic principle of the Judaic ethic. Oscillation between two contrasting feelings demonstrates a shallow personality and a lack of truthfulness.

When we speak of a dialectical emotional experience, we are referring to the *feeling awareness*. When a person becomes aware of his condition, when he listens to the stirrings within his soul and begins to reflect upon them, when emotions are accepted or rejected, moral values intuited and intelligible patterns fitting the personality established—only then does the antithetic experience assert itself. It comes to the fore not in the emotion itself, but in the awareness of it, through which one interprets, assimilates or disowns the emotion, and through which one discovers the freedom of self-formation and self-actualization. Only the awareness, in its interpretive performance, runs through the whole gamut of our emotional responses. The pure, primitive, unintelligible emotion is wholesome and solid without being subjected to the dialectical analysis.

Even in the intellectual sphere, Aristotle distinguished between intuitive and discursive thinking. While the first form of cognition expresses itself through an immediate, almost compulsive responding to a challenge from the outside, the second represents thought formulated in logical judgments. When one enters an illuminated room and exclaims, "Light," he actually means to say there is light in this room. However, the logical gesture was unintended; it came almost as an intuitive reaction to an external stimulus. It is not yet knowledge. It is, as Edmund Husserl says, "a source of authority for knowledge, that whatever presents itself in intuition in primordial form is simply to be accepted as it gives itself out to be . . . " (*Ideas: General Introduction to Pure Phenomenology* I, section 24). Only when the logos awareness directs its attention upon this hyletic datum is knowledge born. The direct approach presents us with primordial data; the reflective awareness engenders knowledge.

The same is true of our emotional life. There is the primordial emotional datum, and there is the interpretive awareness which impresses form upon and molds this *hyle*. The dialectics of the emotional experience belong to the interpretive, not the primordial intuitive sphere. That is why we must not speak of ambivalence in a Freudian manner—since the emotions themselves do not interpenetrate. Only the emotional awareness turns its attention to the opposites. The awareness follows an old logical-mathematical rule that the apprehension of a continuous series cannot be a part-performance. Either one gives his attention to the whole as such, or he gives up his attempt of interpreting. This is particularly true with respect to the unitary time consciousness. One cannot experience the present moment alone, since time is a three-dimensional continuum. The "now" is only one aspect of the time awareness; it is always bounded in by "before" and "after," and one who tries to survey the area of the now must *ipso facto* direct his attention to the boundary line, in both retrospect and prospect. On the other hand, if one engages in recollecting, he cannot limit himself to the past; in the reliving of the bygone is implied the experience of the "now" and the "not yet existing." The same is true of the visionary fixing his glance on the distant future—he cannot divorce his attention from the present and the past. If you enter the realm of time, you must behold this continuum in its glorious wholeness. Partial vision or apprehension is an absurdity.

In light of the above, we may understand the distinction between the *pure emotion* and the *emotional awareness* with regard to the dialectical character of our existential experience. The pure emotion may confine itself to the present instant, without relating itself to the other two dimensions. The immediate emotion has not yet been placed within the time scheme or directed at basic experiences. Therefore, the total involvement in the continuum is lacking. When the emotions are arranged within the personal time perspective into the meaningful whole of our existential experience, then the detached, isolated emotion is suffused with moral significance, expressing the whole cycle of affective life.

Continuity of Religious Emotion: The Examples of Joy, Remorse and Grief

Since the religious experience is not limited to one sector of existence, but rather is an all-inclusive affair (its objective reference extends to the totality of being, to finitude as such in its relationship to the Infinite), it must respond not only to one event, but to an unlimited multiplicity of occurrences. It must encounter a multifaceted reality which can be interpreted only by a strange diverse experience, in defiance of the law of consistency and self-identity. When the *homo religiosus* sees the beautiful, he enjoys it fully. This unlimited pleasure is experienced only at the level of the non-rational primordial emotion. However, at the plane of the cognitive emotion, the ugly looms on the horizon, bounding in the feeling of the beautiful, and the paradoxical looms as the periphery of the knowable, revealing and veiling reality. The emotional awareness directs its glance upon the whole of life, human destiny fraught with the tragic and the comical, the great and the small. Thus, when the *homo*

religiosus views life through the prism of the emotional awareness, his response is complex and full of antithetic motifs.

Judaism holds the view that the isolated emotion within the
affective awareness, completely detached from the emotional
continuum, is a low mood, unworthy of the dignified person.
Only in the paradoxical unity of contrasts is an emotion
redeemed from its primeval qualities. Joy, for instance, is a
great feeling if it is separated from its antithetic emotion, sadness, not by a sharp line but rather by an infinite series of gradations, like the transitions in the rainbow—thus not breaking
up the continuity of communication between both ends of the
table of emotions. When completely bounded in and isolated
from the adjacent areas of emotional activity and related to only
a single existential aspect, joy forfeits its worth and significance. In such a case, it turns into hilarity, an emotion which
loses sight of central realities and helps man escape responsibilities. Judaism has discriminated between absurd gaiety and
meaningful joy, between *holelut* and *simhah*. "I said to the wanton men (*hollelim*), Do not be wanton (*taholu*)!" (Ps. 75:5). Very
illustrative of this view is a peculiar talmudic passage
(*Berakhot* 30b-31a):

> "Serve the Lord with fear and rejoice with trembling"
> (Ps. 2:11). What is meant by "rejoice with trembling?"
> Rabbi Ada the son of Matna said in the name of Rav: In
> the place where there is rejoicing, there should also be
> trembling . . .
> Mar the son of Ravina made a marriage feast for his son.
> He saw that the rabbis were growing very merry, so he
> brought a precious cup worth four hundred *zuz* and
> broke it before them, and they became serious. Rabbi
> Ashi made a marriage feast for his son. He saw that the
> rabbis were growing very merry, so he brought a cup of
> white crystal and broke it before them, and they became
> serious.

> The rabbis said to Rabbi Hamnuna Zuti at the wedding of Mar the son of Ravina: Please sing us something. He said to them: "Woe unto us, for we are to die; woe unto us, for we are to die. . . ."
>
> Rabbi Yohanan said in the name of Rabbi Shimon the son of Yohai: It is forbidden for a person to fill his mouth with laughter in this world, for it says, "Then will our mouth be filled with laughter and our tongue with singing" (Ps. 126:2). When will that be? At the time when, "They shall say among the nations: 'The Lord has done great things with these'" (ibid.).

The Talmud did not intend to recommend suppression of the sense of joy and to replace it with a feeling of gloom. Our sages did not even try to temper the exultation at a wedding party. We know how much the Halakhah appreciates the joyous excitement and cheerful disposition of wedding guests. Gladdening a bride and groom is an important norm in our code of sociability. Many laws have been constructed whose prime purpose is the planned manifestation of our great joy and solemnity on such an occasion. The blessings recited at a wedding indicate the centrality and dominance of the feeling of cheer. There is no doubt that the Halakhah did not intend to check the spontaneous outbursts of gladness and delight, in their first naive and uncritical stage, of which these blessings speak in glowing accents:

> There will yet be heard in the cities of Judea and in the streets of Jerusalem the sound of joy and the sound of gladness, the voice of the groom and the voice of the bride, the sound of the grooms' jubilation from their wedding-canopies and of youths from their song-filled feasts.

However stately the joy should be at the level of the uncritical emotion, when it is raised to the critical plane (where the awareness commits it to an existential moral order within the personal time experience) the joy cannot endure in isolation from the total life-experience of the person about whom this particular emotion centers. The stream of events is reflected not in one state of mind but in the full spectrum of feelings, and the emotional awareness at a certain instant is a microcosm, mirroring not only the dominant emotional motif—such as joy in the case of a marriage celebration—but the whole range of the emotional cycle. First, the unchecked reverberating joy passes gradually into calm and quiet, touched with that solemn melancholy which befits one attending a great festival at which two destinies merge into one. Naively, the person surges forward, unharnessed and uncontrolled, but immediately the critical awareness intervenes and the withdrawal takes place. The central emotion is joined by its antithesis at the periphery.

With regard to the institution of marriage, Judaism was always aware of the paradox involved in this sacred union of two strangers. The drive for matrimonial companionship is, among many other factors, enhanced also by the human experience of our tragic destiny, which ends in death. There is no doubt that the drive for procreation is basically the desire for perpetuation of our own finite existence. The longing for a child is basically the outcry of a lonely soul groping in the dark for salvation and eternal life, and finding instead the wet and dreary fall to the grave. In the marriage event, the critical emotional awareness sees the tragedy of human destiny. It drives two strangers to unite in order to combat a dreaded fiend—death. In the midst of carefree and unrestrained merrymaking and jubilation, the vision of the loneliness of man is beheld. The antithesis of joy emerges from the peripheral distance. Thus Rabbi Hamnuna Zuti's words at the wedding celebration, "Woe unto us, for we are to die."

This paradoxical awareness is symbolized by the breaking of the glass under the canopy. Regarding the above-cited talmudic passage, Tosafot comment: "From here they were accustomed to shatter glass at weddings" (*Berakhot* 31a, s.v. *aytei*).

The same is true of the feelings of guilt and remorse. If completely removed from its total frame of reference, guilt expresses itself in a destructive and inhibiting state of mind. It results in agonizing impotence and exhaustion. Psychiatry is certainly right when it claims to find guilt at the root of many emotional disturbances. However, if guilt and other feelings of penitence are not torn like a single leaf out of the book of life, and channels of communication are kept open between them and their antithetic emotions (in this case, faith in one's recuperative power and the aptitude for reconstruction), then the same feelings of depression may bring about outbursts of creative energy. Guilt might be the gateway to a greater and richer life. The Halakhah has always emphasized that the feeling of remorse be accompanied by the optimistic faith in renewal and regeneration.

Similarly, the Halakhah distinguishes between *aninut* and *avelut*. *Aninut* signifies the immediate reaction to the death of a loved one, the unrestricted gloom and unsounded depths of excruciating grief which render the mourner speechless and confounded. The impact of the emotion is stupendous. Man becomes aware of the worthlessness and absurdity of life, and his distress knows no limits. The Halakhah does not attempt to check this feeling of bereavement—it lets man sink in the abyss of despair at the first encounter with death. It relieves him of all halakhic duties since, because of the painful experience, he is not free to act. *Avelut* denotes the critical stage of mourning, the grief awareness, and at this level, we will notice at once that *avelut* contains its own proper negation—solace and hope. *Avelut* in the Halakhah is interwoven with *nehamah*, consolation. They are inseparable. The latter is not a frame of mind which displaces grief; there is rather an interpenetration of grief and solace, of forlornness and hope, of mourning and faith. Immediately upon closing the grave, the line is formed and comfort is offered to the mourner. What is the *Kaddish* pronounced at the grave if not an ostentatious negation of despair?

Critical Interpretation vs. the Golden Mean

The dialectical emotional experience has little in common with the Aristotelian doctrine of the golden mean. The latter is based upon the peculiar Greek ideal of *metron*, measure, and their commitment to a bounded and fenced-in reality. Aristotle denied the existence of infinity at a mathematical level, trying instead to interpret the cosmic drama in terms of rounded finite magnitudes, possessing determinable contours and surveyable dimensions. He did not care to cast his glance at an immeasurable existence within which numberless systems of worlds stretch without limit before the mind. The gaze of Aristotle's *logos* [reason] at Being is a fixed and limited one. He disapproved of the unmanageable, indistinct and boundless. Aristotle's worldview was never too wide, since he was afraid that, because of the enormous width, it might forfeit its focus (see Oswald Spengler, *The Decline of the Occident*). This philosophy of the fixed gaze or supreme distinctness also influenced Aristotle's ethics and psychology. Overindulgence in or excessiveness of emotional experiences violates the principle of *metron*. Each emotion must be limited and closed up. Infatuation with the unmeasured emotional expanse is unworthy of the philosopher. Each experience must be narrowed down until it becomes controllable and measurable.

Such a theory, which is sound from a practical viewpoint insofar as it promotes sanity and equilibrium and protects the individual from fits and crises, tends nevertheless to dampen the emotional expressiveness of man and to dull the richness and iridescent beauty of our affective life. An emotion is beautiful and great when it is all-consuming and all-enveloping, when its depth is unfathomable and its sweep unpredictable. The creative emotion from which the religious or even the aesthetic experience flows must possess a boundless energy and dynamic qualities; it must be overpowering, shattering all artificial hedges and fences which convention erects around it, and must possess the impetus of the infinite and unmanageable. I doubt whether the passion of Amos and Isaiah for justice and fairness, or the commitment of Moses to his people and his love for them, conformed to the Aristotelian standards of the golden mean. If they had, human history would not have known these great and majestic figures, because people of limited emotional capacity cannot attain such superhuman greatness.

We have been commanded to love God "with *all* your heart, and with *all* your soul, and with *all* your might" (Deut. 6:5)—in an unrestrained manner, overwhelmingly and unreservedly. The medieval Jewish philosophers, such as Maimonides and Bahya, spoke of an enraptured, obsessed love (e.g. *Hilkhot Teshuvah* 10:3), and Kierkegaard later spoke of such a love as the Divine madness. The Aristotelian Nicomachean ethic rejected emotions of such an ecstatic nature. It felt that the ecstatic experience is to be shunned, whereas Judaism recommended an unrestrained love for God. Emotional depth is irreconcilable with the theory of the golden mean, and Judaism as a religion could not content itself with a shallow and restricted emotional experience. Infinity is a basic category of religious thinking, and our emotional response to events must not be limited and watered down.

What Judaism wants to attain with its principle of the dialectical emotion is not a restrained emotional experience, but a critical one. The depth of the emotion and the power of the experience have not been limited by Judaism. The primordial emotion is not purged or even restrained for the sake of remaining within the boundary of the tangible and practical. We allow our naive emotions to flow naturally, without trying to stem their onrush. Only after a while do we raise them to the plane of critical interpretation, at which they are interwoven into the fabric of our time-continuum. Thereby, they are connected with events in which we are not directly involved at present, and with experiences which warrant the release of a rival antithetic emotion. However, even at this level there is no golden mean, nor is there any attempt at moderation or restraint deriving from the notion that intoxication with a feeling is something unworthy of human dignity. The depth of the emotion is not diminished by our critical gazing, nor is its impact on us affected by its relatedness to the total existential experience. All we achieve is an integrated emotion, one which is not detached from the time continuum and moving in an illusory world of its own.

Imitatio Dei

However, the main reason for our dialectical approach to the affective sphere is an ethical one. Judaism believes that the emotional experience is suffused with ethico-moral meaning. Axiological structures and moral ideas are intuited through our emotional experiences. Contrary to the prevailing opinion (held by Kant and many of the medievals) that either the intellect or the will beholds the ethical universe, Judaism has maintained that the aboriginal discovery of the moral law and ideal was made by the "heart," by the feeling, not by the *logos* or the *voluntas*. The aboriginal moral challenge is encountered by the heart, notwithstanding the fact that the later decoding, interpreting and implementing of the message contained in the challenge are carried out by the intellect and will.

Let us not forget that the basic moral norm is contained in the idea of *imitatio Dei*, which we derive from the verse, "*Vehalakhta bi-derakhav,* You shall walk in His ways," (Deut. 28:9), or from the verse, "*Zeh E-li ve-anvehu,* This is my God and I shall exalt Him" (Ex. 15:2), reading *anvehu* as *ani ve-Hu,* I and He (see Rashi, *Shabbat* 133b). This desire to be like Him, to fashion our deeds after a Divine design, is understandable if seen against the background of a relationship based on passionate love. This emotion expresses itself in an overpowering longing for the complete identification of the lover with the beloved. The mystics, in their speaking of the "steep stairway of love" by which one ascends to union with God, have focused their attention upon the most central idea in the love experience, namely, the indomitable yearning or thirsting for merger with the beloved. The institution of marriage in erotic love, and the idea of spiritual commitment to and ecstatic union with the Absolute in the religious mystical universe, demonstrate a common motif of the emotion of love: the inner striving for identity and unity, when the lover passes utterly into the beloved and sinks his own will, thought and feeling into the depths of an existence not belonging to him. Self-adaptation to and assimilation of the way of life of the beloved on the part of the lover stems from the powerful urge for identification. Since the lover wants to unite himself with the beloved, to be him or her, to lose himself in another existence (something which can never be attained), he tries, while engaged in the venture of an endless ascent to complete union, to remake himself in the image of the person he loves passionately by assuming the modes of behavior observed in the beloved.

The categorical absolute in Judaism is anchored in the love of God. Since this fundamental law is revealed to the heart and not to the mind, the entire moral universe reveals itself to the inner eye of a person with a warm heart, and is experienced emotionally as fascinating and redeeming.

Egocentric Emotion

However, on the other hand, we must take into consideration another aspect of the emotional life. We said above that the emotional experience, like the intellectual gesture, must be considered a response to a challenge mostly originating in the outside world. This is true. Yet there is a basic discrepancy between the intellectual or cognitive gesture and the emotional experience. The former is not only object-directed but is also a completely selfless performance. The attention is focused on the object; my gaze is fixed on something which lies beyond the bounds of my sphere of existence. The cognitive response is thus object-centered. Its validity or cogency is entirely independent of the responding person's affective relationship to it—whether or not the image of the object to which the intellectual act is related is pleasing or irritating to him. The impression the cognitive deed leaves upon the soul of the knower is irrelevant; only the objective content of the response is of importance. In the scientific and philosophical vernacular, this is what we call objectivity.

In the emotional sphere, however, the arrangement undergoes a basic change. There is a response infused with some logical content; there is also an attempt at evaluation of the event or object which the person encountered. But all these acts, although object-related, are not object-centered but self-centered. The question which the "heart" tries to answer is not, "What is this object as an entity in itself?" in a manner reminiscent of the intellect, but rather, "What does it mean to me?" The basic inquiry aims at finding out whether or not this particular event or object will promote or block my most vital interests. Let us remember that emotions, even at their highest level, are nothing but reclaimed and refined instinctive drives, converted crude and primitive physiological impulses and energies. As such, they all can be traced back to the parent instinct in the biological world, namely, self-preservation. There is no doubt that this most potent impulse finds its expression in our emotional responses, even when their sublimation process reaches an advanced stage. Self-anxiety and self-caretaking are guiding criteria in our emotional life.

This is certainly true of the intransitive emotions, which are limited to the "agent" who feels them and are not directed upon someone or something outside of him (notwithstanding the fact that these emotions have objective reference, or correlation with some event that impinged upon the "heart" and attracted its attention). Joy, for instance, is an intransitive emotion. I may find delight in or be overjoyed over something, but the experience of joy does not involve me in any external relationship with others; it certainly does not spell out any moral obligations, nor does it compel any action with regard to someone else. The experience is self-contained and does not alter my attitude or action toward the thou. The same is true of grief, remorse, pride, humility, etc.

However, the egotistic theme is extant also in the transitive emotions, whose objective reference is to be understood not only in causative terms, but also in those of outwardly directed relatedness, such as love, admiration and sympathy. The person whom I love is both the motivating factor of my love feeling—meeting him stirred my soul—and also the object of my emotional acting, which expresses itself in unique patterns of feeling or behavior concerning him. The emotion usually manifests itself in action affecting the person one loves. In other words, the experience steps out of the unique private world of the lover and moves on toward the outside. But these transitive feelings, despite their inner urge for merger and passing off into the other person, are self-centered. What one is longing for is his own self-fulfillment, which he believes he will find in his union with the other person. The emotion leaves its inner abode in order to find not the "you" but the "I." (Adler's term "conjunctive emotion" does not connote selfless emotion. It only indicates that, because of self-interest, the person is committed to a state of mind which, regardless of one's self-centeredness, promotes goodwill and unites people.)

In *Repetition*, Kierkegaard describes the love of a young man, in whom a young woman aroused a creative talent, in terms which are indicative of the self-centeredness of the love experience. (Otherwise, the whole problem Kierkegaard depicts would not have developed, and the young man would have been able to attain both his poetic aptitude and the consummation of his love.)

> So again the girl is not a reality but a reflection of the movements within him and their exciting cause. The girl has a prodigious importance, he actually will never be able to forget her, but what gives her importance is not herself but her relation to him. She is, as it were, the boundary of his being . . . What concerns him is attained the very instant it proves possible to redeem his honor and regain his pride.

The same is true of an erotic relationship between two lovers. The ego never recedes into the far distance of communal existence.

Judaism, contrary to Adler's opinion, believes that if emotions are left as detached, closed-up experiences, they can never become conjunctive, since the person refuses to emerge from his egotistic shell and is not ready to give up his self-centrality. He judges the world only as it is reflected upon his own life-screen, as something which can be apprehended only in relation to the self. A boy and girl are in love; they are engrossed in themselves, paradoxically shut up within themselves. Both are self-minded and ego-centered; they desire only to find themselves in each other's company. With regard to the whole world, they display emotional indifference. They cut themselves loose from contact with others. Parents, friends, relatives—associations they cherished for so long—are meaningless to them while they are engaged in their love affair. The sight of an unfortunate woman who lost her husband, a young mother mourning for a child, a daughter for her parent—the sight of misery and agony engages their attention for just a fugitive moment and then, with a cruel motion of their hand, they dismiss the stir in their soul which one of these scenes has caused, as if it had no right to interfere with their happiness and bliss. Love, many a time, cancels warm feelings of sympathy.

On the other hand, despair and grief may desensitize a person completely to the suffering of others and instill in him cruel indifference. I still remember vividly the remark made to me by a young widow who could not forget her deceased husband, at the funeral of her best friend's husband, who was killed in a machine accident. "Rabbi, I wish I could feel sorry for her. I know she loved her husband dearly. But I cannot. She is not better than I am. I sustained this dreadful loss and survived. Why can't she?"

Ethicizing Emotion

Only when the critical awareness shifts the emotion into the total life experience and directs the glance of the person toward the outside, do the emotions become ethicized, endowed with meaningfulness, not confined to oneself. The other, the thou, is drawn into our inner emotional world and we permit him to share our attention. There, something wonderful happens: the wall separating individuals is torn down and free communication of feeling is made possible. If a boy has fallen in love with the girl he chose and he feels how overpowering his love is for this person, he should at the same time realize what he means to his parents, how unselfishly they love him, how important his reciprocation is to them and what an agony they live through when his response to their devotion is one of indifference and misunderstanding. One should interpret his own feelings and place them within the all-embracing life experience. Then the barriers which he erected around his emotional self are done away with, and the other is invited to join him in his moment of bliss.

The same is true of the feeling of despair. It should open up the closed-in individual existence and make it accessible to others. Grief must not enhance one's self-regard and self-care and render him completely oblivious to the suffering of others. The grieving person must also be disturbed by the pain sustained by his fellow man. He should share the other's burden, even though he seems completely preoccupied with his agonizing private burden. What Judaism requires is the communization of the individual existence. This is achieved by directing the self-centered emotional life toward the outside, or, if we wish to state it differently, by letting others from the outside enter our inner life. Judaism has assigned an educational task to the critical feeling awareness. It must enlighten the human personality living in retreat—introverted and insanely self-centered, out of contact with the outside, with the thou—that there are other existences, microcosms, that are as important and meaningful as he is, and whose experiences are similar to his. Whatever is the epistemological explanation for cognition of the thou—whether it is achieved through analogy, or through immediate insight and intuition, or through an empathetic gesture—the feat must be credited to the feeling awareness. This discovery of the thou takes place in the emotional world. This is possible only if emotions are placed within the unitary time-continuum and redirected toward their antithesis.

As a halakhic illustration, let us take the precept of *simhat ha-regel*, rejoicing on a festival, which the Halakhah has associated with the feeling of sympathy with the unfortunate and destitute. Wherever the Torah tells us to rejoice, it couples this with a commandment of charity.

> And you shall rejoice before the Lord your God, you and your sons and your daughters and your menservants and your maidservants and the Levite who is within your gates; for he has no portion or inheritance with you (Deut. 12:12).
>
> . . . And you shall rejoice before the Lord your God in all that to which you put your hand. Take heed to yourself that you forsake not the Levite as long as you live upon the earth (Deut. 12:18-19).

. . . And you shall rejoice, you and your household. And the Levite who is within your gates, you shall not forsake him, for he has no portion or inheritance with you (Deut. 14:26-27).

And you shall rejoice in your festival, you and your son and your daughter and your manservant and your maidservant and the Levite and the stranger and the orphan and the widow who are within your gates (Deut. 16:14).

Remember that you were a servant in the land of Egypt (Deut. 5:15).

Maimonides codifies the law thus:

. . . [W]hile one eats and drinks [in celebration of a festival], it is his duty to feed the stranger, the orphan, the widow, and other poor and unfortunate people. For he who locks the gates of his courtyard and eats and drinks with his wife and children, without giving anything to eat and drink to the poor and the bitter in spirit—his meal is not a rejoicing in a Divine commandment but a rejoicing in his stomach. It is of such persons that Scripture says (Hos. 9:4): "Their sacrifices shall be to them as the bread of grief, all that eat thereof shall be polluted; for their bread is for their own appetite." Rejoicing of this kind is an abomination for those who indulge in it, as Scripture says (Mal'akhi 2:3): "I will spread dung upon your faces, even the dung of your festival sacrifices" (*Hilkhot Yom Tov* 6:18).

Maimonides here introduces the term *simhat mitzvah*, rejoicing in a Divine commandment, and contrasts it with *simhat kereso*, selfish joy, which he identifies with *lehem onim*, the bread of grief, and *kalon*, abomination. The dialectical motif manifests itself here. Of course, the emotion of joy may be aroused by various experiences. However, it goes without saying that the emotion with which the Pentateuch deals is engendered by self-assertion and self-contentment. It is the result of the natural feeling of satisfaction which one derives from a job well done, from the successful completion of a task, from attainment, from the awareness of not having labored in vain. The festivals are periods of joy mingled with thankfulness for the Divine blessings bestowed upon the people, for abundance and plenitude. The farmer and the shepherd celebrate the holiday and rejoice in their achievements.

> . . . And you shall rejoice before the Lord your God in all that to which you put your hand (Deut. 12:18).
> You shall surely tithe all the increase of your seed that the field brings forth year by year . . . And you shall bestow that money on all that your heart desires, on oxen or sheep or wine or strong drink, or whatever your soul requires (Deut. 14:22, 26).
> And you shall keep the Feast of Weeks to the Lord your God with a tribute of a freewill offering of your hand, which you shall give, according as the Lord your God has blessed you (Deut. 16:10).
> You shall observe the Feast of Tabernacles seven days, after you have gathered in your corn and your wine (Deut. 16:13).

The Torah stresses that on occasions such as festivals of ingathering or harvesting, or when one brings his *ma'aser sheni* (second tithe) to Jerusalem, the fundamental note is one of joy aroused in man by the feeling of security. It is the delight of a serene mind at peace with itself and with nature. However, Judaism saw to it that this festival gladness and enthusiasm would not fortify man in his separateness and existential isolation but, on the contrary, would bring him into closer contact with his fellow man. Sympathy—which is intrinsically an experience of pain, the apprehension of misery, destitution and want—was infused into the glorious joy. Only through the critical interpretation, interweaving the antithesis into the experience-texture, does joy ascend from merely selfish, instinctive, harvest merrymaking into the higher, humane, existential sphere, where emotions are provided with values, and joy is socialized as a service to one's fellow man.

As a matter of fact, charity in general is a manifestation of our dialectical awareness. The Torah has tied the norm of charity to the feeling of happiness, security and pride in one's accomplishments. "As the Lord your God has blessed you" (Deut. 16:10) is the motif which is conjoined with the commandment of charity. Compassion is the socialized expression of joy. A person is summoned to serve God by serving his fellow man when he is least inclined to place himself at the disposal of others, when he is preoccupied with himself and the only service to which he attributes any value is self-service. He is contented with himself; he has been successful, he rejoices at his own great achievements, and he is ready to shut out the whole world in his exultation over his marvelous self. Exactly then, the call to service sounds. Man suddenly realizes that there is another side to life which he overlooked in his excessive joy; there are frustrated hopes, suffering and failure, and as long as destitution, poverty and pain prevail, no one can consider himself happy and successful. Out of the dialectical experience, the feeling of sympathy emerges.

At the level of the unethicized emotion, the withdrawal involved in the experience of joy is not directed toward the outside; it is more an anxiety about oneself. There is still in that antithesis no freeing from self-concern. Both the basic emotion—joy—and the inverted experience are self-centered and self-related. Using a Kierkegaardian example, I would say the departure is experienced in the embrace.

He was in love, deeply and sincerely in love; that was evident, and yet at once on one of the first days of his

engagement, he was capable of recollecting his love [as something great which had already passed and vanished]. Substantially, he was through with the whole relationship. Before he begins, he has taken such a terrible stride that he has leapt over the whole of life . . .
He longs for the girl, he has to restrain himself by force from hanging around her the whole day, and yet at the very first instant he has become an old man with respect to the whole relationship.

All this transpires at the level of a bounded-in existence, which is not in communion with others. However, Judaism has elevated this dialectic to a higher plane. Through the emotional thrust into the antithesis which the individual experiences, he frees himself from self-absorption; his awareness expands, and he begins to see the other fellow, in whom he finds the personification of the contradiction, of the inverted experience. By encountering the negation in the thou, the I opens up, and a community of existence is formed. The whole problem portrayed by Kierkegaard would have been solved if the dialectical experience had been ethicized. Religious subjectivism, without placing the inner experience in an ethical perspective, leads to a paradoxical way of life, to insoluble problems and impossible conclusions. The ethico-moral inquiry saves the *homo religiosus* from reaching the nauseating experience of absurdity so common among existentialists.

Hesed

The critical interpretation of our emotional experiences and their ethicization expresses the most uniquely Jewish ethical idea, namely, *hesed*. Basically, the categorical norm within our ethical system, *imitatio Dei*, is correlated with the ideal of *hesed*. In the final analysis, God's act of creation manifested the attribute of *hesed*—He is "*rav hesed ve-emet*, abundant in *hesed* and truth" (Ex. 34:6). Furthermore, God's revelation to His finite creation is realizable only through the medium of *hesed*.

What is *hesed*? It is almost impossible to translate it literally. The conventional English equivalent of *hesed*—lovingkindness—does not convey the gist of the idea. What is intriguing and strange is the fact that in Hebrew, the word *hesed* is applied in an antithetical manner, semantically denoting two mutually exclusive extremes. On the one hand, *hesed* signifies the ideal ethical deed, bordering on the superhuman; on the other hand, it also has the connotation of the most sordid and base behavior. It is needless, of course, to introduce passages from the Bible in which *hesed* is used in the positive sense; the Bible abounds in them. It would help if we would point out the passage in the Pentateuch in which the word *hesed* is employed to condemn something ugly and abominable. The crime of incest is termed *hesed* by the Bible:

> If a man shall take his sister, whether his father's daughter or his mother's daughter, and see her nakedness, and she see his nakedness, it is a *hesed*; and they shall be cut off in the sight of their people. He has uncovered his sister's nakedness; he shall bear his iniquity (Lev. 20:17).

What does this strange usage of *hesed* indicate? The answer was given by Maimonides in the *Guide* (III:53):

> In our commentary to the Sayings of the Fathers, we have explained the expression *hesed* as denoting an excess (in some quality). It is especially used of extraordinary kindness. *Hesed* is practiced in two ways: first, we show kindness to those who have no claim whatever upon it; secondly, we are kind to those to whom it is due, but in a greater measure than is due to them. In the Bible, the term *hesed* occurs mostly in the sense of show-

ing kindness to those who have no claim to it whatever. For this reason, the term *hesed* is employed to express the good bestowed upon us by God—"I will mention the *hesed* of the Lord" (Isa. 63:7). On this account, the very act of creation is an act of God's *hesed*—"The world is built by *hesed*" (Ps. 89:3); i.e., the building of the universe is an act of *hesed*. Also in the enumeration of God's attributes, Scripture says, "And abundant in *hesed* and truth" (Ex. 34:6).

In his commentary to the Sayings of the Fathers (*Avot* 5:6), Maimonides says as follows:

> The *hasid* is the wise man who has inclined somewhat to an extreme in his ethical attributes, as we have explained in Chapter Four [of the Eight Chapters which preface the commentary to the Sayings of the Fathers], and his deeds are greater than his wisdom. Therefore he is called a *hasid*, in the sense of excess, because exaggeration in a matter is called *hesed*, whether the exaggeration is for good or for bad.

Maimonides again emphasizes that *hesed* means excess, both in the positive and the negative sense. Therefore, whenever one transcends the normal bounds of the good and excels in his deeds beyond the call of ethical duty, he acts in accordance with the norm of *hesed*; and whenever the situation is reversed and one engages in the perpetration of an abhorrent and offensive action, denying all standards of decency and losing his sense of moral shame, his behavior is stamped as *hesed*—limitless depravity and evil.

However, Judaism has raised the idea of *hesed* to an existential level. Fundamentally, *hesed* denotes the opening up of a personal, unique, closed-in existence. Self-transcendence and the surge towards the other are called *hesed*. In other words, an overflowing existence—a human being endowed with aptitudes, creative talents, a rich inner life and bubbling energy—faces two alternatives: either to contain himself and retain a shut-in, isolated existence, or to abandon the barrier separating him from others and let the thou share not his money or external comfort but his own self, let him participate in his unique, one-timely, subjective existential experience. The Jewish mystics speak of *hesed ve-din*, of expansion and contraction, of out-reaching oneself and then complete retreating into the self.

The norm of *hesed* demonstrates itself first within external deeds. I am duty bound to aim my efforts at the good of others, not only at my own welfare. However, *hesed* is not limited to the external sphere of human activity, but reaches into the spiritual life of man. His total existential experience must be an all-inclusive awareness, embracing himself and others, sharing with them the riches of his inner world. *Hesed* means a community existence of two individuals (or more), feeling each other's troubles and joys, each giving the other whatever he cherishes as his most precious possession: joy, grief, pride, etc. If you exult about something, impart your joy to others, since this feeling of gladness and delight is, at this moment, the focus of your personality. On the other hand, if your friend is grieving, try to lighten his burden by mourning with him and displaying genuine compassion for his tormented soul. You must give of your emotional life as freely as you give of your money, and per-haps even more generously, by presenting the other person with the most beautiful gift of all: your emotional experience, in which your existential adventure finds its most poignant expression. One's emotions must mirror not only the inner movement of his own soul but the tender stir in another soul as well. One expands his own existential sphere and admits others to partake of his experiences.

Interesting is the Maimonidean theory of education or teaching. What is a teacher, if not one who has found a great treasure which he cherishes with all his might and passion, yet does not want to enjoy the marvels of his find alone? Instead, he invites others to share in this great adventure called knowledge, because he feels that his experience is not full unless he discloses its beauty and splendor to others. Why is a man driven to preach, to publish books, to tell stories, if not by the inner drive of *hesed*? This drive forces man to step out of his prisoner's isolation-cell and embrace others, since his existence is overflowing; like a river in spring, his existence oversteps its bounds and inundates the environs. "Behold, I will extend peace to her like a river, and the glory of the nations like a stream in flood" (Isa. 66:12). And what is the prophet, if not the person to whom God has granted a great, overwhelming, intoxicating and dynamic existential experience—rich in color, magnificent in its contours and fascinating in its majesty and glory—who carries in his heart a great eternal truth and in his hand a flaming torch, and who is overcome by an indomitable impulse to give away everything he has, to let others in on his secret, to share his spiritual possessions with others? The prophet is the man who has succeeded in performing the feat of transcendence, freely spending his inner life on others; he is the man who has realized the ideal of community-existence. So are the teacher and preacher. Teaching and preaching are acts of *hesed*, of self-giving and sharing, of establishing an ontic fellowship [fellowship of being]—as when Elijah threw off of his mantle and Elisha wrapped himself in his master's garment. The life or existence of the prophet, teacher or preacher is public; privacy is abandoned.

There are people who are capable and gifted, yet are deprived of the drive of *hesed* for a very obvious reason. The existential grant which they received from God is too limited. Their experiences are shallow and calm, lacking in depth, passion and impetus. The person is not pressed to move toward others. He can well afford to be a miser, since he has very little to dispense. What he knows, he keeps for himself; what he feels is hidden in his selfish world. He is a microcosm, sealed and tight-lipped, who can never dream of turning into a macrocosm. Spiritually and emotionally, he is a miser. There is no outcry at the pain of containment, no spontaneous revelation to others, no embrace and no communal existence. Such people can never become prophets, teachers or preachers. The Bible calls them *benei ha-nevi'im*, sons of prophets (II Kings 2), who exulted in their own private world, in their seclusion and retreat, without commitment to others and without responsibilities for the people. Maimonides writes (*Guide* II:37):

> It is well known that the members of each class [of those receiving the Divine influence] differ greatly from each other. Each of the first two classes is again subdivided and contains two sections, namely, those who receive the influence only as far as is necessary for their own perfection, and those who receive it in so great a measure that it suffices for their own perfection and that of others. A member of the first class, the wise men, may have his mind influenced either only so far that he is enabled to search, to understand, to know and to discern, without attempting to be a teacher or an author, having neither the desire nor the capacity; but he may also be influenced to such degree that he becomes a teacher or an author. The same is the case with the second class: a person may receive a prophecy enabling him to perfect himself but not others; but he may also receive a prophecy as would compel him to address his fellow men, teach them and benefit them through his perfection.
>
> It is clear that without this second degree of perfection, no books would have been written nor would any prophet have persuaded others to know the truth. For a scholar does not write a book with the object to teach himself what he already knows. But the characteristic of the intellect is this: what one person's intellect receives is transmitted to another and so on, until a person is

reached who can only himself be perfected by such an influence, but is unable to communicate it to others, as has been explained in some chapters of this treatise.

It is further the nature of this element in man that he who possesses an additional degree of that influence is compelled to address his fellow men under all circumstances, whether he is listened to or not, even if he injures himself thereby. Thus we find prophets who did not leave off speaking to the people until they were slain; it is this Divine influence that moves them, that does not allow them to rest in any way, though they might bring upon themselves great misfortunes by their action. For example, when Jeremiah was despised, like other teachers and scholars of his age, he could not, though he desired it, withhold his prophecy, or cease from reminding the people of the truths they rejected. "For the word of the Lord was unto me a reproach and mocking all day, and I said I will not mention it, nor will I again speak in His name; but it was in my heart as a burning fire, enclosed in my bones, and I wearied myself to keep it in, but did not prevail" (Jer. 20:8-9). This is also the meaning of the words of another prophet: "The Lord God has spoken, who shall not prophesy?" (Amos 3:8).

Hesed and Mishpat

However, in the prophets' *hesed*, existential transcendence is always coupled with its rival aspect, *mishpat*: "Righteousness and *mishpat* are the foundation of Your throne; *hesed* and truth shall go before You" (Ps. 89:15). In the vernacular of mysticism, this rival aspect is referred to as *gevurah* or *din*. The mystics have defined *hesed* as *hitpashtut*, expansion, and *mishpat* or *gevurah* as contraction, limitation, *tzimtzum*. Apparently, the ideal of *hesed* must have at its side its opposite aspect, its sheer contradiction—*tzimtzum*, withdrawal and shrinking. The two are inseparable. The thesis, paradoxically, is complemented by its antithesis. Our ethical experience runs back and forth between these two poles. Why? In order to surge forward toward the thou, to widen the circle of one's ontic experience and to share it with others, one must first undergo opposite movement of retreating into himself, of contracting his own egotistic existence, of displacing and removing himself from the center of reality and taking up a peripheral position. Without this movement from the center to the periphery, a performance of self-limiting in order to allow others to enter—*hesed* is a fantasy. The commitment to others requires self-denial (in an axiological sense). Otherwise, the movement towards the thou would be that of the low form of *hesed*, whereby the I, proud and adventurous in a daemonic fashion, reaches out for the thou, not for the purpose of sharing the best and finest I have in my possession, but in order to promote my own good. In that case, contact with the other is not *hesed* in the sense of mutual participation, but in the sense of conquest and exploitation. Erotic passionate love is characteristic of *hesed* which is not preceded by *mishpat*, of expanding without contracting first, of reaching out for something which does not belong to the I. Before one transcends himself, he must retreat first into the most abstruse seclusion within himself. That is the great ethical drama which the dialectical experience unfolds before us.

❧ Index of Topics and Names

D

daemonic personality, 154–56
David, 109, 160–61, 175, 179
Decalogue, public reading of, 14–15
death
  Abraham's reaction to Sarah's, 35
  as conclusion of divine service, 150
  as consequence of human imperfection, 6
  as consequence of sin, 6, 35
  contradicts God-man relationship, 47
  evil only if viewed narrowly, 127
  extricates man from egocentrism, 132
  fear of, 128
  as good, 98–99
  increase in knowledge as death is closer, 97–98
  its inevitability questioned by modern scientific man, 104
  by a kiss, 98
  knowledge of vs. existential awareness of, 130–32
  as opportunity to display heroism, 4
  as part of biological process, 157
  topical *Halakhah*'s attitude towards, 100–1
  trailing behind every man, 1, 4
defeat
  and dignity, 109
  and image of God, 110
  man accepts courageously, 133
  and mental health, 114
  need for man to experience, 107–14
  prayer as consecration of, 167
Delilah, 156
de Gaulle, Charles, 38
democracy, 148
Descartes, René, 164
despair
  contrary to *avelut de-rabbim*, 29–30
  inherent in human existence, 92
  as a legitimate emotion 12, 36, 101
  opens individual to others, 202–3
dialectical characteristics
  advance and recoil, 109–13
  of *akedah*, 113–14
  of emotion, 138, 186–90, 204–7
  expansion and contraction, 213–14

expiation (*kapparah*), mourning as, 6, 8
Ezekiel, 29, 144–47

F
faith
   born of suffering, 118
   fraught with absurdity, 116–117
   of the Jewish people, 100, 103–4
fear
   of God, 108–9
   explanation of, 177–78
festival
   community's rejoicing cancels mourning, 71
   eating meat and drinking wine on, 65
   High Priest's year-round status is like Israel's on festival, 51–52, 78–85
   menuddeh's practices on, 53–54, 70, 74–75
   metzora's practices on, 52, 53, 55, 74–75
   mourning on, 50, 51, 52–53, 56–59, 65–84 *passim*
   not counted towards *shiv'ah*, 71
   rejoicing on (*simhat ha-regel*), 53, 65–84 *passim*, 203–5
   and sympathy, 203–6
finitude, human
   humanistic answer, 156–57
   religious-metaphysical answer, 157–58
freedom of the will extends to emotion, 166–67
Freud, Sigmund, 188
friendship, 154

G
Gandhi, Mohandas, 103
genuflection, 172–73, 174–75
ger ve-toshav (stranger and sojourner), 39
gevurah (in mysticism), 213
gifts, Jewish view of, 40
God
   cleanses and redeems us, 47–48
   departure from man, 8
   distant yet experienced by man, 143–44
   encounter or communion with man, dialectical characteristic of, 106, 121–22, 127–28
   Ezekiel's vision of, 144–47
   fear of, *see* fear of God
   glory of (*majestas Dei*), 135–36

I

remorse
  and guilt, 194
  and joy, 192–93
repentance, *see teshuvah*
resurrection of dead, 5
R. Reuben, 175–76
revelation
  apocalyptic needed as atonement for ignoring divine gift, 138
  apocalyptic in prophecy, 142–47
  apocalyptic and suffering, 118–25, 132
  apocalyptic in Temple, 144
  in contrast to natural ethic, 119–20
  cosmic vs. catastrophic, 137–38
  need for awareness of catastrophic, 140–41
  opens man up to suffering, 120–25
  twofold nature of revelational experience, 121–25
  in whirlwind, 128
Rosh, *see* Asher b. Yehiel
Rosh ha-Shanah
  joy on, 68–69
  liturgy of, 67–69
Rothschild, Alain de, 38
Rothschild, Edmund de, 38

S
Sabbath
  honor and delight as outer actions, 72, 73
  inner *kiyyum* of mourning possible on, 72
  public and private mourning on, 56–57, 72–73
  in topical and thematic Halakhah, 89–90
sacrifice
  leads to catharsis, 129
  of pleasure introduced by revelation, 119
  as relinquishing illusion, 159
  sacrificial offerings (*korbanot*), 65–84 *passim*
  sacrificial offerings and *onen*, 51–52, 65
  shelamim, 67–68
Samson and Delilah, 156
Sand, George, 183
Sarah
  change of name, 33
  as cofounder of *masorah*, 32–33

❧ Index of Biblical and Rabbinic Sources